SURVIVAL READY

LIFE-SAVING SKILLS AND EXPERT ADVICE FOR SURVIVING ANY THREAT AT ANY TIME

CHECK FREEDMAN WITH **BILLY JENSEN**

U.S. SPECIAL FORCES AND GOVERNMENT SPECIAL OPERATORS

TABLE OF CONTENTS

99 MENTAL TOUGHNESS

165 SELF DEFENSE

179 BUSHCRAFT BASICS

203 HELPING OTHERS IN CRISIS

214 URBAN SURVIVAL

228 FIELD MEDICINE

FOREWORD

I FIRST MET Check Freedman and Billy Jensen a few years back when they attended a hostage negotiation class that I was conducting in Lynchburg, Virginia. I was the commanding officer of the New York City Police Department's (NYPD) Hostage Negotiation Team (HNT) before retiring. They say when you can't do anymore, you teach, so that's what I now do, both throughout the U.S. and internationally. Although the students in my classes come from diverse backgrounds, they are each a member of law enforcement or military hostage negotiation teams, or aspire to become one.

I always begin each class by going around the room and asking for a quick introduction from each student to get a flavor of the class makeup. I then give a quick introduction of myself in return. When it came time for Check and Billy to introduce themselves, I noticed that both were quite modest and a bit aloof in doing so. Frankly, I was a bit stymied at what appeared to be reluctance to speak openly in front of the class. I consider myself a pretty good judge of character, perhaps because of my 34 years of policing experience with the NYPD and being part of the tactical team and a hostage negotiator. In fact, I sensed that I had two exceptional people in my class based on how they carried themselves. I knew there had to be more to them than what they were choosing to reveal. I was reminded at that moment of the true martial artist who is so confident in their ability that they never have any reason to boast.

In the interest of moving the class along, I let it go and continued on to the other student's introductions. When I returned to my hotel room that evening, I Googled their names. I started with Check and was blown away by what I saw. It was like reading a page out of Wonder Woman's bio. She holds black belts and instructor ranks in 11 different martial arts styles. In addition, she is a technical scuba diver, a multi-engine instrument pilot, private investigator, private detective, certified missing and exploited child investigator and locksmith, amongst many other skills and abilities. She is even a crisis hostage negotiator, a skillset near and dear to my heart. I was in awe of how this modest and unassuming woman could have accomplished so much. I understood, however, why she had no need to boast—a true martial artist, indeed.

I then turned my search to Billy Jensen. Billy can take a page out of former Special Forces operative Steve Rogers's bio, (a.k.a. Captain America). Billy, like the fictional Rogers, was a member of the U.S. Army's Special Forces—the elite Green Beret fighting force—spending more than a decade in that assignment. During his time with the Green Berets, Billy underwent intensive training in combating terrorism, criminal network analysis, irregular warfare, evidence-based operations, technical surveillance, biometrics and threat vulnerability, amongst other highly concentrated and rigorous areas of study. This unique resume enables him to serve as the CEO of the Captive Audience Prevention Training and Recovery Team, where he works alongside Check, Captive Audience's COO.

Their collaborative work, *Survival Ready: Life-Saving Skills and Expert Advice for Surviving Any Threat at Any Time*, is exactly what the title describes. It navigates you through hundreds of extraordinary and unexpected life encounters—ones in which you might easily find yourself when you least expect it.

Check and Billy provide situational awareness and survival strategies to help you fully understand the dangers of your environment and make the right decisions during stressful confrontations or under life threatening conditions. In short, this book will enable you to be confident in your personal safety, no matter what circumstances you might find yourself in.

After spending many years with the largest municipal police agency in the U.S., I was certain of my ability to detect hazardous environments wherever they existed. After reading this book, I realized that I still had a lot to learn—and I will never book another hotel room the same way again. Neither will you.

—*Jack Cambria, NYPD Hostage Negotiation Team Commander (Ret.)*

INTRODUCTION

LIVING IN CONDITION YELLOW

IF YOU ARE reading this, you want to be survival ready. You want to be prepared for whatever life may throw at you, whether it be a common occurrence or completely unpredictable disaster.

Your journey to survival readiness begins with a commitment to situational awareness, a mindset that enables you to be prepared for any life-threatening scenario. Simply put, situational awareness is the ability and willingness to take note of the world around you. Consider this series of questions:

What did you wear yesterday?

What time did you eat this morning?

What kind of car does your closest neighbor drive?

How many exits are there wherever you are right now? Where are they?

Without looking, what shoes are you wearing right now?

Having situational awareness means you live in a state of paying attention to details and noticing trends. These details inform your state of alertness to danger, which can be defined as four "conditions": white, yellow, orange and red. An example of condition white is a person who is texting while crossing the street. They are totally oblivious to the world around them, its opportunities and its dangers. Condition yellow means being relaxed but aware. This is where you are comfortable in your setting and you understand what and where the likely problems or dangers may be. Next is condition orange, a heightened state of awareness. You may or may not be able to identify a specific threat, but you do not like the way the situation feels. You are prepared to react if necessary and you are probably already somewhat on edge. Condition red, then, is an identified threat and the need for immediate action. You have spotted a dangerous individual and recognize that you cannot afford to stay put and ignore their actions.

We want to live in condition yellow, even at home. This does not mean living in fear. Instead, this means living in moment-to-moment awareness of the world around us and being prepared to take action on our own behalf.

Establishing good situational awareness will enable you to live comfortably in condition yellow, staying safe and avoiding danger more easily and effectively than ever before. The lessons in this book take situational awareness a step further. When conditions change for the worse, to orange or red, you will recognize what is happening, know what to do and how to survive, no matter what threat comes your way.

You will be survival ready.

SURVIVAL 101

BASIC SKILLS FOR ALL SEASONS AND OCCASIONS

THESE ARE THE straightforward skills every savvy survivalist should know. Whether you're a beginner or a seasoned pro, brushing up on your fundamentals is always a good idea. From living in the gray to prepping your gear to maintaining the steel trap mindset of a conqueror, these timeless tips will help you focus on enduring just about any scenario and overcoming threats to your well-being. Learn how to train, pack, lead, thrive and lay the groundwork for your journey to self-sufficiency.

ADVANCE PREPARATION OF THE BATTLE SPACE

In military terms, advance preparation of the battle space means "an analytical methodology employed to reduce uncertainties concerning the enemy, environment and terrain for all types of operations." That makes sense. No one goes to war without preparing the troops, producing equipment and gathering intelligence on the enemy, environment and terrain.

The security savvy man or woman would be wise to do the same. Where is our battle space? Where are our own battles won and lost? Is it at work? At home? In our relationships? In the logistics of our hectic lives? At the destination end of a trip? Reintegrating at home after an extended absence? I say no. I propose to you that our battle space is our mind.

The entire purpose of this book is to arm you with the things you may need in order to survive a multitude of situations. Whether you are building a fire and an emergency shelter after getting lost or defending yourself against an attacker, you are taking action to save your own life and preserve your safety. Remember that survival is the byproduct of action. Taking action on your own behalf encompasses many things. It could mean building a fire, running away, changing a tire, applying a tourniquet, finding water, hiding, jump-starting a car, performing CPR, navigating, fighting unarmed, winching a vehicle out of a trap, packing a wound, building a shelter, making an improvised weapon, stopping a coolant leak, applying a pressure bandage, trapping, pulling a knife on an attacker, treating for shock, hunting, using a firearm in self-defense, performing the Heimlich maneuver, fishing, de-escalating a tense situation, making a raft, negotiating for freedom, employing a found object as a weapon or many, many other things. The point is, you need to have all of these skills. You never know what life will throw at you. Therefore, you must be prepared for anything.

However, nothing I can teach you could possibly be as important or as valuable as advance preparation of your battle space: your mind. Do you wake up one day and decide to run the Marine Corps Marathon that same day? Do you jump in with no training, no conditioning and no prior planning and see how you do? Of course not. You decide to do it well in advance. You plan a training schedule that will take you from where you are to where you need to be by the day of the marathon. When that day arrives and it takes everything you have, you emerge victorious because of your advanced preparation of the battle space.

There are three types of people: Victims, Survivors and Conquerors. Victims encounter adversity and succumb. They require intervention, but they never fully bounce back to the whole person they were before. Survivors encounter adversity and resist. Although they require intervention, with time and help, they will eventually recover. Conquerors encounter adversity and fight. They refuse to give up or surrender. They fight until they overcome. They require no intervention and they return to full strength and vigor in short order.

What is the difference in these people? Is it personality? Advantaged situation? Privileged upbringing? Genes? Faith? Why do some people succumb without resisting while others fight for victory? I propose that it all comes down to how well they have prepared their battle space, their minds, before adversity struck. People who are allowed to fail and recover show the most remarkable levels of resiliency. Through their failures and recoveries, they figure out how to think. Each failure and subsequent recovery is an opportunity to practice their skills, and skills are not developed nor sharpened without practice. Deciding to get back up when you have been knocked down 100 times takes incredible stamina, endurance and a will to overcome.

Consider kidnapping, something we can all agree is one of the worst things that can happen to someone. It is an egregious attack on the security of a family and an emotional inferno of the first magnitude. However, we cannot counter the problem by ignoring it. Believing that "it can never happen to me" will not make this growing human-rights violation cease to exist. So, knowing that it could actually happen to you, and knowing that advance preparation of your battle space, you mind, will mean the difference between being a victim or a conqueror, what should you do?

Your training begins now. You have just joined a gym for your psyche and worldview. Each day, you must put measures in place and make decisions in advance of the need so that, when you do encounter adversity, you will already have the tools you need to conquer it. Here are a few ways to prepare your mental battle space.

TAKE RISKS

No, I do not mean crossing the street while texting. I mean go for something when you might not succeed. Try out for a team when you might not get selected. Audition for a part in a play when you might not get cast. Tackle a personal project when you might not meet your deadline. Take up a hobby that is challenging and difficult. Take a chance that you might fail. This will do two things: it will increase your confidence as you realize just how much you can already do, and it will give you the priceless opportunity to fail and recover. Learn who you are. Fall back, regroup and attack the problem again with renewed energy and determination. Look at the problem from another perspective and find a different solution.

LEARN FROM YOUR MISTAKES

Analyze what went wrong, why it did not work and what might work instead. Evaluate the results. Look for object lessons all around you. They abound to the one who has the eyes to see them. I reached down to pet a stray cat one day while I was out walking. I felt bad because I had no food to give her. As I walked away, I realized I did not need to feel bad about what I did not have to give: food. Instead, I could feel good about giving what I did have: affection. That applies everywhere in life. If I am giving all I have to give, why should I feel sad about what I do not have to give? Object lessons abound.

At the end of each day, ask yourself what you learned. Do not be content with the status quo. Learn something every day. Look for and celebrate small victories. If all you have is the fact that you stood back up every single time someone knocked you down, that is a victory. Note it. Celebrate it. Resist the temptation to give up. Insist on surviving. Insist on thriving. Insist on conquering. Fight! You are worth it. You are worth the ordeal, the effort, the pain, the cold, the hunger, the fatigue, the nightmares. Your life is the most precious thing you have. It is worth preserving. It is worth fighting for.

CONDUCT YOURSELF HONORABLY

You will have to live with your decisions and actions for the rest of your life. You are the one who will have those memories forever. What can you live with? Make some pre-made decisions. Use the word WHEN and not the word IF. "If" allows room for doubt and negotiation. "When" is a solid, non-negotiable. "WHEN I get out of here" will do far more for your morale than "IF I get out of here." Decide to conquer.

Conduct yourself according to your moral code and make that non-negotiable. No one can decide your convictions but you. They are the boundaries within which you choose to live. They provide the rules of engagement along the way and give you a compass by which you can navigate when everything else is dark and confusing.

PRACTICE FAITH

People of faith are far more likely to be conquerors than those who believe in nothing. It is really your faith that will sustain you. Your faith is the place from which you draw those convictions and morals. Your faith can fight for you when your body is too weak. Your faith gives you hope and something to believe in beyond the adversity that is obscuring your view.

PRACTICE GOOD MORALE

Lift your spirits and everyone else's around you. Maintain excellent hygiene. It is amazing how much better a simple shower or brushing your teeth can make you feel. Smile. Speak a kind word. Look for 10 reasons a day to say thank you. Open the door for others. Greet people. Laugh.

Advance preparation of the battle space means you must do these things now. The system will fail you if you wait until adversity strikes to put these things into practice. Now is the time to get yourself ready so that, when the day of adversity strikes, you will be a conqueror.

THERE IS ONLY ONE SHADE OF GRAY

Have you ever heard the term "Gray Man"? Do you know what it means? Being gray is blending into your surroundings, choosing not to stand out, moving around freely and escaping everyone's notice. This is the same principle as hundreds of identical fish schooling together in the ocean; they think and act and move in unison because instinct tells them that those who stand out or stray too far away will be the first to be picked off by their predators. When sharks inevitably circle a school, each fish is doing its best not to stand out in any way. Before you travel to a new place, be it domestic or international, you should always take the time to do a bit of research on the local population. Who are they? What do they wear? How do they use their hands? What is their posture? What is their body language? How fast do they walk? Do they look around? What do they eat? What hours do they keep? What do they do for pleasure? Does the business community dress in suits and ties? Do women go out unaccompanied?

There are so many questions you can ask. The key is to get to know the baseline attitude, behavior and look of the local population and then pack accordingly. Asking these questions is the key to situational awareness, one of the most foundational pillars of survival training. Another pillar? Not standing out. Do not draw any unnecessary attention to yourself. Do not be loud, different, noticeable or memorable. Blend in until you disappear.

One of the most difficult and expensive parts of this plan is footwear. Shoes are distinctive and quite different from place to place. Even when a person changes hats, a jacket, glasses and a backpack in an effort to quickly go gray, his or her shoes will usually stay the same and give them away. Make sure to know and obtain local footwear if you decide to blend in. Go online and look at photographs of local people and try to copy what they wear in terms of headgear, clothing, shoes and accessories like bags, purses, briefcases, messenger bags, backpacks, etc. Depending on your destination, it might not be that different from what you already own.

If you know anyone from that area, study their gestures, mannerisms, facial expressions, body posture, body language, speed of movement and verbal expressions. Are they different from yours? How so? If you do not know anyone from that region, try to find an online video of human interaction from the people of that region and practice what you see. For instance, if you travel to Italy and try to order an iced coffee or espresso drink, the words will not yet be out of your mouth before they peg you for a stranger.

Speed of movement is not an intuitive thing of which most of us are aware, but it is absolutely crucial to blending in. You may come from Manhattan, where everyone looks straight ahead, does not smile and walks with purpose. The average speed of a Manhattan pedestrian is quite fast. In Tijuana, however, you will see a much slower pace of life. People walk at a much more relaxed pace. They browse. They smile at strangers. The baseline is entirely different. Which is to say, if you are from Manhattan and want to go gray in

Tijuana, you absolutely must slow down.

There is only one shade of gray: the shade that works, the one that successfully conceals your differences and allows you to blend in and become undetectable.

THE IMPORTANCE OF OPSEC

OPSEC is an acronym that stands for Operational Security. In short, OPSEC is about knowing what not to say.

Not talking can be very difficult. When we know something good, interesting, exciting or special, we naturally want to share it. However, when it comes to security, knowing what not to say is an even more valuable skill than knowing what to say.

Imagine a widespread catastrophe scenario. You can make it any event you want: an earthquake, a blizzard, an electromagnetic pulse attack, a terrorist attack, etc. Any event will suffice. Now, imagine that, because of the event, you and all of your neighbors are sheltering in place at home for a week. You have been reading, planning, studying, preparing, amassing gear, laying in food and water stores, and living in a general state of readiness. Your neighbors have not. You are prepared to feed your household for a month, whereas your neighbors have three days worth of food in their pantry and no water stores at all. How will you proceed?

OPSEC would dictate that you have been making all your preparations in secret, not announcing to your neighbors that you have a veritable convenience store and a camping supplier in your basement. OPSEC would also dictate that you do not cook food outdoors or create tantalizing smells. If you have power from a separate source, like a generator, and everyone else is using candles for light, you will probably want to use candles too.

By no means am I telling you to not help your neighbors—kindness, generosity and helpfulness are survival skills unto themselves. By all means, do whatever you can for whomever you can whenever you can. However, the OPSEC part comes in by not allowing a security breach in the information concerning the location and amount of your provisions. No one else needs to know how well prepared you are; knowledge about the amount and location of your provisions should be treated as classified. In adverse situations, when people are worried about feeding their family, you are putting yours at risk by effectively advertising your readiness.

Likewise, OPSEC comes in very handy as you travel. Do not announce that you are going to be out of the country for two weeks, i.e., that your house will be empty. Do not post your daily routine on social media. Consider these tidbits of information to be security risks in the wrong hands and guard them carefully. Remember: Do not live your life in fear but live boldly in wisdom and security.

EVERY DAY CARRY

Do you know what it means to become a hardened target? It means making yourself a difficult person to victimize. It starts with situational awareness, but there is more to it than that. One of the hallmarks of a hardened target is preparedness.

Every Day Carry refers to the things you will physically carry on your person every day, and the list works both at home and abroad. You must, however, familiarize yourself with the local laws in order to decide what you are allowed to carry and where. Bear in mind that laws vary from country to country, state to state, county to county and town to town. Know the laws and do not carry anything illegal in any locality.

There is a school of thought that says, "Survive out of your clothes, fight out of your gear, live out of your pack," meaning you need to keep anything necessary for your survival in your pockets and on your person. You need to be able to handle the situation out of your purse, backpack, messenger bag, etc. You need to be able to live out of your bug-out bag (pg. 22). For now, we are going to focus on surviving out of your clothes.

CLOTHING

- Have a baseline-appropriate head covering with you, even if it is not always on your head, to help you change your look quickly.

- Have eyeglasses or sunglasses with you for the same reason.

- Dress in layers so you can shed, reverse or relocate pieces quickly.

- Choose a shirt and pants that are flexible, comfortable, rugged and filled with as many pockets as possible. Concealed carry shirts with hidden pockets and cargo pants are optimal. Again, remember the baseline of your locality.

- Shoes must be comfortable and rugged for walking, running and fighting.

- Keep a jacket with you. It is always good to have for the purpose of changing your look quickly. It also provides extra pockets. It can be tied around your waist, slung over your arm or stuffed in a backpack whenever you do not wish to wear it. It can function as a method of concealing something, and it can also become a tourniquet if one is ever needed. A jacket can be converted into a bag for carrying things and can even be employed as a weapon.

TOOLS

For a list of specific gear recommendations, see pg. 50.

- **POCKETS** Ideally, you should have pockets in your shirt, pants and jacket, and you will need to find a methodology for distributing your tools across your pockets. I strongly recommend that, when you find a configuration that works for you, you be consistent. You need to know where each thing is without thinking when the moment of adversity strikes.

- **KNIFE** This is employable for all kinds of routine uses, so I recommend that it not only be easy to access but—and this is almost just as important—not physically alarming to anyone who might happen to see it. For example, a machete anywhere outside of the jungle or the outback categorically does not fit the baseline.

- **TACTICAL PEN** Likewise, this useful tool functions primarily as a pen, so it should also be kept in a location that is easy to access. Tactical pens are usually made out of steel, aluminum or titanium. They can function as a stabbing, trapping, pressure point or joint control weapon and they often come equipped with a glass breaker; some are even fitted with a multi-tool, flashlight and whistle. At the very least, yours should have a glass breaker. As a simple pen, they are allowed in government buildings, but they are a powerful weapon in the hands of someone who takes the time to learn and practice the necessary skills.

- **BUTTON COMPASS** These are pretty small these days; I personally like one that is about the size of a nickel. They can be clipped off anywhere. If you purchase one from a well-respected brand, it will be every bit as reliable as a full-sized compass. This tiny device can ultimately be responsible for directing you out of harm's way.

- **PARACORD** This is the most amazing tool in existence. It has 101 uses and I cannot over stress its importance. Consider keeping a small amount (about 10 feet) on you. These days, it comes in line strengths of 550-pounds, 750-pounds, 850-pounds and more. Be sure to get a good quality paracord that does all that you need it to do.

- **LIGHTER** This is also a tool with daily use as well as tactical use so again, I recommend keeping this in a place where you can access it easily. Should you get caught in an avalanche, the flame will show you which direction is up.

- **BOBBY PIN** Yes, a bobby pin. This is the Mighty Mouse of tools. It has many uses and can be easily carried and concealed. It is not illegal anywhere and you will never feel it in your clothes. These little gems can be turned into lock picks, shims, screw drivers, clips, leads, antennae, conductors and more. There is no good reason not to carry one, two or even three.

- **CELL PHONE** I do not have to tell many people to remember to carry a cell phone anymore. This will, quite often, be your one-stop-shop for getting yourself rescued, so you should always keep it charged.

- **WATCH** Most people like to rely on their cell phone for the time but I still wear a watch. It is not something that needs to be concealed and it requires no pocket space. It is useful all day long and never gets in the way. Knowing the time and being able to time things are necessary survival skills.

- **MAP** If you are in an unfamiliar area, I recommend having a map. Should you need it, the map and the compass will be your ticket home.

- **FIREARM** Personal choice. Open carry. Conceal carry. Brand. Size. Caliber. Having one on you can make you an incredibly hard target, but do not become myopic. You are carrying many tools. Some are for survival, some are for fighting and some are for avoiding or escaping a bad situation. Use all the tools available to you and always prioritize them in this way: Avoid. De-escalate. Escape. Fight.

• **SIGNALING DEVICE** This is most often a whistle. If you get trapped somewhere and need to be found and rescued, it is far easier for you to blow on a whistle for a long period of time than it is for you to yell for a long period of time. Your voice will give out. A whistle will not. Whistles can also be heard from a much greater distance than can a human voice.

• **CASH** This is the true universal multi-tool. It is not subject to the availability of electricity. It can buy help. In an emergency, it can bribe. It can expedite transactions. It stays off the radar. It can be used to procure survival gear or transport. It is accepted everywhere. Never leave home without it.

One of my mantras dictates that "two is one and one is none." This means that if I am going to need something, I have to count on losing it, breaking it or having it stolen. Therefore, I must carry a backup. If you need it, whatever item that might be, take two. If you do not need it, do not carry it. Keep it simple.

THE BUG-OUT BAG

There are many schools of thought on "go bags" or "bug-out bags." However, most agree on the core essentials that must be present. For all you campers out there, this will not be very different from the gear you take with you every time you go camping. There may be some additions, though. There is also bound to be a difference in the recommended quantity.

There are bug-out bags and there are Every Day Carry bags (pg. 19). There are also cached bags. I personally keep nine fully-stocked bags. One is always in my house. One is always in my vehicle. One is in my office. One is for search and rescue. One is for climbing and rappelling. One is for emergency medical response. One is for the range. One is for camping. One is a floater—something I can cache at a location of my choosing. I can take it with me when I travel. I can quickly equip another person. I can use it as backup for my main gear. These nine bags are my personal system. I realize this might seem terribly redundant but I actually do use it all (and sometimes I loan things out). Every person in the house has at least one bug-out bag, always packed, fully stocked and ready to go.

I have learned what is worth carrying and what is not. I have learned what brands I like (pg. 50) and which do not stand the test of time. I have learned which materials are the warmest and how many backups I need. I have also learned there are two often overlooked categories that are of premium importance to humankind: Morale and hygiene.

Hygiene is critically essential and plays directly into morale. When we are clean and fresh, we simply feel better. We have more self-confidence and more self-respect. Good hygiene contributes to overall wellness and health. It helps to prevent disease and infection. It allows us freedom of movement. It is a victory we can celebrate each day we practice it.

After securing safety, shelter, fire, water and food, I turn my attention to

MY BUG-OUT BAG PACKING LIST

- Book
- Deck of cards
- Money
- Passport
- Wallet/ID
- Emergency medical kit
- 850 paracord
- Flint
- Matches
- Lighters
- Knives (fixed blade and folding)
- Rappelling rope
- Leather gloves
- Carabiners
- Cams and wedges
- Tubular nylon webbing
- Figure 8 descender
- Rescue 8
- Harness
- Mylar blanket and tent
- Water purification tablets
- Water bags/bladder
- Trail soap
- Towel
- Flashlight

- Batteries
- Hand crank flashlight
- Hand crank radio
- Solar powered lantern
- Pencils
- Pencil sharpener
- Waterproof paper
- Knife sharpener
- Lock picks
- Tactical tomahawk
- Cargo pants
- Shirts
- Base layer
- Wool socks
- Underwear
- T-shirts
- Ultralight 850-count down jacket
- Folding shovel
- Leatherman multi-tool
- Hiking boots
- Compass
- Fishing line and hooks
- Ziplock bags
- Toilet paper
- Deodorant

- Lip balm
- Sunblock
- Toothbrush
- Toothpaste
- Sunglasses
- Hat for sun
- Hat for warmth
- Blousing bands
- Kettle
- Eating utensil
- Bowls
- Stove
- Fuel
- Hammock
- Straps
- Dehydrated food packs
- Water
- Energy bars
- Solar charger
- Water filter
- Down blanket
- Handgun
- AR Pistol
- Ammo for both of the above

morale. Once the essentials of life are obtained, morale needs to be assessed and raised, if needed. That is why I bring reading material and a deck of cards. I do not want to add unnecessary weight to my bag, so I confine myself to one book and one deck of cards. However, I do consider them minimum necessary equipment, just as I do a knife or a compass. Mindset is everything. If, by some small measure, I can keep my spirits (as well as the spirits of those around me) up, I am achieving victory. I am conquering.

You will need to decide what to bring and what to leave. While I can share the contents of my bags with you, it ultimately comes down to personal preference and experience. Whatever you do, do not leave the planning for when disaster strikes. Now is the time to get ready. These things can be costly, so even if you start with a skeleton kit and add to it slowly over time, you are doing something in advance of the need. Plan and execute as much as possible now and you can sleep the sleep of the prepared.

SHELTER IN PLACE

When it comes to catastrophic weather events, terrorism, social or political unrest and epidemics, it may not be advisable to grab a bug-out bag (pg. 22) and go. Instead, the smart thing to do may be to shelter in place wherever you are. If you have already put together a bug-out bag, you will have many of the essentials and even the comfort items covered. However, that only works when you can get to your bag.

When people hear the term "shelter in place," they naturally think of home. That is the absolute best place to be, because you have all of your own possessions for both comfort and survival. However, you may not be home when disaster strikes. You could be at a hotel, a friend's house, a store, at work, in a shopping mall or anywhere else. You might even be abroad. No matter where you are, here are some things that will make your stay more bearable.

FOOD STORES

This is an obvious essential. At home, you can prepare by stocking up on canned, frozen and dry foods. Buy more than you need and rotate through what you eat and replenish to keep everything reasonably fresh. Conversely, at a friend's house, a shopping mall or elsewhere, you cannot decide what they keep in store. It is not a bad idea to have energy bars on your person, in your backpack or in your car as a matter of course. I keep enough food in my car at all times to feed me for 72 hours. I check the dates, eat from my stores and replace items on a regular basis so that they never exceed the date stamp. I keep the same amount of food at work and use the same system.

WATER

As mentioned above, keep lots of fresh water on hand at home. If you have any advance notice about an event that will keep you housebound, fill all your bathtubs with water. I keep 10 five-gallon drums of spring water at home. I keep a case of bottled water in the car. I keep a case of bottled water at work. If you get stuck in a building of some sort, look for containers and a water fountain or sink and start filling them right away.

METHOD OF COOKING

This is easiest at home, even if you lose electricity or gas. If you have a yard, you can build a fire and cook outside. If you put a camp stove in your bug-out bag, you can use this outside as well. For most of the long-term food stores, you will need a way to boil water. For all the scenarios where you are not at home, I recommend ready-to-eat food stores such as energy bars, crackers and cookies, dried fruit, nuts, candy bars and other similar foods.

HEAT AND/OR WARM CLOTHING

If you are at home and you lose electricity and gas, you still have all your clothes, jackets, coats, blankets and sleeping bags. You will be able to withstand any outside temperature because you have shelter and warm clothing/blankets. But if you get caught elsewhere, you will need to improvise. Obviously, a shopping mall will have stores with warm things for sale. In an office building, however, you will have to think outside the box. Hopefully, if it is autumn or winter, you already have a jacket or coat with you. Since you are now practicing Every Day Carry (pg. 19), you also have a lighter. You may have to find a safe place to build a fire. You can also use plastic trash bags to line your clothes. This will trap the body heat you generate inside with you instead of letting it escape. You can also line your clothes with newspapers or magazines. This functions on the same principle, but is less effective.

MEDICAL SUPPLIES

A first-aid kit is a must at home, at work and in your car. You should also have one in your bug-out bag. If you are dependent on any medication, you will need to think ahead and decide how much you can keep on hand to weather a shelter-in-place event. Keeping over-the-counter medications on hand can also add to your quality of life. You might want a pain reliever, cold medicine, decongestant, fever reducer, eye drops, etc. Only you can decide what you are willing (or physically able) to do without.

DUCT TAPE

This is like the Force—it has a light side and a dark side and it binds the universe together. Duct tape has abundant uses limited only by your own imagination. It can be used to seal, fix, create, bind, repair, stabilize, treat, mark and many other things (pg. 252). It is a fantastic multi-tool which should be found in your home, car, bug-out bag, office and just about every place you routinely spend time.

LIGHT

At home, you may choose to use candles. I recommend a head lamp, a hand-crank flashlight and a solar-powered lantern in your bug-out bag, at work and in your car. A flashlight and a headlamp are small and easy to carry but they only have a directed beam of light. If you need to light a wider area and be free to use both hands, a lantern works very well. You can set it down and it keeps the area illuminated and leaves your hands free.

BOOKS AND GAMES

Packing a book and a deck of cards will help alleviate boredom and boost morale. Boredom can set in quickly and lead to deteriorating morale. At home, you will have all your books, games and projects to keep you occupied. You might want to consider a pack of playing cards in your Every Day Carry kit or at least in your car. There are plenty of card games that can be played alone and even more that can be played with others. Cards are small, light and require no electricity. A book is also a good idea. Do not allow yourself to succumb to defeat solely because of boredom.

SPACE TO EXERT

Speaking of morale, people need to exert energy. We all need to work out. Fortunately, we can work out without a single piece of equipment if all we have is a little space. Running in place. Jumping jacks. Push ups. Sit ups. Stretching. The list is practically endless. As important as it is to plan against boredom and occupy your mind, it is equally important to plan for your body's need to exercise. Staying active, fit and strong goes a very long way toward living as a conqueror.

HYGIENE

Make sure to prioritize your own health and sanitation. Even if the running water is turned off or unsafe, use the bathtubs full of water to refill flushed toilets and take sponge baths. Keep your body clean. Use deodorant. Brush your teeth. Insist on maintaining the same standards of hygiene you use on normal days.

SECURITY

When disaster strikes, panicked people do crazy things, opportunistic people do illegal things and criminals do evil things. Pay attention to your surroundings. Form friendships quickly through kindness, helpfulness and generosity. Band together for mutual protection. Keep your knife handy. Remember to be situationally aware. Choose a lookout to keep watch while everyone gets some sleep. Diffuse tense situations and avoid getting into arguments. Exercise self control. Use patience. Stay away from unpredictable or hot-tempered people. Be cooperative.

There are so many things for which we cannot plan. We will not know which kind of disaster we may face or where we will be when it happens. However, if you live with these measures in place, you will be set up for maximum provision and comfort so that, when the day of adversity strikes, you will be a conqueror.

FORCE MULTIPLIERS

A force multiplier is anything that increases effectiveness and efficiency. For example, a car will carry you over a distance much faster than walking. Thus, the car is a force multiplier. There is a mathematical equation in this science: if you walk at three miles per hour and you drive the same route at 30 miles per hour, your force multiplication factor is 10. See how that works?

Anything, if used correctly, can be a force multiplier: personnel, tools, technology, information, intelligence, equipment, facilities, etc. We all tend to gravitate toward things that make our lives easier and allow us to do more in less time. Instinctively, we are looking for force multipliers all the time. We may not be thinking in those exact words, but that is nevertheless what we do. Take heating and air conditioning, for example. Companies that provide this equipment are forever researching and developing ways to make units smaller, lighter, less costly and more efficient. They are chasing force multipliers. How about computer technology? Every generation seeks to make smaller, lighter, faster, more capable machines with more memory for less money. Force multipliers.

The ultimate force multiplier is the smartphone. Think about it. It is a telephone; a GPS; a video game system; a mobile office; a library of books; a calculator; a data base; a text and email platform; a calendar; an address book; a phone book; a compass; a journal; a fitness coach; a search engine; an encyclopedia; a camera; a clock; a translator; a cash register; a planner and many, many more helpful things. Imagine if you had to carry all of those with you separately.

Now, how can we use this? If you find yourself in a survival situation, you will automatically begin to prioritize what to take and what to leave behind. It helps if you understand which pieces of gear are force multipliers. A tiny, folding pocket knife has very limited uses, but a larger, fixed-blade knife has many uses: it can be used in self-defense; to field dress a kill; to fillet meat or fish; to cut or chop small branches for firewood; to hack through undergrowth. It can be used as an ice pick and as a pry bar. See? Instead of having to carry all of these tools individually, one fixed-blade knife can be your force multiplier.

Self-defense techniques can also be prioritized by their force multiplication capabilities. If your time to study is limited, you can learn just a few techniques that have lots of power and many applications rather than learning every possible kind of strike. Some strikes are highly specialized, take lots of time to master and cannot generate much power. Instead of learning those, learn a few powerful techniques—such as front kicks, elbow strikes and knee strikes—which can be used on any body part in any orientation.

What about cash? Cash can be a force multiplier unto itself, but different countries use different currencies. In non-emergency times, credit cards are the universal currency. However, in a survival situation, you may want to take gold with you instead of paper. Gold is valuable in every country and will be a force multiplier.

How about a deck of cards? We have already discussed the importance of morale. Having something to do to stimulate your brain and pass the time is an excellent idea. We can assume that cell phones are not working at this point and that we do not want to carry around boxes for Monopoly, Life, Sorry, Pictionary, Clue, chess, checkers and backgammon. A simple and relatively tiny deck of cards can be slipped into any pocket and the games contained within are only limited by your imagination.

Now that you are thinking about the concept, try to imagine all the force multipliers you would choose to prioritize in an emergency, disaster, survival scenario or whenever adversity strikes. Thinking about these things now will help you decide what to grab when it is time to go.

LEAD, FOLLOW OR GET OUT OF THE WAY

By now, you know that I am trying to convey to you the importance of acting on your own behalf, being self-sufficient and capable of self-rescue. When disaster strikes, you are your own first priority. Fire and rescue services may or may not come; they may be obstructed from movement or they may have a thousand other calls besides yours. It is your responsibility to live in a way that is trained, equipped and prepared to look after yourself. After you have ensured your own safety, you will then be in a position to ensure the safety of others. Remember that survival is a byproduct of action.

In order to be in a position to rescue yourself, ensure your own safety and survival and help others to do the same, you need to put some critical things in place. The first thing you need is a sound knowledge base. You are already taking action to obtain that by reading this book. You need to know what could happen, what your options are and how to employ your skills.

You also need to spend time practicing the things you learn. Theoretical knowledge is better than none, but actually performing the skills in a non life-threatening situation first will give you the confidence that you can, in fact, do these things. Additionally, you will have the comfort of knowing that because you have done it before, you can do it again.

Decide upon and obtain whatever gear you feel you will need. Test it, practice with it and know how to use it well before you need to. Do the same with provisions. If you intend to use a camp stove to heat a can of ravioli in a disaster, give it a try now and understand how it works. Iron out the wrinkles.

When the day of adversity comes, be prepared to think, decide, take action and even lead others. People will look to the one with apparent knowledge and experience. When they see your level of readiness, they will suddenly want to be your best friend. Be prepared to answer questions, help treat wounds, find safety and shelter, secure or share provisions and make decisions for action. Be prepared to turn into a friend, parent, medic, scout, grocer, morale officer, diplomat, police officer or commander. The need for you to become these things may come up one at a time, but it will be in rapid succession until you are wearing all of these hats simultaneously.

Doing nothing is never the right answer. As stated above, it is the worst thing you can choose. Please do not mistake staying in place for doing nothing. Sheltering in place (pg. 24) might prove to be the best option. However, you arrive at that decision by analyzing the available data and making a choice. I guarantee that, even if you shelter in place, you will be doing plenty to treat medical needs, stay warm, stay safe, prepare food, eat and drink, keep arguments from turning into fights, provide for hygiene, cure boredom and boost morale.

No, we are not the responsibility of EMS, fire or search and rescue services. We are our own responsibility. How much is your life worth to you? Probably more than it is to a rescuer who has never met you and does not even know your name. If that is true, act like it. Prepare yourself and your loved ones with the right knowledge, experience, mindset and gear to handle adversity. Survival is not just about gear. It is about decision and action. Equipment does not save lives. Action saves lives.

THE FULCRUM PRINCIPLE

Every person has a fulcrum upon which their balance rests. It is composed of three parts: Physical, Emotional and Spiritual. Each of these three is equally important, and if any one of these is neglected, the entire person is out of balance. Each part must be invested in, protected and provided for in order to ensure a whole and healthy person.

PHYSICAL

Every person needs three main things, physically speaking: food, sleep and exercise. Not only does each person need these things, they need them in moderation. Eating is not all there is to food. A person's intake must be of nutritional value in healthy amounts. It does very little good to eat only junk food, just as it does very little good to eat only lettuce. Sleep is another input that must be moderated. We adults have terrible habits at times and often stay up way too late before getting up way too early. However, sleeping for 12 hours a day is no good either. Exercise can be just as tricky. Some of us are gym rats who cannot seem to work out enough for our own tastes, while others of us sit in the car on the way to work, then sit in front of our computer for eight hours, only to come home and sit in front of the television until bedtime. We all need good quality food, sleep and exercise in healthy amounts.

EMOTIONAL

It is important for us to do things that bring us happiness. That may be spending time pursuing a hobby, cultivating relationships or serving the world in some fashion. We need to allow ourselves to spend a moderated amount of time on the things that help us to relax, laugh and feel connected and useful. Again, too much time spent here leads to an imbalanced fulcrum, just as too little time does.

SPIRITUAL

Everyone believes something. Whatever your beliefs, dedicate time to practicing them. Set aside time to pray, meditate, read, reflect, worship, learn and grow. Neglecting the practices and tenets of your faith will also result in an imbalanced fulcrum.

If you prioritize your own fulcrum and invest time into all three categories on a regular basis, you will find yourself strong, resilient and ready to take on the challenges of adversity and emerge as a conqueror. Remember, advanced preparation (pg. 13).

SELF-SUFFICIENCY

The concept of self-sufficiency is not one we talk about much anymore. For some reason, we as a society have left that concept largely in the past. We enjoy an interconnected life, dependent on doctors for medical care, grocery stores for food, utility companies for electricity, dry cleaners for laundry, television for entertainment, mechanics for maintenance, department stores for clothing and specialists for everything. We do not repair things—we replace them. Gone are the days when most people knew how to fix and maintain everything they owned. Now, we make more money so that we can hire people to protect, provide, teach, defend, heal, fix, feed, clothe and shelter us. This works very well in our disposable society so long as nothing goes wrong. It is a system which cannot be upheld in the rest of the world and it patently will not work under certain kinds of adversity.

If you experience a widespread power outage for two months, how will you handle it? Will you be able to figure out a solution for refrigeration and freezing? How about heating or air conditioning? Light? Cooking? Plumbing? Cleaning? Sanitation? Hygiene? Entertainment? Do you have the knowledge base, training and skill set to improvise? Fix what is broken? Find a work-around solution? Defend your home? Feed yourself?

Figuring out how and why things work is a necessary data set. If you can understand the concepts at play, if you can understand how the world works, you can figure things out. I would rather understand general concepts and principles than I would try to memorize "how to" lists. A list tells me only which steps to take and in what order. Understanding concepts, on the other hand, helps me to figure things out on my own. If I understand the concept that watts divided by amps equals voltage, or that volts divided by amps equals resistance, that will help me troubleshoot and solve electrical problems. It is far more helpful to me to know principles than to memorize data for data's sake.

Sure, there is always the possibility someone will be there to help you. You may have a member of your own household—a neighbor, a friend or a relative who works in the right field—who can help you out of a bad situation. Then again, you might just find yourself completely alone. Suppose you are hiking or camping and you get separated from your companions and become hopelessly lost. Do you know everything you need to know in order to fend for yourself? Can you survive without help?

In technical scuba diving, we have a team concept called independent/interdependent. It means each member of the team will be trained, equipped and qualified to meet 100 percent of their own needs, even in an emergency. Although the team may have a common task, it is a team of solo divers. This is not meant to imply that we would not help a teammate out however we possibly could. It simply means everyone is trained for the difficulty/skill level of the dive, that everyone is carrying their own redundant gear and 1.5 times as much gas as they need to complete their dives. In an emergency, yes, the team is right there, standing by to be of assistance, but the diver in trouble is his or her own primary problem solver and rescuer.

This all goes back, of course, to advanced preparation. Take the time now to ensure that you have the understanding, knowledge base, skill set and tools to be your own problem solver and rescuer. It may prove to be the very best investment you will ever make.

PACE PLANNING

Have you ever heard of a PACE plan? It is meant to teach us how to think as we plan for anything. PACE stands for:

P - Primary

A - Alternate

C - Contingency

E - Emergency

The more options you have, the higher your chances of success. Since the potential cost is so high when dealing with a threat to life, limb, eyesight/hearing, freedom or property, you will want as comprehensive a plan as possible. A proper PACE plan allows the user to move seamlessly from one part of the plan to the next, mid mission.

To give you an idea of how this works, say that I am planning a hiking trip to a remote place, well out of cell coverage. I will need a communication-oriented PACE plan.

PRIMARY I may choose to use a satellite phone as my primary means of communication with the outside world.

ALTERNATE I could use a handheld radio as a backup to the satellite phone.

CONTINGENCY I might opt to use a PLB (personal locator beacon) to send a distress call.

EMERGENCY I will pack some flares, signal mirrors and whistles while also relying on my ability to make fire and smoke should I need to attract attention.

All in all, PACE planning comes in very handy for just about everything. It helps us think through our objective, the possible problems we may encounter and what we intend to do to overcome them, while telling us what to prioritize and how to pack.

THE OODA LOOP

OODA stands for Observe, Orient, Decide and Act. It is the process we go through in order to make an intelligent decision and ensure that our actions bring about the desired results.

O - OBSERVE

This is the part that usually gets short-changed, especially when timing is critical. In an active shooter situation, we do not have all day to observe—we have seconds. We have to fly through the steps in the OODA Loop and get to A (Action), because lives are on the line. However, in most situations in life, timing isn't quite as critical. Usually, we have more time to observe than we take.

O - ORIENT

This is my favorite step. This is when you have observed all the inputs you can, and now you need to determine how they impact you. What is your position, relative to your choices? For example, if you are lost and you pull out a map to help you get home, the very first thing you need to do (after observing that you are lost) is to orient yourself to the map. You have to observe the terrain and visual clues and then find that place on the map.

D - DECIDE

Easier said than done, right? Your observation and orientation gives you data from which to make your decision. Is it enough? What happens if it's not? When people do not feel that they have enough data to make a good decision, they naturally go back to the first step: Observe. Then they move on to Orient. This is a sound plan, as long as you continue to move on to the next step: Decide. Many times, I have seen people bounce back and forth, caught between Observe and Orient and unable to Decide and Act. This is exactly what is happening when someone freezes in fear. All they are doing is moving back and forth between steps one and two, unable to move on.

A - ACT

This is the part we like. Everyone likes to take action. It makes us feel better. We took in information. We figured out how it impacts us. We made a decision based on that information. Now it is time to carry out our decision: Act.

Then what happens? You guessed it! We go right back to step one: Observe. That is why it is called a loop. As soon as we get through the last step, we evaluate what we just did. That takes us back into observation mode.

This entire loop can occur in only a few seconds or, in the case of something like buying a house, it can take months. Being aware of the process can help in your decision making itself. Knowing the steps can clear confusion, calm chaotic thinking and slow the impulse to rush through things. Just knowing what your brain is up to can allow you to take control and decide things based on data instead of fear.

TRAIN, TRAIN AND TRAIN SOME MORE

None of us expects that after sitting on the couch for three years, we can instantly pop up, enter a competitive sport and win with no training. Or do we? Sometimes the decisions we make about life belie the fact that we think we have that ability. All of us want to win, perform and achieve. But very few of us want to put in the necessary work to make that a reality. I can think of many times in my life where I have expected perfection and a flawless performance out of myself when I have not yet put in the time to master the skills. Why should I expect to be able to watch someone do something and perform it myself with no mistakes on my first try? When you put it that way, it sounds ridiculous, yet we do it all the time.

Since 1992, I have studied 13 different combat arts styles from all over the world, including Korea, China, Philippines, Japan, Israel and the United States of America. I also have black belts, or their system equivalent, in 10 of those styles. I tell you this because I am by no means an inexperienced rookie; my opinion is drawn from more than two-and-a-half decades of firsthand experience. Of all the places where I have studied and trained, Kore Self Defense and Krav Maga in Ashburn, Virginia, is my absolute favorite. Aside from teaching my favorite style, Krav Maga, the personnel and facility at Kore are unmatched. Kore was established by Dr. Tammy McCracken, a psychotherapist. Her professionalism, love of learning, attention to detail, eye for quality and in-depth knowledge of human behavior show through in every single class. Kore is a physically and emotionally safe place to train in a curriculum that can keep you uncomfortably close to your classmates. It is tightly focused on skills, professionalism and being a good student and training partner, all of which have contributed to my ongoing drive to keep training after so many years. I know that I must keep up with my training if I expect to be able to handle a crisis when it comes.

All of us want to have a sense of personal security, to know that if we were attacked, we would be able to protect ourselves. That if there was a disaster in our immediate vicinity, we would be able to run. We expect we can already do these things, which is why we may not actually take the time to learn and train. Can we go straight from being couch potatoes to running for our lives or fighting off an attacker? Perhaps adrenaline alone might carry us a certain distance. But if we do not train, we will not have what we need when adversity strikes. It is that simple. Again, I harken back to advanced preparation of the battle space, but in this particular case, I am referring to our physical body.

If you want to have the stamina, speed and split-second decision making skills available to you, now is the time to begin cultivating them. Get into a routine and train. Ideally, you will need a combination of cardiovascular exercise and full body (muscular) exercise to achieve well-rounded results.

RUN - This is the easiest, cheapest, most simple workout you can do anywhere you go.

FIGHT - Take up some sort of fight training: combat/martial arts, boxing, wrestling, self-defense, etc.

SWIM - This low-impact activity is amazing at working all of your muscles against a small but constant resistance. It also improves coordination between thought and action.

LIFT WEIGHTS - This is the secret to keeping yourself toned and to burning fat.

ISOMETRIC EXERCISES - These require no equipment and practically no space. You can do these using only your body, the floor and perhaps a wall.

GET A HEAVY PUNCHING BAG AND SPAR WITH IT - Practice fighting from your feet and from the ground, drag it or hoist it to practice carrying a full-sized person.

Only through training do we learn and perfect skills. Only through training do we commit skills to muscle memory, condition our minds and bodies and break through our own limitations. If we are not willing to train, we have no just cause to believe we will have what it takes to survive if we ever need to run or fight.

DECIDE TO ACT

"The best thing you can do is the right thing. The second best thing you can do is the wrong thing. The worst thing you can do is nothing."

—PRESIDENT "TEDDY" ROOSEVELT

When action is required, these words of wisdom could not be more true. This applies to all four phases of adversity: preparation, during the event, the aftermath and the rebuilding. In all four stages, action is required. Why? Preparative action means you are thinking and planning for a stressful situation which may cause a temporary lapse in judgment or an inability to think clearly. You are calculating and acting in advance to ensure you are as ready as possible. We know if we do nothing in advance, we will not be as ready as we can be.

During the event, you will find yourself battling your instincts of fight, flight or freeze. Fighting, running and hiding might be necessary. However, all of these things are decisions and actions. It may be enough to simply get off the X—in other words, you may be able to walk away—but even that requires action.

In the aftermath, there is more action required. Sorting through the wreckage, physical or emotional, will help you find the things that are salvageable. This is the point at which we take stock of what we have left and decide how to use it wisely. We look for force multipliers (pg. 28). We begin to value each and every person and item as we never have before.

The rebuilding stage is arguably the most difficult. This is where we must make the conscious decision to live, to focus on what it is we are living for and face the future. This is where we opt not to wallow in what happened but to take actions that will set us up for healing, recovery and a new life. We must choose to be future-focused and move in the direction in which we orient ourselves. This takes fortitude, a strong constitution, resiliency and action.

Action does not create itself. We must take it after assessing our situation, gathering intelligence, exercising sound judgment and making decisions. Remember the OODA loop (pg. 35)? Observe. Orient. Decide. Act.

Prepare for action.

CHECK YOUR GEAR

So... camping. I will start with a story. The forecast was for rain but I am not faint of heart, I have no heartburn with rain. In fact, I love to listen to the rain from inside the tent. All one has to do is take the necessary precautions to ensure that all is waterproofed. Well, I decided to take some gear I had not used in almost exactly a year, a two-person tent and a single-sized air mattress. The road trip was 10 hours and I arrived at my destination with just enough light left to set up camp and settle in. I checked in and headed to my site. In the midst of setting up my tent, I tore a no less than four-inch hole in the top. Brilliant. Next, I unrolled the air mattress and hooked it up to my manual, plunger-style hand pump. I am tough and reasonably strong, and I began the lengthy task of putting air into the mattress. As it was raining, there was no evaporative cooling.

I worked hard. I panted and sweat and would not relent. I must have pumped away for half an hour. I had never used this pump with this mattress before and I was amazed at how long it was taking. An electric pump fills it in one minute flat. For what it is worth, I had recently inflated some 22-inch ball chairs and those took about 1,000 pumps each, and I was determined to be patient and have a good attitude about it. The rain came down harder and I moved the mattress inside the tent to keep it as dry as I could. I took a break from my inflating work and turned my attention toward the tear in the tent. After a quick once-over, it dawned on me I was missing a key piece of equipment. Remember: two is one and one is none. I know this. I live by it. It is deeply ingrained in my code of conduct to buy and keep ready three to five backups of each piece or gear on my minimum equipment list. I had moved my duct tape to a different gear bag than the one I had brought with me. Grrrr. But OK, I thought. Not insurmountable. I headed out to buy a tent repair kit. Although I got the kit, it was absolutely no help whatsoever. It refused to adhere to either the inside of the outside of the tent. Alright, time to think outside the box, I told myself. I will just use one of the tarps I brought to create a watershed over the tent. Now, where are those tarps? Oh dear. They are 10 hours away, back at the ranch. No worries. What else do I have? Ah, a plastic tube tent. That will work.

I cut the tube open and stretched it over the top of the tent. I knew I brought paracord but could not locate it and time was ticking. The sun was going down. I located my bungee cords, cut them, fastened them to the corners of the plastic and then staked them to the ground. One item down. Now, how about that mattress? I went back into the tent and it was totally flat. So much for all my hard work. My 8,000 repetitions on that plunger, my sweat and exhaustion were all for naught. Being the person of action I am, I set about the task of filling that air mattress with renewed vigor. I put in another 8,000 repetitions and still only managed to get it filled half-way. What on earth was wrong? Forget it. New focus. I went to the store (again) and bought some duct tape. I managed to seal the hole in the tent, which was now under plastic. But I soon noticed I was getting hungry. I needed a fire.

The wood was wet, so I wound up spending time slicing off shavings and creating a feather stick. True to my code, I had a lighter, matches and flint with me; I opted for the lighter. Without too much trouble, I did manage to get a nice fire going. I sat down to enjoy my dinner and proceeded to do the anti-smoke dance. Everywhere I went, there it was. I was trying to enjoy my dinner without burns and excessive smoke inhalation. OK. Dinner accomplished. Now, back to that mattress...

There it lay, flat and lifeless, taunting me. It must have a leak, I reasoned. I put more air into it and listened carefully. If I could find the hole, I now had

MASTER TACTIC

Whatever time it takes to double or triple-check your gear cannot possibly compare to the headache (or even potential danger) you will face should you fail to notice your gear needs fixing. Take the extra minute or five. Prep now or pay later. The choice is yours.

the duct tape to patch it. No noise. The air disappeared but there was no clue about its source. Now completely exhausted, I abandoned the idea of sleeping in comfort and resigned myself to a night on hard, wet, cold ground. As I lay there listening to the sound of the rain hitting the roof of the tent, I had to laugh at myself. Here I am, survivor extraordinaire, and I am paying the price for breaking my own rules.

Two is one and one is none. Make sure you have multiples of everything you need so that you are never without the means to solve your problems.

Check your gear regularly. Had I taken the time to check them after a year of non-use, I would have known the air mattress had a hole and the tent fabric was stuck in a hinge.

Attitude is everything. The battle space is first and foremost the mind. Stay calm and reason your way out of tough situations. Think outside the box and be willing to use conventional items in unconventional ways to solve your problems.

Be willing to work hard.

Make sure to leave yourself enough daylight to set up your site and factor in additional time in case you encounter problems to solve.

Be willing to cannibalize your gear if it will keep you safe, dry, warm, watered or fed.

YOUR BODY

Preparing and training for survival does no good if you are not taking care of yourself right now. Advanced preparation applies as much to your body as it does to your mind. We have talked at length about preparing your mind as well as training your body. But how about the way you live? Do you make daily decisions that will establish a pattern of strength and effectiveness now? It will not magically appear when you need it unless you have been cultivating it in advance.

None of this is rocket science. We all know the importance of getting enough sleep, eating a healthy diet and exercising. What about the "little" decisions? Are you a little too dependent on caffeine, alcohol, nicotine or tobacco? What about vaping? How about over-the-counter medications like aspirin, ibuprofen or acetaminophen? What about sugar? How about the number of hours dedicated to watching television, or web surfing or social media? Is your cell phone an addiction? In what ways are you saddling yourself with too much extra weight?

All of these things can take a toll on your physical health. If we live for today and indulge our every craving, what will happen in a crisis when those things are unavailable? What happens if you enter that situation with notable dependencies? Anyone who suddenly finds themselves thrust into a survival situation wants to be on top of their game. Trying to deal with an unfolding crisis is enough of a challenge without it being compounded by withdrawal symptoms from an unfulfilled dependency. Combining the two is likely to make you a liability to your team as you struggle to function let alone survive.

Now is the time to evaluate your physical body, make some decisions and take action.

RABID CHIPMUNK

In the United States, there is an 85 percent drop in survival rate when a kidnap victim allows themselves to be moved to a secondary location. Sometimes what begins as a robbery or mugging culminates with a kidnapping. Aside from places along the Texas/Mexico border, the United States has almost no kidnappings for the purpose of gaining a ransom. Instead, the kidnappings that occur here are for much more gruesome purposes. Sadly, most U.S.-based kidnappings are perpetrated with the ultimate intention of committing human trafficking, rape and/or murder.

If someone pulls a weapon on you and demands your valuables, the smart thing to do is to relinquish your valuables and let the perpetrator get away. However, if anyone tries to take you into their custody and move you from the place of the initial encounter to any other location, then by all means, FIGHT! DO NOT allow yourself to be moved! Do whatever it takes.

Imagine having an encounter with a rabid chipmunk. How would that animal behave? What would they do? Though tiny, the thought of that kind of an encounter is enough to strike fear into even the most stalwart of hearts. Can you out-maneuver a mad chipmunk? Is there anything you could do to be just as savage and downright crazy?

If you are accosted in the United States for the purposes of kidnapping, become a rabid chipmunk. Fight. Kick. Growl. Claw. Roar. Punch. Scream. Bite. Squeeze. Strangle. Pummel. Stab. Do absolutely anything it takes to prevent your attacker from dragging you to another location. Go crazy. Make noise. Strike Strike Strike Strike Strike until they let go. Do not stop until they collapse or run away in fear. Do not allow yourself to quit. Your life depends upon your ability to harness your inner chipmunk.

PRIORITIES

Throughout life's seasons, our level of effectiveness is determined by our ability to set and maintain our priorities. It does you no good to set priorities and then abandon them in times of adversity. That is when we need them most! In aviation, there is an expression: "Plan your flight and fly your plan." This means to stick to the plan you developed, even in the midst of chaos, uncertainty and doubt. Is there a time and a place to re-evaluate your plan? Absolutely. There are things that may force you off course and you may have to rearrange your plan, but keeping your priorities intact will help you find your way in the midst of confusing inputs.

Remembering these priorities in this crucial order will help you stay calm and focused. It will give your chaotic situation some structure, build your morale as you accomplish important things for yourself and give you the most efficient system by which you will increase your own chances of survival to the maximum extent.

SURVIVAL PRIORITIES IN ORDER OF IMPORTANCE	
IN COLD/WET WEATHER	**IN WARM/DRY WEATHER**
• Remove wet clothes, then find dry clothes	• Getting found or self-rescue
• Medical treatment of wounds or injuries	• Medical treatment of wounds or injuries
• Warmth	• Water
• Shelter	• Shelter/shade
• Protection	• Protection
• Water	• Food
• Food	• Getting found or self-rescue
• Getting found or self-rescue	

COMBAT BREATHING

All of us seek ways to lower our stress, anxiety and blood pressure. In a survival situation, this needs to achieve immediate results. There is a technique called combat breathing. It is something snipers use before taking their shot. It is something skydivers use before jumping. It is something combat divers do, real-time, as they lay mines and traverse through zero-visibility waters. Performers use it, too, before walking out on stage. Acrobats use it before engaging in death-defying stunts.

This is a ridiculously simple technique that slows the heart rate, calms the nerves and focuses the mind.

1. Get into a physically comfortable, seated position.

2. Close your eyes and imagine yourself in a peaceful and beautiful place where there is perfect safety and security.

3. Put your hands on your knees.

4. Breathe in through your nose for 4 seconds. Imagine yourself filling your belly, not your lungs, with this air. Let your stomach expand.

5. Hold your breath in that stomach-expanded position for 4 seconds.

6. Breathe out through your mouth for 4 seconds. Let your imagination show you that your in-breath fills you with light and peace. Your out-breath expels darkness and turmoil.

7. Repeat this technique for 5 or 10 minutes, as time allows.

It may seem too simple to be effective, but give it a try. You will feel calm, tranquil and relaxed immediately upon finishing.

If you see the problem coming and have the time, this technique can be used in advance of the problem's arrival. If you have no advanced warning and must deal with the problem first, this technique can help you recover and decompress. In a hyper stressful situation like self-defense or survival, this technique will help you focus. It will allow you to get ahead of your fears and clear your mind to support good decision making.

A MEDIUM OF EXCHANGE

In the South Pacific, the people of Yap, an island in Micronesia, have predicated their culture on betel nuts, which stain your teeth a dark shade of burgundy and produce a noticeable high when chewed. To intensify the effects, they add tobacco, mint and lime dust from coral which has been baked for three days. Consuming these nuts is seen as a rite of passage, a visible signifier of adulthood for both men and women, and men have been known to chew as many as 70 a day. Culturally, the Yapese people label everyone with white teeth a child, as people are expected to begin eating betel nuts at 12 years of age (and to keep eating them for the rest of their lives). Anyone with white teeth is believed not to have learned how to be respectful yet. The darker the teeth, the more the respect. It has become their standard of measure.

I had no idea this addiction was so incredibly ingrained and that part of their very culture is derived from it. I wonder what we have in our culture that addicts us the same way. Could it be alcohol? Television? Video games? Sugar? Caffeine? Instant gratification? Cell phones? Social media? When the people of Yap come here, what do they see? Do the cultural impacts of our addictions make as little sense to them as betel nuts make to us? How would these things help or harm us in a crisis or survival situation?

But Yap is known for more than just its betel nuts. One thing, above all, makes it famous: stone money. The Yapese have disc-shaped stone money, each with a hole in the center. Even more remarkable than the material out of which the money is made is the sheer size of it. Some of the coins can fit in your hand, whereas others are 10 feet tall. Going to a Yapese bank, I felt a little like I was about to meet Fred Flintstone. Seeing the coins towering above me, my first thought was that it made no sense. No one can even move them, let alone carry them. How could they be considered money? Then it occurred to me. It makes about as much sense as carrying around pieces of paper in our wallets that we can exchange for food, toys or anything else we want. The paper money we carry has no inherent value as paper alone. A piece of paper could never be worth as much as a television. So, how does it really differ?

We have all agreed to value the little pieces of paper in our wallets the same way that the Yapese people have agreed to value the stones (and betel nuts, for that matter). Owning a stone or a share in a stone is like having cash in the bank. You can use a debit card or write a check to represent the physical money you have, and use it to buy whatever you need. The person receiving the payment accepts the check or debit card in exchange for their goods or services and the transfer of money from your account to theirs is made later. Does it matter if the money is paper or stone? Neither one is used for anything beyond representing wealth. Everyone agrees to value the money the same way and, as a result, it can be used as a medium of exchange.

It used to be much tougher to make a sale. Before money, you had to have something to offer in trade that the other person wanted. If I wanted a chicken and I had a blanket to offer, I would have to find someone who wanted a blanket who also had a chicken to sell. Having that medium of exchange meant that the person with the chicken to sell could accept the money and then use it to get whatever they needed, whenever they needed it. A much easier system in my opinion.

So why bring this up? Whether in a survival situation or in international travel, we must be ready to trade in a currency that works in that place and situation. Not every place on earth accepts electronic transactions. Not every place takes

MASTER TACTIC

Consider not only what valuable items or goods you have but what worthwhile skills you could offer should a crisis arise. What could you do for others that would have value and worth if money suddenly meant next to nothing?

U.S. dollars. And in a catastrophic situation when electricity is gone and banks are down, paper cash almost immediately loses its appeal. There are situations and times where having something like silver or gold will be met with much more universal acceptance. However, in a true survival situation, even precious metals are devalued. Imagine a man who has been lost in the desert for three days. He is weak, dehydrated and sunburned. If you cross paths with him and offer him a bar of gold or a gallon of water, which one do you think he will choose?

This is where we go back to advanced preparation. I know there are some folks who stock up on things like ammunition because they believe, in a widespread disaster, bullets will have more value for trade than money. One well-placed bullet can fell a deer that can feed several families. Other people stock water and food for trade. Still others stock paracord, matches and knives. Some convert cash to precious metals. What really matters is that you have a plan. Think about being thrust into a situation where the paper in your wallet is worthless. You may be entirely self-sufficient, but I suspect you will need something more than you can grow, hunt or provide at some point. What will you use as your medium of exchange?

LAYERED SECURITY

Layered security is a concept that can be carried out anywhere: at home, at work, in your car, in your neighborhood or on your person. It can even be expanded out to include your geographic area.

We alluded to layered security on your person in the Every Day Carry section (pg. 19), which explored what tools to carry and how to carry them effectively. The underlying concept, of course, is layered security. If you have a firearm on your belt, a knife in your boot and a tactical pen in your pocket, you have just layered your security. Likewise, if you have a taser in the glove compartment of your car, a knife in the armrest and a gun in the trunk, you have layered security. The same is true if you have firearms in your house, in your car and safely geocached elsewhere.

One of the most effective ways of layering your security is through relationships. Make friends with your next door neighbors. Then make friends on your street. Then make friends in your neighborhood. Make friends in your town. All of these friend circles will serve as an integrated threat detection and early warning system for you. If you take cookies to your neighbors, if you use your snowblower to clear their driveways as well as your own, if you invite their kids to come over and play with your kids, you are developing and maintaining layered security. These folks will go out of their way to tell you if something is amiss in the neighborhood. Perceived threats will be shared and discussed. That is exactly how neighborhood watches are formed.

We all know the old adage, "Don't put all your eggs in one basket." It may be provincial but it really is quite sage advice. We have already learned that "two is one and one is none," which means we need more than just one tool upon which to rely. Taken slightly further, we also need those tools spread across multiple locations. I may not be able to get to my trunk, but I can get to my glove compartment or my armrest. In a fight, I may not be able to get to my belt, but I can easily reach my breast pocket. This is layered security.

At work, you may have a locked entrance that requires a badge to access. You may have a metal detector screening all incoming personnel. You may have cameras mounted outside and inside the building, security guards and locked doors. Even Common Access Cards (CAC) are part of it. Perhaps you have access to vaults and Sensitive Compartmented Information Facilities (SCIFs). All of these things are examples of layered security.

Your security is only as good as the thought, time, effort and preparation you put into it. Whether that means training in self-defense, preparing a geocache of gear or carrying tools on your person, no one will take your security as seriously as you will. Spend a little time educating yourself, practicing skills and procuring gear and you will breathe easier as you reap the benefits of living securely.

IN A MULTITUDE OF COUNSELORS, THERE IS SAFETY

I readily admit I am not the be-all and end-all of safety, security or survival. That being said, I do know my way around these subjects very well and have been studying, training, practicing and living them for many years. However, now is the time for you to seek counsel elsewhere as well. I am not going anywhere, nor am I suggesting that you forget about all I have told you. What I am suggesting is that you get as much feedback from as many knowledgeable sources as you can.

Right now, in the midst of normal life, when all is well, is the perfect opportunity to go out and talk to people. Go to your local outdoor store and see what the latest tips and tricks are for campers and backpackers. Go to the range and talk to the firearms instructors about the performance, cost and reliability of various products. Visit preparedness websites and ask your questions. Read about the goings on in the world on one of the State Department's sites like *OSAC.gov* (Overseas Advisory Council). Search YouTube for life hacks that might come in handy in a pinch. Take a class at a local martial arts school. Join a gym. Go camping or hiking. Try your gear. Make sure you know if, how and in what scenarios it all works.

Why do I say this? Well, different experts have different opinions. When you take the time to talk to people from a wide range of backgrounds, you can gather a wide range of opinions. Then you can try the skills and the gear and begin to select the tools with which you craft your tool kit. There are things you will like, agree with and understand. Integrate those. Likewise, there are things you will not like, agree with or understand. Feel free to consider them for a moment, then set those aside. There are also what I call neutral things. Trust me, you have lots of room in that tool kit. You might as well include things that are neutral to you. Who knows, you may find them handy someday. The key is to act now. Prepare now. Educate yourself now. Practice now. Do not wait until crisis time. That will always be too late.

Always remember advanced preparation of the battle space (pg. 13).

GEAR RECOMMENDATIONS

These are, hands down, my all-time favorite brands. I have field tested them for many years and come to rely on them so often that I can say I have literally staked my life on their reliability.

CAMP STOVES: Esbit, BioLite

PARACORD: Tough-Grid

KNIVES: Spyderco's Police, Benchmade's SOCP Dagger, Cold Steel's Espada and Spikes and Emerson's Super and Combat Karambits, CRKT's Provoke Karambit and Fox's Karambit

BEACON: SPOT

TACTICAL PENS: Cool Hand, 5.11 and Smith & Wesson

PISTOL: SIG Sauer (P320)

HOLSTER: Safariland

TOURNIQUET: RATS Medical

BANDAGE/DRESSING: QuikClot

ISRAELI PRESSURE BANDAGE: First Care

TRAUMA SHEARS: Leatherman

EMERGENCY MEDICAL SUPPLIES: Adventure Medical Kits

DEHYDRATED FOOD PACKS: Mountain House, Ready Hour, ReadyWise, Patagonia and My Patriot Supply

BLANKET: Get Out Gear

SLEEPING BAG: Marmot

SOLAR CHARGER: Sunkingdom

WATER PURIFIER: Sawyer Products

BACKPACK: Gregory, Deuter and Marmot

DECK OF CARDS: Gemaco

EMERGENCY BLANKET/ TENT/SLEEPING BAG: Don't Die In The Woods

FLINT: UST BlastMatch

FUEL CELLS: WetFire, Expedition Research and Esbit

MATCHES: UCO Stormproof

LANTERN: Mpowerd (Inflatable Solar Lantern)

RAPPELLING ROPE: Black Diamond and Blue Water

WEBBING: Blue Water

LEATHER GLOVES: Petzl

CLIMBING/RAPPELLING CARABINERS: Black Diamond

FIGURE 8 DESCENDER: Black Diamond

HARNESS: Black Diamond and Misty Mountain

HEAD LAMP: Black Diamond

WATER PURIFICATION TABLETS: Taharmayim (Israeli)

WATER BAGS / BLADDER: CamelBak

TRAIL SOAP: Sea to Summit

TOWEL: Sea to Summit

FLASHLIGHT: Pelican

BATTERIES: Duracell

HAND CRANK FLASHLIGHT: Secur

HAND CRANK RADIO: iRonsnow

PENCILS: Paper Mate

WATERPROOF PAPER: Rite in the Rain

KNIFE SHARPENER: Smith's

TACTICAL TOMAHAWK: SOG

CARGO PANTS: L.L.Bean

SHIRTS: L.L.Bean

BASE LAYER: Smartwool and Patagonia

SOCKS: Smartwool

HAT FOR WARMTH: Smartwool

FOLDING SHOVEL: SOG

MULTI-TOOL: Leatherman

JACKET: Mountain Hardwear

GORE-TEX OUTER SHELLS: Mountain Hardwear, Columbia and North Face

HIKING BOOTS: ASOLO

COMPASS: Suunto

FISHING LINE AND HOOKS: Best Glide and Grim Survival

GALLON/QUART BAGS: Ziploc

TOILET PAPER: Cottonelle Wipes

LIP BALM: Vaseline

SUNBLOCK: Banana Boat

SUNGLASSES: Costa Del Mar

BLOUSING BANDS: U.S. Army

KETTLE: GSI Outdoors

EATING UTENSIL: GSI Outdoors

METAL CAMPING CUP: Snow Peak

BOWLS: Guyot, Outdoor Research and Mountain Hardware

HAMMOCK AND STRAPS: Eagles Nest Outfitters (ENO)

ONE-PERSON TENT: Eureka!

SLEEPING PAD: NEMO

CANDLES: UCO

PONCHO: Helikon-Tex

TARP/EMERGENCY SHELTER: Free Soldier

SURVIVAL CARDS: Grim Survival

EMERGENCY WATER PACKS: SOS

LOCK PICKS: SouthOrd

CALM IS CONTAGIOUS BUT PANIC KILLS

Panic is abandoning logic and reason for unthinking instinct. In most cases, instinct is a very good thing, designed to keep us safe. However, when dealing with panic, the things our instincts drive us to do can get us killed.

I was scuba diving on a closed-circuit rebreather system, designed to extend bottom time and shorten decompression obligations for technical diving. It uses a closed breathing loop comprising oxygen, a diluent gas (in this case air) and a scrubber which removes carbon dioxide and allows only oxygen to pass back through to the diver. This feels very different than open circuit and I had just gotten certified, so I was utilizing a trip to the Caribbean to get comfortable with the feel of it.

I had carefully transported it and painstakingly set it up for diving the night I arrived. For the first half of the first day, my buddy warned me I had a small leak coming from my over pressure valve. This valve is exactly like the ones found on all dry suits and does the same job: automatically relieving my loop when there is too much volume. My buddy tried to troubleshoot it underwater. No dice. He asked me if I wanted to continue the dive or abort. I opted to continue and planned to have a closer look at it once we were back at the dock. I finished that dive without further issue.

At the dock later that day, I took the valve out to inspect it visually for cracks. Nope, no cracks found. Nothing noteworthy to report at all. After my buddy put a bit of plumber's tape on the threads and reinstalled it for me, I headed back out to dive. I admit I did not closely inspect the valve once it was replaced. (We will call this mistake number one.) When I put the unit back on, I reached behind me and turned my cylinders on, one small twist each. (Wrong! Mistake number two.) The oxygen cylinder requires only one small twist, yes, but the diluent cylinder is the same as an 80-cubic foot open circuit tank. This cylinder must be opened up wide to allow for any flow at all under pressure.

I splashed first and began my swim toward the anchor line. All of a sudden, I realized two things at once: I was taking water in through my mouthpiece and I felt like Wile E. Coyote when someone hands him an anvil. I have never felt so heavy! As I plummeted toward the bottom, I switched to open circuit via my bailout valve, a device mounted on the mouthpiece of the loop. With one 90 degree twist, the user can switch back and forth between open circuit and closed circuit modes. In the open circuit mode, I was drawing directly from my diluent bottle. You know, the one I had failed to open all the way. Nothing happened. In closed circuit mode I got water. In open circuit mode, I got nothing at all. While my mind was ripping through possible causes at a mile a minute, I realized I did not have any flotation either. The diluent cylinder is plumbed into the Buoyancy Compensation Device and supplies the gas for flotation, the same as it does on open circuit. As I descended uncontrollably, breathing became a secondary concern and I swam for the anchor line with all my might.

When I finally reached it and arrested my descent, I was able to ditch my loop and switch to my open circuit bailout cylinder. This is a standard part of every rebreather diver's gear. It is an entirely independent cylinder, usually slung on the side of the diver. It provides backup gas in case it should become necessary to abandon the closed loop. I was instantly engulfed in clouds of bubbles from my exertion and heightened anxiety level. I pulled myself up the line, struggling to calm myself down and troubleshoot at the same time. I knew that I HAD turned my diluent on. I could remember doing it. Why couldn't I access it? I pulled myself hand over hand to the surface. As my head broke the surface of the water, the dive master on the boat asked me if I was OK. I shook my head no.

The waves were still breaking over my head and I was not willing to part with my regulator yet. When I brought myself under control, I realized that I would have to let go of the line in order to swim to the ladder. Not doing! I still had no flotation. I seriously considered ditching my unit when I decided to try opening my diluent valve further. The sea state was about six feet, so it took me a minute

---

MASTER TACTIC

Panic sets in the moment we believe we are no longer in control. Every second is an opportunity for action. You do not have to immediately give in to instinct. Remember your training. Keep a cool head and the rest will follow.

of fighting to let go of the line with my left hand, make a space between my bailout cylinder and myself, find the valve and open it. Now, I had flotation. I was able to inflate my BCD, let go of the line, make my way to the ladder and re-board the boat. When I broke the unit down, I found the scrubber canister flooded to the top, as well as the breathing hoses.

Needless to say, I was quiet and introspective for the rest of the day. I scrutinized what had happened. I can only surmise that the over pressure valve itself had gotten stuck down or cross-threaded during reinstallation. I should have made a close visual inspection of it, but more importantly, I should have done another round of positive/negative pressure checks before getting back in the water. These checks are done before the first dive of every day and whenever the loop seal is broken for any reason, and they are designed to show the diver the system is truly closed and ready to dive. I also realized that while I had turned my diluent on, I had only opened it by half a turn, meaning it was no good to me under pressure for bailout gas or flotation. I also never anticipated having two dramatic problems at once; having no flotation and nothing to breathe at the same time is not fun. I did learn, though, that it does not have to kill you. Ultimately, my training kicked in just as it was designed to. Although I admit I was scared, I did not panic. I knew what I had to do—I had been trained to handle a flood and I did it. Admittedly, I was never trained to handle a no gas and no flotation scenario, so I had to write a few protocols on my own.

I took some very important lessons away with me that day. The buddy checks that had been so critical when sport diving seemed to have faded to the background when I turned the corner of technical diving. Those should be more important to me now than ever. I have more gear and more technology on me than I used to. Two sets of eyes should make sure that everything is good before I splash. I need to take the time to inspect all my gear thoroughly and to make sure all of my gear actually passes the pre-dive checks before getting in. I need to set my unit up the way I was taught to before every dive; diluent all the way on!

I also learned the things that I had done right: I did not panic. I retained my ability to think and reason through the situation instead of giving way to animal instinct. I attribute my ability to handle the situation to the fact that I had such good instruction and the fact that I had only just come out of the course. I am a big believer in practicing the skills I was taught. We had gone over the flood drill more than any other skill in the class. As a result, I had the knowledge and ability to handle a real one. Since these drills were so fresh in my head, I did not hesitate to carry them out. If it had been years since my training, the outcome might have been very different. This reinforced the theory that it is necessary to practice all life-saving skills on a regular basis.

Naturally, I must assume all of the responsibility for what happened that day. I know that the entire incident was user error. I know now what I will and will not do again. I also assume the credit for a successful self-rescue. I did not panic. I was focused and remained calm. Because I was calm, my dive buddy was calm too. If I had panicked, he might have done the same, and the outcome would have been significantly different. It gave me confidence in my instructor, my training, myself and in the system. I can now attest to the fact that what you are taught truly does work and might save your life. Calm is contagious but panic kills.

ALWAYS BE KIND

It would never occur to most of us that kindness can be a survival skill. In fact, we might think exactly the opposite. My mind rushes to situations where we are being attacked and our gear is being demanded of us. It seems kindness is the very last thing we should show in a nightmarish situation like that. Kindness equals weakness, right? Have you ever heard of the phrase "enlightened self-interest?" It means seeing how something could possibly benefit you even when it only appears to benefit someone else.

Imagine this. You are traveling overseas and planning to stay a while. You initially meet people at your destination and you treat them kindly. You smile. You help. You laugh. You make friends. You give. You develop relationships. You begin to become part of the community. But one day, bad guys begin to show up and case the area. They are looking for lucrative targets and asking around. Their intention: kidnapping for ransom. Which of your friends or neighbors is going to care enough to protect you? Will they give you an early warning of the danger and advise you to leave or hide? Or will they callously aid the bad guys in your abduction?

Think back to any movie you can recall where there has been an antagonist throughout the story, someone who lives selfishly and treats everyone poorly. The viewing audience is not the least bit upset when that person gets swallowed up by a volcano or pushed over a cliff or eaten by a monster. In fact, they are relieved and downright glad to see him or her gone. They might even cheer. Now, think about the contrast in the reaction when a beloved character gets killed. There is great sadness, shock, anger, even tears. Why? One character lived by kindness. One character lived by selfishness. In the end, it makes a massive difference.

On the surface, kindness may seem to only benefit the recipient. But in reality, its long-lasting benefits are for the giver. Showing kindness is like making a deposit into a savings account—the funds will be there for you to draw out when you need them. Spend time showing intentional kindness during times of normalcy. When the day of adversity comes, those to whom you have been kind will care enough to help you in whatever way they can.

ASK

We humans have an aversion to asking for help. We all want to be seen as strong and self sufficient. No one wants to humble themselves by admitting that they have any sort of need. Some people take it so far that they will not even go see a doctor when they are sick or injured. That is the opposite of advance preparation of the battle space.

In a travel or survival situation, you might forget that your best resource is going to be other human beings. You must learn how to ask for what you need. In fact, you should ask for more than you need, just in case. Who knows? You might get it. If not, asking for more than you need gives you wiggle room for negotiation, should it come to that.

Of course, if people are unaware of your need, they cannot be expected to offer help upfront. Your humble request makes them aware of your need and appeals to them to get directly involved. "Ask and it shall be given to you." When in need, ask. It might just save your life.

PERSONAL PREPAREDNESS

TIPS FOR LIVING IN "CONDITION YELLOW" ALL YEAR LONG.

WHEN IT COMES to survival, the best thing we can do is practice our skills as often as possible. For many of us, that means incorporating our alert mindset into our daily habits any way we can, secure in the knowledge that when danger inevitably strikes, we will already know exactly what to do and can jump into action. From knowing how to assess and mitigate risks to trusting your instincts to varying your routes in case you suspect you are being followed, these helpful habits will maximize your level of personal security seven days a week.

LIAR, LIAR

Have you been to school for kinesics? Most of us have not. Do you know what it is? It is the study of the way in which certain movements and gestures serve as a form of nonverbal communication. In other words, the study of body language and facial expressions.

It doesn't take a whole lot of imagination to understand why it is important to know when someone is lying to you. If you are in need of a ride, and a stranger tells you he is an Uber driver, what do you do? If someone offers to sell a valuable item to you at an alarmingly low price, what then? If your teenager tells you they are going to be at a friend's house studying, how do you know if that is true?

There is a simple, straightforward way to determine if a person is recalling data or creating data as they speak to you. Start by asking the person a series of innocuous questions for which they must recall data. You might ask them what they had for lunch today or what time they went to bed last night or what they wore yesterday. When they answer, pay close attention to what they do with their eyes. Do they close them or keep them open? Do they look up and right? Up and left? Down and right? Down and left? Straight up? Straight down? Do they keep level eye contact with you the entire time and never look away?

People's brains store and recall memories in one place and create information in another. This usually shows up physically when they respond to questions. If I ask my children what they had for dinner last night, I can watch their eyes: they look down and left. "What did you do today?" They answer while looking down and left. One more question just to be sure. "Did you have coffee this morning?" Their eyes go down and left. Now I know where they need to look in order to access their memory centers.

Now, on to the creativity center. I might ask them what they would recommend I do to decorate the walls on the main floor at home. I then watch their eyes. Their answer requires creativity, and I watch what they do. As they ponder their answer to my question, they look up and left. I now know how they access their creativity center. The data recall center and the data creativity center are NEVER in the same place. So, I now know when they are trying to recall something, they look down and left. When they are trying to create something, they look up and left.

So, when they tell me that they are going to study at their friend's house, I watch their eyes. For their sake, they had better look down and to the left. Truth is recalled. Lies are created.

TRUST YOUR INSTINCTS

Years ago, I was taking my instrument check ride with the Federal Aviation Administration (FAA). I had been flying my airplane for a few years already at that point and I knew it very well. I was flying a brand new type of aircraft and I was the first person in history to do my instrument training and check ride in this particular kind of airplane. There were no established performance numbers yet. We had to discover them. My instrument flight instructor and I had taken great pains and copious amounts of time to establish all the performance numbers associated with both precision and non-precision approaches. In fact, we were the ones who provided these new numbers to the aircraft manufacturer. I knew exactly what numbers I needed to set on the manifold pressure and the RPMs in order to get a certain airspeed and descent rate. After conducting weeks of testing, we had the numbers down to an exact science. Once they were proven, we used them over months of training. We made a quick-reference card for the cockpit so that we would always use the same settings. There is a saying in aviation that "perfect numbers produce predictable performance." The saying is accurate, and it had always worked for me until...

The day of my check ride. We had gone through all of the in-flight maneuvers and were moving on to flying approaches. But for whatever reason, I could not get the performance out of the airplane I knew I should be getting. I had been the researcher who discovered the numbers. I had been the test pilot who proved the concept. I had flown by these numbers for a long time and they had never let me down. However, as I was trying to fly some non-precision approaches on my check ride, the performance of the airplane was noticeably sluggish. I went over everything in my head. I had the numbers memorized, inside and out, but I compared them to my reference card, just in case. They matched. I asked myself about the payload. The fuel level was the same as usual. The FAA examiner was within 10 pounds of being the same size as my instructor. There was no extra cargo onboard. What was wrong? I kept pushing the manifold pressure and RPMs higher and higher to get the same performance I should have gotten at much lower numbers.

The examiner noticed my consternation and asked me what was wrong. I explained the problem and he suggested that I was nervous because this was a check ride. He told me to stop chasing the problem and look for trends. I did, but the trends just proved my own conclusions. Something was wrong. The numbers were not working that day. I told the examiner all of this and he patiently told me to establish new numbers and fly the approaches. I did, but I kept a serious eye on everything and made a mental note of exactly how much extra power I was using to get the same performance as usual.

I finished the check ride carrying higher power and RPM settings and landed back at my home airport. When I got out of the plane and walked around it for a post-flight inspection, I noticed a huge black scorch mark on the cowling around the engine. Alarmed, I had maintenance come and tow the airplane down to their hangar and pull it apart. What they found was that I had cracked a manifold in flight. By the scorching, they could tell that if the flight had lasted much longer, we would have had an in-flight fire. I had been right all along: something was wrong. I knew my airplane and I knew the numbers, and because of that, I knew what I should have been getting and that needing so much extra power meant something was seriously amiss. It pains me to say, but I should have trusted myself and followed my own instincts that day. Instead, I deferred to the superior wisdom and experience of the FAA examiner, a well-meaning move that nonetheless could have easily spelled disaster for us both.

In a security or survival situation, always trust your instincts. If you feel that something is wrong, it probably is. Go with that. Act according to your own good judgment and do not be bullied or manipulated into following someone else's judgment when you disagree. The life you save may be your own.

LEFT OF INCIDENT

There is a useful concept called Left of Incident. This is the core concept in the prevention of violence. In English, we write from left to write. Therefore, left means before and right means after. Left of Incident, then, refers to the time before an incident occurs. This can be minutes before, days before, weeks before, months before, years before or decades before. Because history teaches us so much about what to expect in the future, we can predict certain events with accuracy.

For example, psychologists that conduct studies in the prison system have the chance to interview inmates extensively about their crimes. From these interviews, they have learned why people do the things they do. They have been able to reconstruct crimes, going all the way back to determining what it was that put the criminal in the frame of mind to commit a crime in the first place. They have followed the progression from the initial emotion all the way through the planning and execution of the crime. This helps them tremendously when they set about the task of preventing crimes; they can look at the entire picture and all the details involved and begin to forecast where things will go.

Obviously, these kinds of extensive studies require massive coordination, effort, permission and incur a great deal of cost. They are used for federal, state and local law enforcement to train and to get ahead of the problem. The results and the data from these studies eventually make it out to the general public, where it continues to be useful.

We are all familiar with the phrase, "If you see something, say something." It has become our mantra since September 11, 2001. Many people began to

> ## MASTER TACTIC
> Living in condition yellow means keeping an eye out for the well-being of your friends, family, colleagues, neighbors and others. If something seems off, check in with them.

elevate their situational awareness from condition white to condition yellow. They started taking notice when things did not look right, feel right or seem right. Because they began paying attention to details, they began to see patterns unfolding accordingly. Abnormal patterns and behaviors began to stand out more easily. People began reporting suspicious activity and many plots were foiled before the perpetrators were ready to act.

I admit that this is not how things should have to be. We should not have to live so vigilantly for the sake of ensuring our own security. But it is as clear today as it was on 9/11 that we live in a dangerous world. It is a shame people ever have to call the police because of a neighbor's suspicious activity, and I am sure that we all wish things were different. However, we must accept things are the way they are. Not wanting things to be this way does not alter reality.

For most of history, when a bank hired a new teller, that new person was taught how to spot counterfeit money. Prior to modern technology, the only way to identify a counterfeit bill was by look and feel. How did the banks train these people? Did they give them samples of every kind of counterfeit bill to study? No. They had the new person spend a generous amount of time familiarizing themselves with real money. They got to know every shade of every color, the nuances of the texture, the exact size, and the look and feel of real money. It was only by becoming intimately familiar with the real currency that they could quickly spot the differences in a counterfeit.

If you go to school or to work every day, you too can be alert to the abnormal behaviors and patterns around you. You already know the look and feel of normal behaviors, attitudes, words and gestures. You already understand how the people of your school or office typically communicate. You know the personalities of your co-workers and friends, and you know if something is out of the ordinary. Remain alert. If someone is showing signs that something is wrong, do not ignore them. Ostracizing people never makes the problem go away. It only defers it to a later time. Be a friend. Ask the person what is wrong. Ask if you can help. Listen to their words. Advocate for them. See if you can get them the help they need or at the very least point them in the right direction. If we all practiced this neighborly awareness as a way of life, I am convinced we would see a dramatic shift in our society for the good.

MONEY!

There was a test conducted by a Krav Maga school a few years ago. They chose a hotel and put a large man and a petite woman into an elevator together. Each time the doors opened and there was a person waiting to board, the man acted like he was attacking the woman and she in turn cried out for help. They played the scenario out 100 times in a row. Out of more than 100 people who saw the elevator doors open to reveal an attack taking place, only seven people intervened. Yes, you read that right: seven. That means that 93 out of 100 people witnessed the commotion, then simply backed away and let the doors close, choosing not to get involved.

Sadly, it has been shown through many different kinds of studies that shouting "HELP!" or "MURDER!" or "RAPE!" or "FIRE!" will not get you the help you need when you are in distress. People are either too scared, uncertain, oblivious or disinterested to get involved in the clearly distressed call of a total stranger. However, there is one word that gets everyone's attention the very first time it is said. No one is disinterested or oblivious if they hear a shout that says, "MONEY!" At that point, it seems like everyone cares enough to get involved.

If you are ever threatened or attacked in public and you need to attract attention, shouting "MONEY!" or "I FOUND MONEY!" will draw the attention you need, (hopefully) prompting the more level-headed and proactive observers to call 911 on your behalf.

A GOOD NAME

A good name is more desirable than riches. Why? Well, if you have a good name, you have set yourself up for success. You can get the things you need more readily if people trust you. If your good name precedes you, people are already cooperative before they ever actually meet you.

Think about any time when you have finally met a person about whom you have heard a great deal. If what you heard was good, were you inclined to cooperate with the person to the fullest extent of your ability? If what you heard was not good, were you reluctant to get involved at all? That is one of the ways in which a good name serves you well.

If you have a good name and a crisis unfolds, people will look to you for leadership and comfort. They will listen to what you have to say and follow your instructions. They will trust that you can and will help, and they will go along with what you are trying to accomplish.

The only way to find yourself in this position is to make sure that you are living in such a way as to build your good name now.

- Always tell the truth, but be diplomatic
- Help your neighbors
- Live up to your own principles
- Have a good attitude
- Be cooperative
- Be even tempered
- Be approachable
- Be transparent
- Always keep your word
- Smile
- Put people at ease
- Be a calming influence
- Bring peace to tense situations
- Only speak up when you know what you are talking about
- Be squared away in your own knowledge base, skill sets, equipment and readiness
- Never stop learning
- Be humble
- Genuinely care about people
- Be willing to sacrifice
- Be patient

If you live according to these "rules of engagement," you will find that people will be willing to do just about anything for you. Imagine how magnificent that will be when adversity strikes and it falls to you to lead the way and make a difference.

TOXICITY

Toxicity is the exact opposite of resiliency. Toxic people not only hamper their own resiliency but obstruct the resiliency of everyone around them as well, sapping the life out of the people with whom they come into contact. They keep themselves and everyone around them from being happy, achieving goals, healing, progressing, growing, feeling grounded or understood, having self-confidence, developing independent decision making, trusting their own instincts and living in freedom. In fact, the very nature of a toxic person creates the polar opposite of all these desirable traits.

If you have a toxic person in your life, you will know it by some combination of these signs. If you have...

- A feeling of guilt for every decision you make that is not centered around them.
- A feeling of fear if you have allowed too much time to go by without checking in.
- A feeling of dread about saying or doing the wrong thing and causing an explosion of anger.
- A feeling of being chronically misunderstood.
- A feeling of anxiety if that person is too quiet for too long.
- A chronic expectation of an impending emotional fallout.
- A feeling of being constantly manipulated into actions you do not want to take.
- A fear that every decision that does not directly benefit that person will cost you.
- An inability to fully enjoy anything because fear and uncertainty are never far away.
- A need to walk on eggshells in order to keep the peace.
- A feeling of hesitation to introduce that person to anyone else you know.
- A chronic worry that you are going crazy.
- Suicidal ideations.
- Depression.
- Anxiety.
- An inability to communicate effectively with only that person.
- Fantasies of breaking free from that relationship.
- Nightmares of being trapped, stuck, smothered, cornered or caught.
- A debilitating feeling of obligation to make that person happy at the cost of your own happiness.
- A feeling that the only time when you are not really yourself is when you are with that person.

- **A feeling of desperation to get out from under the load imposed upon you by that person.**
- **The knowledge that yours can only ever be a one-sided relationship.**
- **Physical symptoms of extreme stress, such as tunnel vision, hyperventilation, nausea, heart palpitations, shakiness, night sweats or insomnia.**
- **Space to breathe and relax only when that person is absent.**
- **A feeling that there is no way for you to measure up or ever be good enough to satisfy that person's expectations.**

There are three types of people: victims, survivors and conquerors (pg. 14). Toxic people are emotional hostage-takers. They create learned helplessness in others and allow it to fester in themselves. They excel at stripping people of their joy and their sense of freedom. Most importantly, toxic people create victims out of their hostages. Some psychology studies show resiliency is directly related to the presence or absence of toxic influences. In other words, if there are only toxic influences and no positive influences in a person's life before and after a traumatic event, the person is likely to remain a victim. However, if there is a mix of both toxic and positive influences on a person's life, they are likely to become a survivor. Best of all, if there are only positive influences on a person's life, they are likely to emerge as a conqueror. Therefore, abandoning toxic influences becomes a matter of survival.

Do you remember the Fulcrum Principle (pg. 31)? Imagine how resilient we would all be if we removed the toxic influences from our lives and invested in all the components of our fulcrum every day. Now that is the ultimate in advanced preparation of the battle space!

BAD COMPANY

Bad company corrupts good character. We have all been taught this simple pearl of wisdom. But did you know this can present a security issue? Who we choose for our companions will determine a lot about the outcome of our lives. I have heard it said we are a product of the five people with whom we spend the most time. He who walks with wise men will be wise, but the companion of fools will suffer harm.

Toxicity is clearly damaging to the innocent. Of course, I am well aware that we cannot choose our family members. To a large extent, we cannot choose our classmates or coworkers, unless we change schools or jobs. However, we can choose our friends. When you choose your friends, do you consider their attributes? Do you ask yourself about their character? Do you watch them to see if they get into any kind of trouble?

People who get into trouble tend to take others with them. No one will get into trouble alone if they can help it. How many stories do we know about an innocent person whose friend got them into trouble, whether directly or indirectly? If your friends demonstrate lapses in sound judgment and show questionable moral character, it is only a matter of time before they bring you trouble.

How does this factor into security? There was a man who fell in with bad company. He did not do anything wrong when he was with them, but he knew that they were up to a lot of things that violated his conscience. He always held out, unwilling to engage in their disreputable activities, but unwilling to sever the relationship either. One day, they asked him to drive them to the bank. He obliged, never suspecting their real intentions. He waited in the car while they went in and, in time, they came flying out, jumped into the car, and yelled at him to drive away as fast as possible. He did. It turned out that they had robbed the bank and shot the security guard. To make matters worse: he had just driven the getaway car. They were all caught and this young man was sentenced to life in prison for being an accessory to an armed bank robbery and murder.

This is a true story. If he had given a little more weight to his feelings, he might have chosen differently earlier on. If he had paid attention to the fact that his conscience was being violated every time he hung out with those guys, he would be a free man. He should have recognized the security risk he was taking by choosing to expose himself to their influences repeatedly, and he has paid dearly for his poor judgment ever since.

You will become like the people with whom you spend your time. Troublemakers bring trouble back upon themselves and everyone else around them. If you value your personal security, peace of mind, safety and freedom, choose your companions with care.

COMMUNICATION IS CRITICAL

Communication is, arguably, the most important tool people have at their disposal. We depend on it. It is what distinguishes us from the rest of creation. Yet how many of us study it? How many of us put time and effort into cultivating it?

As humans, we have many types of communication: verbal languages, bodily posture, facial expressions, hand gestures, written, recorded, musical, etc. We have intentional and unintentional communication.

What do people need in order to communicate? We need a common frame of reference. It could be a shared language, or even a shared understanding of what a smile means. Both people need to agree to ascribe a certain meaning to a word or gesture or facial expression. When people ascribe different meanings to the same attempt at communication, we run into trouble.

For example, what happens when I smile in an attempt to communicate friendliness, but the recipient of my smile interprets that as flirting? What about when I laugh in an attempt to lighten a mood but the person I think I am laughing with believes I am making fun of him? Trouble. We both need to agree on the meaning of the smile or the laughter in order to truly communicate.

There are three distinct aspects of any communication: the transmitter, the receiver and the message. It is the responsibility of the transmitter to ensure the message is correct and clear, and that the receiver receives it. If the message is garbled, incorrect or false, or if it never reaches the receiver... trouble. It does not get any simpler than that.

Let us ascribe just a little responsibility to the receiver as well. In this next scenario, let us say someone is talking to me. That someone is the transmitter, and I am supposed to be the receiver. I could aid the transmitter a bit by paying attention, by engaging in active listening. Or I could let my mind wander. I could use the time while they are transmitting to formulate my rebuttal to their message. I could assume I know what the rest of the message is going to be and choose to interrupt them. I might even tune them out. Again...trouble. The communication attempt has failed and I contributed to this outcome.

What is the first step toward effective communication? I would submit it is the art of listening. A good place to start is by giving the transmitter and the message my undivided attention. If I wish to be a good listener (receiver),

I need to put as much importance on the message as the transmitter does. I need to listen actively, not passively. I need to apply my brainpower to hearing and digesting the message as it is being relayed, not waiting in boredom until the full message is finally transmitted.

There are myriad ways that I can communicate the fact that I am actively listening. I can silence my phone and put it away, and I can look the transmitter in the eye. I might sit forward or nod at intervals. All these

THE ART OF ACTIVE LISTENING

Active listening is exactly what it sounds like. Truly listening to someone requires your active participation. People know the difference between an active listener and a passive listener. If you want to encourage someone to talk, here are some things to keep in mind:

- Put all your electronic devices away and silence their noises. This conveys where the speaker ranks in their priority order to you.
- Look the speaker in the eye. This indicates that you care.
- Lean forward, toward the speaker. This indicates that you are listening with rapt attention.
- Summarize their words intermittently. This shows them that you are making an effort to truly understand.
- Parrot their words and movements, not to excess, but subtly. If done properly, this conveys they can trust you and makes them comfortable with their own mannerisms and word choices.
- Give them "minimal encouragers" as they speak like a nod, a smile, a verbal "mmm, hmm" or anything else that tells them to keep going. This conveys you are not getting bored.
- When appropriate, respond with words of sympathy and encouragement like, "I am so sorry" or "I can see why you feel that way". This normalizes and validates their feelings.
- Ask questions. This shows an active interest in the topic.
- Ask how you can help. This conveys a willingness to stay involved and connected.
- Thank the speaker for trusting you enough to confide in you. This shows you take their confidence in you seriously and that you are trustworthy.

non-verbal methods of communication convey that I am hanging on the transmitter's every word. They show how I am focused solely on the message and nothing else, that I have placed a number one priority on the transmitter and the message. To the transmitter, that is quite compelling.

That being said, what causes the receiver to malfunction? What erodes the receiver's ability to receive the full message in its intended spirit? To put it bluntly: disrespect. This can take many forms: intentional deviousness, bullying, whining, arrogance, long-winded lectures, belittling the receiver's intelligence, talking down, yelling, swearing, temper tantrums, etc. All of these convey a distinct lack of respect for the receiver.

What other kinds of things get in the way of communication? There is a concept called the Signal to Noise Ratio. This is defined as the ratio of signal power to that of noise power. The signal is the real message, while the noise is everything else that can interfere with or otherwise overpower the signal. Noise can be anything at all. If someone is talking to me but I hear music playing at the same time, obviously the music is noise because it may interfere with my ability to hear the message. But remember what I said about disrespect? If the transmitter is disrespectful to me, that alone may be enough to prevent me from fully understanding or accepting the message, due to my negative feelings about the transmitter. The disrespect is noise.

Being able to tune out, turn down or overlook the noise will help me to be the best possible receiver I can be. Doing everything I can to prevent or minimize the noise will allow me to be the best possible transmitter I can be.

In a crisis or a disaster, the ability to communicate with those around you will be critical. In travel, communication is critical too. Now is the time to develop some strategies for communication (a comms plan) for those demanding and stressful situations. Do not wait until you are thrust into an adverse situation to come up with your comms plan with total strangers. Decide what you will do and practice some advanced preparation.

It is amazing how much people will tell to a good listener. When adversity strikes, one thing you will need in abundance is information. Being an active listener is the best way to encourage people to share their information with you. If you find yourself leading a group, actively listening to your people is imperative for good morale and for gaining vital intelligence.

ELICITATION

You never know when you might need to get someone to tell you something. Invoking someone's urge to talk is known as elicitation. No need to worry, though—it is not a threatening technique. In fact, if done properly, the subject will never know it is happening.

This is simple to do, and chances are you engage in variations of these techniques all the time. Combining them will make even the most tight-lipped stranger more willing to share a little info with you, even if it's offhand.

- Ask open ended questions instead of questions that can be answered with one word.
- Put aside all distractions and give them your undivided attention.
- Use body language that conveys that there is no one in the world more important than they are at that moment in time.
- Hang on their every word.
- Be polite.
- Massage their ego. Inflate their position and importance.
- Make inaccurate statements for them to correct.
- Ask about their work and show you are impressed by what they do.
- Exude calmness and trustworthiness.
- Make meaningful eye contact.
- Smile when you say their name.
- Use their name often.
- Always look genuinely glad to see them.
- Care about them as a person.
- Meet their needs.
- Let them know how valuable they are.

These are just some of the things that will get a person talking about themselves. According to Dale Carnegie, author of *How to Win Friends and Influence People*, a person's name is the sweetest sound in the world to their own ears. People enjoy conversation that is all about them. It will not be difficult to get them talking about themselves. Once you have them on a roll, smoothly transition to the subject about which you really need to know.

AN ODD ENCOUNTER

I had an odd encounter when arriving at work one Friday morning. There are six options for parking at my building: a lower lot, an upper lot, a side lot, street parking and two parking garages. I randomly oscillate between them, always striving to be as unpredictable as possible. (I said I practice what I preach!) That day, I opted for the lower lot. As soon as I made the turn into the lot, an SUV appeared out of nowhere and turned in behind me. It seemed to have been waiting for my arrival. Odd, I thought. I peeled off to the right and made my way around the lot. The SUV peeled off to the left and made its way around to the same spot, taking the other path. It stopped as I began to park and just lingered where the driver could see me. There were many parking spaces available and I chose one. As soon as I pulled into my space, the other vehicle circled behind me, made one loop around the lot, and departed to park in the upper lot. I noted the strange encounter and immediately raised my awareness level to orange. I got out of my vehicle and headed to one of the entrances to my building.

I then noticed that the driver of the SUV had parked, got out and began heading to the same entrance at the same time, bypassing the closest and most convenient entrance. I stepped back and allowed her to enter first. As I walked in behind her, she said, "Good morning" and I responded in kind. She asked me if I work in this building. I answered in the affirmative. She asked me where and I gestured down a particular hallway. She seemed unsatisfied and pressed me again. She asked me if I work in this building. Once again, I answered yes. Once more, she asked me where. I said, "Down there," pointing to the same hallway and not offering any more of an explanation than that. I did not wait, I turned to leave and walked off in a third direction, not the one I had come in by and not the one to which I had gestured. She seemed frustrated and simply called out to my back, "Have a good day." I returned her well wishes without stopping, slowing down or turning around. I headed off to the restroom and she got into the elevator.

This was highly suspect to me and definitely out of the ordinary. I had the distinct impression that she was trying to find out exactly who I work for and the exact location of my office. This was an attempt at elicitation—at my place of work, no less. My chosen method of handling it was a cross between ignoring it, evading it and out-maneuvering. I inferred by my abrupt departure that I did not have the time to chat with her (evasion). I identified the information she wanted from me and acted as though I knew nothing of her intention (ignoring). I answered her questions with one word and a gesture, offering no details (out-maneuvering). I did not engage her, which is the fourth option.

You can actually practice this stuff in routine conversations. Just make a game out of seeing how you can choose from the four methods as you navigate routine communications. The more you practice, the easier the real thing will be to spot and to handle.

TO ANSWER OR NOT TO ANSWER

This is the question: When the doorbell rings, do we open it wide to see who it is?

Your answer is probably predicated on two things: whether or not you are expecting someone and the nature of your specific community. If you live in a small town and know just about everyone, you probably feel safe opening the door to find out who is calling. On the other hand, if you live in an inner city, you probably look through the peephole and call out "who is it?" before you are willing to open the door. In fact, neither choice is wrong. All that matters is you make an informed choice.

Times are changing, and we certainly do not live in the same world in which our parents grew up. To be quite honest, we do not live in the same world we knew less than two decades ago. It is unfortunate that we must enact so many security measures just to go about our daily lives. Deciding how to treat an unannounced visitor is one more level of security about which you will have to decide.

MASTER TACTIC

Introduce yourself to your neighbors and get a feel for the neighborhood. Offer help to those who might need it. Make friends and allies you can count on should an emergency arise.

There are those who take this layer of security so seriously that they never order pizza or have packages delivered to their home address. They will use a rental box through USPS or FedEX or UPS or Amazon to receive their mail and packages, and they will pick up their own pizza. In fact, their household rule is that if they have not invited someone over, they will not answer the door. Period. They will post a "No Soliciting" sign conspicuously at the front door, usually right above the doorbell, and they will never open to anyone whom they are not expecting. Is this inherently wrong? I would say we cannot judge that decision. They are making an informed decision and they realize the tradeoff is being seen as antisocial and un-neighborly, missing opportunities, and coming across as paranoid. However, since they are willing to pay that price, the payoff is their own ability to breathe easier, feel more secure at home and have complete control over their family emergency plan.

Naturally, there is the opposite mentality as well. There are those who never lock their cars or their homes, who leave the main door open all day with only the storm door closed, who frankly cannot remember where their house keys might be, who call out "come on in!" whenever the doorbell rings, and who might as well put a revolving door in for all the neighbors who come and go at all hours. The obvious upside is the old-fashioned lifestyle of trust and wonderful social relationships. The obvious downside is what an easy target they and their house would make should someone wish to do them harm.

Most of us live somewhere in between. We will look through a peephole or a window when the doorbell surprises us, but will go ahead and open it if we see a delivery or utility uniform. In most cases, that has proven to be a safe thing to do. However, criminals get smarter and more sophisticated all the time and they are fully aware people tend to trust uniforms. One of the classic ploys when a burglar is casing a neighborhood and gathering information about people's schedules involves donning a uniform of some sort and ringing doorbells to see who answers. This gives them two data points. The first is they assume that a non-answer means no one is home at that time of day. The second is to see who will go ahead and open wide when they ring. Now the criminal has two options: they can either discover which houses will be empty and when, so that they can burglarize in solitude, or they can use the fact the occupant unlocked and opened their own front door to their advantage and force their way in.

There is an important difference in the mindset of a burglar who knowingly enters a house when the occupants are home and the burglar who specifically waits for the people to be gone. One wants only the items they can steal and they want to come and go undetected, while the other knows they will have to deal with the people they are robbing and often have far more sinister plans while they are there, from kidnapping to rape to murder. That is why you must decide when to open your door and when to leave it closed and locked. Know the risks you are taking versus the reward of living in more freedom. Have a candid talk with your family and decide on some house rules for how to handle an unexpected visitor.

STOPLIGHT RISK ASSESSMENTS

Most of us are familiar with the colors of a traffic light: red, yellow and green. We are also familiar with what they represent: stop, yield and go. Using this same format, we can translate this into a practical everyday methodology for conducting risk assessments.

Before we take an action of note, we conduct an overt risk assessment. Believe it or not, we conduct a covert risk assessment prior to taking any action of any magnitude, whether we realize it or not. However, when the action may be risky or have noteworthy consequences, we stop and take the time to assess the risks and any possible damage we could sustain, then weigh those against the potential gain.

The stoplight analogy is a fantastic tool because it is so easy to remember. Allow me to explain...

GREEN IS A GO
Everything checks out and there are no glaring flaws or risk factors.

YELLOW IS A RISK FACTOR
Risks may be mitigated but three yellows or more means a no-go.

RED IS AN ABSOLUTE NO-GO
One red means there is a potential risk that is simply too great.

We look for these indicators while formulating plans. If all is green, we have nothing to mitigate and we proceed as intended. If we have two yellows or less, we must put mitigation measures in place before we go, but once we do, we can go. Three or more yellows or one red, however, is a game stopper. No-go. Back to the planning board until we can get the proposed activity down to a green or two mitigated yellows.

Too many mitigated risks stacks the deck against you. Let's say you intended to take a long drive after work, at night, when you did not feel well, and had just had a fight with your spouse. How many yellows is that?

1. **You have already worked all day and you are tired.**
2. **Night is dark and it is harder to see.**
3. **Not feeling well puts you behind the power curve in physical reaction time.**
4. **A recent fight puts you behind the power curve emotionally and impairs your judgment.**

We can mitigate risks reasonably to an extent but in order to mitigate all four, your trip would look like this: You drink coffee or some other energy drink for the fatigue. You take cold medicine for your aching body but it makes you sleepy. You take the route which is best illuminated but highest in traffic, and you either ignore your feelings about your spouse or try to make up but you are not physically in the same place, so making up on the phone feels incomplete. The stoplight risk assessment is what we use in jet formation flying and in test flying of brand new aircraft. It has never let us down.

See how it works? Try using it when planning an outing, activity or adventure. If you do, you will find it helps you think logically and objectively about taking risks and provides you with an external unit of measurement to help you make informed choices when you are unsure how to proceed.

COUNTERING SURVEILLANCE

When it comes to surveillance detection, we say that if you see someone once, it is an anomaly. If you see them twice, it is a coincidence. If you see them three times, it is surveillance. Red alert.

The acronym TEDD stands for Time, Environment, Distance and Demeanor. If you see someone three times across time, environments and distance, you are being surveilled, no doubt about it. Acknowledge this, accept it and most of all, do not panic. If you happen to covertly catch them watching you, observe and note their demeanor. It is very difficult to act natural while conducting surveillance. No matter what lengths they have taken to blend in, these people will likely become markedly uncomfortable once they realize you have noticed their presence.

Act natural and leave. Go gray. Do not make a scene or engage in an altercation. If you feel you are in danger, stay in a populated area and contact the police.

SURVEILLANCE DETECTION ROUTES

Whether at home or abroad, situational awareness is a must. If, by your situational awareness, you begin to suspect you are under surveillance, there are many methods available to you which you can use to either confirm or dispel your suspicions. You can:

- Drive a surveillance detection route that takes you both onto a highway and into a neighborhood.
- Drive through a choke point: a place where the road narrows all the way down to one lane, if possible.
- Make a U-turn.
- Drive into a cul-de-sac or dead end.
- Go through a bank or restaurant drive-through.
- If available, go through a formal and manned checkpoint, such as a metered garage, toll booth or military facility.
- Create an accordion effect in traffic.
- Drive through a long stretch of traffic lights, stop signs or stop-and-go-traffic.
- Make three left turns instead of one right turn.
- Make two unnecessary stops for at least five minutes each.
- Switch to public transportation.
- Switch to walking through densely populated areas.

It is much better to lose your tail "naturally" than to engage in high visibility maneuvers which may threaten them into acting prematurely against you. **Never let a surveillance team know their presence has been detected.** Once you have confirmed your suspicions, you can decide whether to call the police or go to a police station, go home, go to a public place like a cafe and simply wait it out or carry on with your plans as usual.

ROUTES

We are all creatures of habit. We also have schedules to keep, which means most of us go to the same place(s) every day. Naturally, we have our favorite route because it avoids traffic or is the most direct path or has the most beautiful scenery. However, using the same route to go to the same place(s) every day is a dead giveaway. All anyone has to do is watch you for a week and they will know exactly where you will be. They can then choose a convenient spot along your route to make contact with you.

Instead of using the same route every day, switch it up. Be unpredictable. Predictability is the cardinal dead giveaway. Keep any potential surveillance completely in the dark about your plans and be as unpredictable as you can safely be.

TIMES

When it comes to keeping our schedules, we not only tend to choose the same route every day, we also leave at the same time. So, if you are under surveillance, not only will they know where you are going to be but when you are going to be there. It could be they will choose a spot along your route to make contact, or it could be that they are simply waiting for you to leave home because it is your house in which they are most interested. Predictable timing is a dead giveaway.

Vary your times as well as your routes. Leave early (this is usually a good idea regardless of whether or not you think someone might be trailing you). Leave on time. Leave late. Change up your schedule whenever you can. Again, be as unpredictable as you can safely be. Keep the bad guys guessing and try to frustrate them to the point that they give up on you as a target.

FLASHY BLING

People take pride in their income and possessions. It is a very human trait to want to have the best and to want to show it off. However, advertising your wealth is a dead giveaway.

If you have the biggest house, the most expensive cars, eat at all the best restaurants, wear the biggest diamond, only buy the best brands, send your kids to the most exclusive private schools, vacation in exotic places, have your own airplane, etc., you are inviting interest from the bad guys who would like nothing more than to kidnap a member of your family for ransom. A target with a rich family is like winning the lottery.

If you have wealth to enjoy, do so with discretion. Instead of making an announcement in all the newspapers about your daughter's debutante cotillion ball, perhaps some direct phone call invitations would be preferred. Rather than talking about your country club, golf game and newest jet in public—where anyone within earshot could begin to take inventory of your wealth—perhaps you could restrict that to the people you really know you can trust. Instead of carrying around status symbols everywhere you go, perhaps you might consider choosing items whose brand is not readily apparent in order to maintain a low profile.

This same principle applies to people who have far less as well. If you can, wear clothes that do not advertise brands. Go gray (pg. 16). Know your surroundings and moderate your choices of what to wear and drive to suit the venue. Be mindful of your image projection and do not make yourself an attractive target.

BE ALERT

Being oblivious to your surroundings is a dead giveaway to anyone who wants to take advantage of your carelessness or naïveté. Bad guys target oblivious people. Period. They are very soft targets because they will never see the danger approaching and will be unprepared when it reaches them. Do not allow anyone to have this advantage over you.

Instead, be proactive. Simply look around. Notice people. Look at their faces, hands, eyes, movement and body language. Observe their gait, style and overall demeanor. Do all of these things and you might just see things before they happen. Most importantly, be aware of people moving toward you and do not hesitate to leave if their presence or behavior make you uncomfortable. If you have no other skills, the willingness to take the time to notice what is going on around you and to respond to it appropriately could save your life.

CARELESS TALK

In England during WWII, there was a media campaign called Careless Talk. They produced posters depicting drawings of soldiers being killed because intelligence had reached the enemy before the soldier did. One of the posters showed a dead paratrooper, barely touching down after a grueling jump. The caption reads, "Careless talk got there first." Even now, when I look at those period pieces, my heart constricts. The message is clear: Careless talk is a dead giveaway. In the United States, a similar campaign generated the phrase, "Loose lips sink ships." You might already be familiar with it, but the message is the same.

This principle is just as valid today. Pay attention to what you are saying and to all the ears who might overhear it. If you are having lunch at a restaurant with a friend, you intend to talk only to that friend. However, be aware there are lots of other ears around. This advice applies to idle gossip as well as personal information like travel plans. If you are excitedly talking about your upcoming vacation and the associated dates, you have just announced that your house will be vacant for more than enough time for someone to plan and execute a burglary.

Know not only your intended audience but also your unintended audience. Be discreet when disseminating information and choose your information, audience and method of delivery with care. At the very least, it could save you a good deal of embarrassment, but you never know—it might also save lives.

COLORFUL LOGOS

Believe it or not, choosing what to wear each day is a personal security decision. On a basic level, items like high heels, short skirts or sagging pants all impede movement in their own respective ways. It is not unreasonable to say that you would sooner twist an ankle than outrun an attacker while wearing stilettos. Putting that aside for a moment, however, wearing anything exceptionally attention-getting, even if it does not restrict movement, is a dead giveaway.

People who wish to go gray (pg. 16) make a habit of avoiding neon colors like highlighter yellow. Your number one priority is to blend in and lose yourself in a crowd, especially if you think you are being followed. Make yourself hard to remember and hard to spot. Wearing bright colors, bold prints, memorable logos and the like make you stand out amidst a throng of people. All someone has to do is look for that telltale color or logo, be it on your shirt, hat, jacket, backpack, etc., and they can stop scanning faces or looking for familiar movements. To make matters worse, they can easily find you again after losing sight of you for a moment.

Make yourself as gray as possible. Be one fish in a school of a thousand identical fish.

BUMPER STICKERS

Much like wearing neon clothing, plastering your car with bumper stickers makes you easy to spot and could easily attract unwanted attention. It makes describing your vehicle to others too easy. To a lesser extent, vanity license plates are also a dead giveaway. By their very nature, they demand a closer look and there is only one of them on each end. However, it should go without saying that anything you do to decorate, accentuate or otherwise make your car noticeable falls under the dead giveaway category.

When a vehicle is under surveillance (pg. 77), it is usually being watched by teams. Because vehicles move so much faster and farther than people do, there are usually teams staged at various points along a route that will hand the target vehicle off to each other as they leapfrog around. Describing your vehicle to the next waiting team is so much easier if it has unique features like bumper stickers and vanity plates. Instead of scanning the road for every single tan Toyota Camry and then, upon spotting each tan Camry, having to scan for the right driver, they can ignore all the tan ones which are not decked out like the target. It makes for a more streamlined search and much smoother handoffs. In other words, it creates a lot of trouble for you.

Take a look at your vehicle. Does it stand out from every other vehicle of the same make, model and color? If so, what can you do to reduce its noticeability and help it blend in? Trust me, those fuzzy dice are not doing you any favors when it comes to personal security.

PARTICIPANT OR SPECTATOR

When I was in school for evasion, I was taught the principles of what works best. We spent time in the classroom discussing techniques and methodologies and strategies. We studied scenarios and talked about case studies. We learned how to think, but it was all academic. Until we actually got out in the field and put our skills to use, we had no first-hand knowledge of how well or how poorly something worked.

The first exercise was three days long. At the end, once all of the students were accounted for, the head instructor began to debrief each of us on our respective performances. He addressed each student in front of the whole class, so that everyone present would have a chance to learn from each mistake and triumph. Needless to say, I learned a lot from the other people. I learned about a great many good decisions that had been made, but I also learned about one particularly bad one. One of the students had disappeared at the beginning of the exercise and was never seen again until after it was over. No trail. No clues. No sightings. Nothing. Each of the other students had been sighted or left clues or a trail. Not this guy.

As the instructor talked about this disappearing act, I was really impressed. I thought to myself how much I wished I was as good at this stuff as he was. I wished I had been able to disappear without a trace. Frankly, I was in awe until the instructor began his withering debrief. As soon as the exercise had begun, this student broke into a car and hid in the trunk where he remained motionless until the exercise was over. He did not accomplish the tasks we had been given. He never made any progress. He learned nothing and knowingly skipped out on a chance to master new skills. Aside from sleeping the entire time, I bet he was pretty miserable in there, too.

He missed the entire point of the exercise! He incorrectly believed the goal was to evade capture by any means necessary. While that basic thinking works in the real world, this was school. The point was to learn how to move about, make progress, accomplish things, close in on a target and leave an area without being detected. The point was to put into practice the things we had been learning in the classroom to make sure that we understood them and that they really worked when we needed them. He learned nothing in the trunk of that car. Clearly, he was a spectator and not a participant.

When it comes to survival, preparedness and life, which will you be? You can amass all the best brands of gear in the world but if you do not get out there and try it out, are you truly prepared? You can read and study all kinds of savvy techniques, life-saving tips and clever hacks, but if you never actually try anything for yourself prior to needing it, how will you know if it works for you? Practicing is your opportunity to fail safely, to learn from your mistakes in a controlled environment. It is your chance to see how easy or how difficult a skill really is to perform. It is your time to make adjustments or improvements and tailor the skill to suit your own needs or abilities. If you wait until you really need it to figure it out, you will be way behind the power curve and the consequences could be expensive if not deadly.

STAND TALL

None of us wants to be mistaken for a victim. How do victims look? Vulnerable. Victims or "targets" have an aura of fear or low self-esteem about them. They look around furtively and they look down. Their head is bent low. Their shoulders are hunched. They will not make eye contact for more than a microsecond. Rather, they project an air that they are incapable of defending themselves. Easy to spot and easy to exploit, these are the people that attract the unwanted attention of bullies. On an even grimmer note, these are also the kind of people who are kidnapped, tricked or coerced into human trafficking and slavery.

If you do these things, remember: you can choose to be a conqueror. This starts by cultivating basic habits that exude self-confidence. When you walk, hold your head up high. Be proud to face the world. Square your shoulders. Swing your arms freely. Use a strong and purposeful stride. Look around like you are surveying for a picnic site—what looks good? Look people in the eye. In many cultures, this nonverbal sign conveys respect. Smile. Breathe deeply and let go of your lesser anxieties. It is far better to overdo it and come across as arrogant and self-assured than it is to be targeted. Be assertive and aggressive if you feel threatened. Show by your posture, body language, facial expressions and words that you do not require the approval of others to be whole. Be your own person. Like yourself. Approve of yourself. This alone will deter most predators and cause them to choose a weaker-looking target.

SEE IT THEIR WAY

One of the most powerful tools for problem solving is the ability to see a problem from the perspective of your opposition. Whether conducting a hostage negotiation, de-escalating a conflict or trying to build cooperation, try adopting the viewpoint of the obstructionist in the room. Ask yourself:

- **What do they want?**
- **What are they afraid of?**
- **What motivates them?**
- **What is their worldview?**
- **What has brought them to this point?**
- **What are they feeling?**
- **How can I solve their problems?**
- **How can I ease their fears?**
- **How can I get them what they need?**

If you can answer these questions and genuinely care, you can reach the heart of the opposition. If you can demonstrate concern for them to be made whole and if you can look out for their interests, you will accomplish your goals. Rarely do we find ourselves in a situation where we genuinely want to come away with everything and for the other party to come away with nothing. We do not actually want the other party to "lose" necessarily. Instead, what we ultimately want is a solution that works for all parties, an outcome where everyone gets something positive out of it. This principle holds true along the entire spectrum, all the way from matters of national security down to property disputes between neighbors.

If you are at a stalemate and the other party is absolutely intractable, ask yourself these questions and then use the answers to generate a solution.

LOW BLOOD SUGAR

Low blood sugar can quickly creep up on you during a busy day and prevent you from making sound decisions, as well as cause you to become irritable or rash.

One thing I keep in my go packs and bug-out bags (pg. 22) are candies made with dextrose. Generally speaking, these are the non-melting sorts of candies like Sweet Tarts, Smarties and Nerds. They take up very little space and I have never known any other sugar source to do as good a job of bringing up blood sugar rapidly and stabilizing it.

From personal experience, glucose and fructose do a sloppy job. They bring the sugar up but they cause up-and-down oscillations that can be hard to manage and can bring about a secondary crash down the road when you least expect it. I recommend finding a dextrose source that you enjoy and tossing a few in your readiness packs. You never know what kind of physically demanding situations you may find yourself in when using that gear, and having a good sugar source on hand could save your life.

BATTLE BUDDIES

Most of us have heard the terms "battle buddies" and "wingman." But do we know what they mean? The premise is that if people operate in pairs, they are far safer than they would be if they operated alone. This is the reason why some churches will only send their missionaries out in pairs. It is a far better system from a security, liability and oversight perspective. Female joggers often run in pairs. Why? They know they are less likely to be targeted for nefarious activity than a solo jogger. We could all take a lesson from them. There is some sage advice which says:

> **Two are better than one,**
> **because they have a good return for their labor:**
> **If either of them falls down,**
> **one can help the other up.**
> **But pity anyone who falls**
> **and has no one to help them up.**
> **Also, if two lie down together, they will keep warm.**
> **But how can one keep warm alone?**
> **Though one may be overpowered,**
> **two can defend themselves.**
> **A cord of three strands is not quickly broken.**

In an uncertain or potentially dangerous situation, there is nothing quite as comforting as having someone around whom you can trust. It makes everything easier, from dividing and conquering logistics to having strength in numbers to having someone to witness your words and actions to having a second set of eyes on the problem.

It is a good idea to take someone with you when you travel or into any other uncertain situation. However, you must be selective about the person you choose. You would not want to take someone hot tempered into a situation where they are likely to cause an incident. You would want a cool head on your team in that scenario. Before you make your selection, ask yourself if you would put your life in their hands, because that is essentially what you are doing. If the answer is no, hard pass. Make a different choice. Having an ally along is more than a good idea. It could be a life saver.

LOYAL OPPOSITION

Do you surround yourself with honest people who may or may not agree with you? Do you surround yourself with "yes people" who will never disagree with you nor think for themselves? Do you surround yourself with "devil's advocates" who love poking holes in whatever you have to say, or do you have an echo chamber of people who agree with you on all fronts? Think about it.

If you really want to improve yourself, if you really want to know if your ideas or plans are the very best they can be, if you really want any shortcomings pointed out to you, what you need is loyal opposition. Loyal opposition is a person you trust and with whom you have a good relationship. When all is said and done, they are on your side. The way they help you become the best you can possibly be is to look for deficiencies and point them out to you. Is it comfortable? Definitely not. Does it work? Yes, and you can trust that it will be accurate.

How does this relate to security? Suppose you are taking great pains to make your home as secure as possible. You buy a guard dog. You install an alarm system. You buy a firearm and spend time honing your skills. You install cameras and motion sensing lights everywhere. Would you rather believe that you are now 100 percent secure and absolutely impervious to crime, or would you rather conduct an honest assessment of the measures you put in place and look for any gaps or weak spots? We call this a threat vulnerability assessment. If you asked someone you trust to try to break in and sneak past your security in order to test your system, that person would be your loyal opposition. Their actual intent is to help you protect your home, not to make you feel badly about anything that may have been overlooked. Whatever weaknesses they report to you can be addressed and fixed so that, at the end of the day, you are in a stronger place.

I have talked about the importance of battle buddies (pg. 85). In selecting that person, make sure that they can think independently and critically. Make sure they are willing and able to speak up if they see you heading into a dangerous situation or making a faulty security decision. Make sure that you can and will do the same for them.

TEAMWORK

Have you ever given any serious thought to who you would want to have around in a survival or security situation? Take a moment to think about it. Who among your friends, family, co-workers or acquaintances would you most want to have close by in a desperate situation? Who would you want to have on your team?

Of course, your team will not build itself. If you plan to travel to a crisis area, who will you take along? If you have a disaster plan for sheltering in place (pg. 24), who do you want to bring into your space? If you need to bug out, where will you go and with whom?

These are pretty important questions. Having a level head and a calming influence on others during a crisis is paramount. Those are the kinds of people you will want on your team. You will also want experienced people with useful skill sets and reliable equipment. They will need to be team players who can take charge if needed but can also follow another leader. They should boost or at least maintain morale, be capable of taking care of themselves and have a proven moral character. The people on your team should be slow to anger, slow to panic, reliable and trustworthy. They should be capable of motivating those around them to keep fighting no matter the odds.

A place on your team should be a place of honor. If you select one or more people and ask them to join you, you are showing your high regard for them and your deep trust. I suggest conveying that to them in no uncertain terms. Tell each person precisely why you are asking them specifically and let them know how much you esteem them, why they matter to you. A good leader will plan for eventualities and form alliances with strong allies in advance of the need. That way, if (or more accurately when) the need does arise, you are all ready to go.

UNTRACKABLE

Living in the gray (pg. 16) and keeping a low profile does not end with your wardrobe when you walk out the door. Smart phones, tablets, computers and even credit cards with RFID chips emit trackable signals which criminals use to steal your personal data. There is an easy way to shield these vulnerable signals with a common household item: aluminum foil. Most modern electronic devices can still transmit through one or two layers, so to be safe, you will need to use four.

1. **Cut four sheets of aluminum foil, then stack them on top of each other.**
2. **Place your device on top and wrap it as you would a birthday present.**
3. **Make sure the foil is tight against all sides and that there are no air gaps.**

Now you can transport your devices undetected.

PVC CACHING

There are all kinds of ways to hide things of value and the sky's the limit when you use your imagination. One of my favorite methods of concealing and protecting gear is to use a section of PVC pipe and some rubber end caps. You will need to select the diameter of your pipe to fit whatever it is you wish to conceal. PVC is quite hard and resists crushing and cracking exceptionally well. It is also very tolerant of extreme temperatures, high and low. It is white, but can be painted to match any surroundings. With the correct sized rubber caps in place, it is also waterproof.

You may already know exactly what you wish to conceal. If not, consider caching some survival gear. In a section of PVC pipe, place:

- **A few hundred dollars in $20 bills**
- **Paracord**
- **A first-aid kit**
- **A compass**
- **A knife**
- **A fire starter and tinder of some kind**
- **A map of the local area**
- **A pair of clean socks**
- **Water purification tablets**
- **A carabiner**
- **A flashlight or headlamp**
- **Energy bars**

Once your kit is assembled, choose a good hiding place. Caching locations are chosen based upon different things. The location needs to be accessible by you in a crisis situation. It needs to be concealed from being found by people and wildlife. It needs to be findable by you. Do not rely on GPS coordinates to find your cache. If technology fails, you will need an alternate way to find this life-saving gear. Draw a map. Write directions down. Mark the spot. Use your ability to pace count to measure distance.

There is nothing wrong with making multiple kits and caching them in multiple locations. Just take the necessary precautions to ensure you can find them, but no one else can.

KNOW THE LAW

Twice now, I have been in zero tolerance no-gun zones and it has come to my attention that one or more of my companions is armed because they did not know the local law. A family friend once got arrested trying to board a cruise ship for his wedding anniversary because he had a few loaded magazines in his bag. He had simply forgotten about them and did not empty his bag prior to packing it. Unfortunately, due to this one mistake, he was prohibited from taking the cruise at all and from traveling with that cruise line forever. Worse, he now awaits an out-of-state trial, all because he did not check his gear or know the law.

It is not worth your freedom, your reputation or a police record, my friend. If you carry, do your homework, full stop. Know the law in every place you will be. Stay vigilant. Check your gear. Do not get complacent. The cost is too high.

THE POWER OF CHOICE

One of the things I was taught throughout the course of my PTSD recovery is that the difference between victims and survivors is that survivors have choices. Victims have none. The thing that depresses people and makes them feel trapped and helpless is that they feel like they have no choices. They feel stuck, manipulated or controlled, and the missing ingredient is options. When a person is in that position, they can begin to reverse their direction by taking control where they can and purposely making choices. Little choices will result in little freedoms. That produces the immediate result of relief. The little freedoms result in bigger choices which produces bigger relief and eventually leads to genuine happiness. As an example, a person who is crying can choose to get up and grab tissues. Once they blow their nose and wipe their eyes, they feel a little better. This feeling of relief might allow them to realize they are hungry, which may then prompt them to make something to eat. Satisfying their hunger produces more relief, which allows them to notice they are tired. They choose to take a nap and awaken feeling significantly better. In this way, little actions add up.

This is especially true after a crisis event. The truth is that you always have options, even when you cannot see them. Just understanding and believing that you have options brings an inherent amount of relief and freedom into one's psyche. It is empowering to know. Exercising the power of choice, making decisions and taking action are the antidotes to learned helplessness.

Do not allow yourself to be frozen in fear. You have choices in every situation. Recognize that and embrace it as a shield against despair and doubt. Wield it as a sword against depression and anxiety. Use it to protect yourself and fight your way out of helplessness and into effective living.

AN EXCUSE TO WIN

Most people make excuses for themselves when they lose or fail. They come up with something that sounds just plausible enough so they can feel less bad about their loss or failure. If they can pin the blame on anything from a poor night's sleep to a twisted ankle to a slow metabolism to a lack of time, they feel justified for not having done their best.

This is not the mindset of a conqueror. You are more than capable of cultivating your outlook on life and adjusting the ways in which you respond to adversity. Why not look for an excuse to win? As we live with a mindset of advanced preparation, we will be able to spot the advantages (excuses) that can help us win and succeed.

If I am planning to rise early tomorrow morning and work out hard, wisdom would seem to suggest going to bed at a decent hour tonight. I could stay up late, cruise the internet, get too little sleep and make an excuse for my poor performance in the morning by chalking it up to a lack of sleep. Well, that might sound valid to others, but can I really admit, deep down, that I gave myself a chance to succeed? Of course not! Alternatively, I can bid everyone an early goodnight, stating that I have to rise early and work out and I need my sleep, then adequately prepare myself for some decent shut-eye. That, my friends, is an excuse to win.

This translates easily into personal security, travel and other survival scenarios where the stakes are highest. Looking for excuses to win is nothing more than seeking every advantage and readily taking it. Make no mistake, I am not talking about taking advantage of others; I am talking about making sound decisions and setting yourself up for success. Do you want to win or do you want an excuse to lose? Only you can make the call. Choose wisely.

PRACTICE WHAT YOU PREACH

I was traveling to teach a course a few states away from mine, and I chose to drive. Three states from home on the interstate, the alternator in my car failed. I coasted to a stop on the shoulder of the highway and called my roadside assistance service. It took three hours of waiting for the tow truck to arrive and I was sweltering in my car. I could not open the windows because they are electric and I had no alternator, which killed my battery. Fortunately, I carry everything I need with me whenever I am on the road. In my trunk, I had a wool blanket and a camping pillow. (This could have happened in the winter.) I also had a tourniquet, pressure dressing, bug spray, a hammock and running shoes. In my back seat I had my 24-hour bag, complete with water and food, as well as an emergency shelter, paracord, signal mirror, whistle, lighter, matches, flint, tinder, flashlight, multi-tool, pen, knife, backup battery for my cell phone, first-aid kit, compass, back up compass, lip balm, mints and toilet paper wipes, in case my situation evolved from a few hours' inconvenience to a days-long fight for survival.

No matter the season, I had everything I needed with me to take care of myself. I was set up to handle heat, cold, hunger, thirst, elimination, sanitation, hygiene and navigation. I used the water, the food, the cell phone and the multi-tool as I waited. (If you are curious, I used the multi-tool to uninstall the battery to see if the problem was in the connection, poured Coke on the connectors to eliminate the corrosion, then reinstalled the battery.) If I had to walk to the next exit to find help, I could have done so with ease and peace of mind. I smiled to myself as I waited, grateful and relieved that I was practicing what I preach. It made a big difference to the stress level the situation created. I was calm and relaxed as I waited, knowing that, no matter how long it took, my needs were met because I had prepared for them in advance.

In the winter, if you have a vehicle, take some time to stock it with everything you will wish you had should you break down or go off the road, far from help. Some of those items might include:

- **A thermal blanket**
- **High calorie foods (jerky, energy bars, etc).**
- **Water (which will freeze and need to be melted)**
- **GORE TEX and down gloves or mittens**
- **Wool hat**
- **Face protection (balaclava, neoprene mask, scarf, etc.)**
- **Boots**
- **Winter coat**
- **Layered clothing**
- **Hand crank flashlight**
- **Hand crank radio**
- **Fire starter (flint, stormproof matches, blow torch style lighter, etc.)**
- **Tinder (fuel cells)**
- **Paracord**
- **Jump-start kit**
- **Snow brush**
- **Ice scraper**
- **Tire chains or studs (where permitted)**
- **Visual signaling device (flares, signal panel, etc.)**
- **Audio signaling device (whistle, air horn, etc.)**
- **Travel-sized snow shovel**
- **Gas can**

- Healthy and fully inflated spare tire
- External battery for recharging your phone
- First-aid kit (with tourniquet and pressure bandage)
- Multi-tool
- Chemical hand and foot warmers
- Thermal socks
- Window breaker
- Emergency shelter (mylar blanket, poncho, tarp, etc.)

This might seem like a long list, but most of us have these things around somewhere anyway. Why not gather them up and put them into your car? Better to take the time to do this now than regret it later. It might save your life.

DON'T WRITE IT DOWN

At the risk of sounding overly simplistic: Do not write anything down. Trust me. As a security conscious person, you must be aware that anything you write, in any medium, can be stolen. If it can be stolen, it can be used for many bad things: ID theft, money theft, home invasion, kidnapping, extortion, blackmail, public humiliation, etc. Any electronic information can be hacked. Anything physical, like paper, can be stolen or copied. This should be in the forefront of our minds when we create and handle data. Unless it is being recorded, a spoken conversation comes down to one person's word against another. It is often very difficult to get to the absolute truth. However, written data speaks for itself.

If you have a reason to protect the fact that something exists, do not text about it, email about it or pass notes about it unless you can communicate in code. Even using an encryption system does not guarantee its security. There are many things we must be willing to allow to be written down. Anyone who has ever gone to college, bought a house, applied for a credit card, taken out a loan or bought a car knows how much personal information is required for that paperwork. There is no fool-proof system. The companies that gather that data on you do their best to protect it while it is in their care. However, we see hacking scandals in the news every month. So, if you have information that must remain secret, the only way to ensure secrecy is keep it in your head instead of writing it down.

NOTHING SUCCEEDS LIKE SUCCESS

In the military, there is a concept known as "confidence targets." This is when newly trained personnel are given an assignment that their leader knows they can achieve. It is designed to allow them to put their brand new skills to work in the real world and prove to themselves that it can be done. Not only can it be done, they have everything they need in order to do it. Once it is accomplished, the rookie gets a huge confidence boost and knows they are fully capable of doing it again in the future. Even if the next task is a bit more difficult, just having the confidence that comes from accomplishment sets them up for success.

This is the way we should train and perform in all our survival and self-defense capabilities. Once we learn a new skill, we should go ahead and employ it in a crawl/walk/run kind of way. If your new skill is in firearms or hand-to-hand combat, you will only want to employ it in a training environment. If it is a survival skill, go ahead and use it.

Unused skills get rusty. Using the things we know how to do keeps them sharp and builds our confidence to reach higher and higher levels of difficulty. Take a moment and consider the goals you can set for yourself on a daily, weekly, monthly or even yearly basis that will set you up for success. Use that momentum to your advantage.

FIRES GROW FAST

The night before Thanksgiving one year, I spent hours toasting eight loaves of bread in the oven in order to make sage and onion stuffing for my family. On Thanksgiving morning, I got up at 4 a.m. to put the turkey in the oven. I prepared it according to our traditions and put it in the roasting pan. I added chicken broth to the bottom of the pan to be sure to have lots of gravy later on. Then I covered the turkey with the lid to the roasting pan, put it in the preheated oven and went back to bed. I woke up at 6:30 a.m., showered, got dressed and headed back to the kitchen to baste the turkey. I grabbed a pair of oven mitts and opened the oven door. Whoosh! A fireball rushed at my face and I jumped back. Within two seconds the fire had spread up the stove, up the wall, up the microwave, up the cabinets and all the way to the ceiling.

I had a gas stove. The bread crumbs from the eight loaves of bread had collected in the bottom of the oven. One turkey leg had popped the lid partially off of the roasting pan and was wicking the oils from the bottom of the pan, up the leg and slowly dripping them over the side. The breadcrumbs and oil were the fuel. The gas stove was the spark. All the mixture needed then was oxygen, which I provided by opening the oven door.

Without thinking, I grabbed the turkey in its roasting pan and pulled it from the inferno and placed it on the counter behind me. Then, I shut the oven door and turned off the gas, certain that cutting off oxygen to my gas oven would contain and eventually smother the fire. I could not have been more wrong. It got too big too fast. Billows of black smoke poured out and filled the room. I threw open the sliding glass door in the kitchen but I could not get ahead of it. By this time, the smoke was down below my shoulders. I dropped to the ground so that I could see and breathe but my exposure had been too much. In that short amount of time, my eyes and my esophagus had been seriously burned. I thrust by face into the crook of my elbow to save my burning eyes, coughing then choking as smoke continued to fill the room. I could not stop. I had to get out.

Blind and choking, I made my way down the stairs and out of my house, something I was only able to do thanks to my level of familiarity with my surroundings. I managed to dial 911 and make my problem known (in what sounded like the voice of a bullfrog) in between gasps and chokes. I fell to the ground in my front yard, and that is where fire and rescue found me.

I learned something very valuable and scary that Thanksgiving day. Fires can grow FAST and smoke can become debilitating in a matter of seconds. I had been schooled on the dangers of fire and smoke and I knew the risks, but the one thing I did not know was the timeline. I was astonished at how fast I went from routinely checking on a turkey to totally incapacitated.

Any time you stay in a hotel or in someone else's home, you are at the mercy of the decisions of the other people in that building. Because that is the place where you will sleep, you are in a state of increased vulnerability. If something catastrophic awakens you from a sound sleep, your survival will depend on your ability to stay calm, make sound decisions and draw from the resources you brought with you. You may have to start dealing with the problem before you are even able to exit your room.

HOW TO MAKE YOUR OWN SMOKE HOOD

There are some hacks you can use to improvise your own, but it takes access to the right materials and prior planning. You will need a gallon sized plastic jug, clear packing tape, a sponge and scissors.

1. Remove the cap and turn the bottle upside down.

2. Cut out a rectangular hole in the "front" of the bottle, large enough for you to see through. (This is the side opposite the handle.) Cut the "back" (handle side) of the bottle away, making sure to leave the actual handle in place. Leave a 2-inch piece of continuous plastic in place from the viewport side of the bottle, which will go over your head and down the back of your head, for stability.

3. Seal the viewport you just created with clear packing tape.

4. Put your head inside the apparatus. The original opening of the bottle (where the cap was) should be under your chin.

5. Seal the entire thing to your face with packing tape.

6. Soak the sponge in clean water and place it in the neck of the bottle's opening, where the cap used to be.

I strongly recommend carrying a smoke hood with you when you travel. A smoke hood would have saved my eyes and esophagus from burns that day and would have saved me from smoke inhalation and depleted oxygen, the effects of which lingered for days after the event. If you carry a quick-donning smoke hood with you when you travel, you maximize your chances of survival in the event of a fire or smoke bomb.

The DIY smoke hood above might be worth the time it takes to experiment with it at home, but you will need to ask yourself how likely you are to take your creation with you when you travel, or have access to the individual components and the time to make one, when the need strikes. In my kitchen that day, I would have had the time to slip into a ready-made smoke hood, but I would not have had the time to build a gas mask from scratch.

IT'S ONLY YOUR LIFE

Whenever I see someone doing something negligent or dangerous, I will say to them, "It's only your life. How much is that worth?" This is my way of cautioning them to pause, think and re-evaluate their plan. It might be telling them to stop being lazy or cutting corners on safety issues. It might mean more work needs to be put in before they are ready. It might mean there is a glaring flaw in their thinking or in their plan, or it might mean that the plan is simply too risky.

For us, it simply means this: The world is getting crazier all the time. Man-made problems and natural disasters abound and they seem to be occurring with increasing frequency. Now, more than ever, we truly need to be prepared for anything. If we know this and do nothing to prepare ourselves, then I would simply ask, "It's only your life. How much is that worth?"

MENTAL TOUGHNESS

YOUR BRAIN: THE ULTIMATE WEAPON.

THE BEST ALLY you have in your fight for survival is usually not a multi-tool, a tactical hand axe or even duct tape. It's that honed bit of gray matter between your ears. Training your brain to prioritize your values, assess your risks and overcome your own internalized biases—to already know what to do when danger strikes rather than default to fight-or-flight—might just be the thing that gets you home at the end of the day. From learning the finer points of principle-based living to understanding how to read the people around you to knowing how your body reacts in crisis mode, these tips will help you make the most of all your mind has to offer.

IMAGE PROJECTION

Image projection is anything you broadcast about yourself by your words, actions, body language, posture and facial expressions. You may or may not be aware of how these things are being read by the people around you, but you can choose to purposely direct what you project.

If you stand up straight, look people in the eye, smile, speak with enough volume that no one has to strain to hear you and pay attention to the people you see, you project an image of confidence.

However, if your posture is poor, you look down, do not smile, do not engage with people, speak in a whisper and keep your hands in your pockets, you project an image of defeat or fear.

Similarly, if your face looks grim, you walk in a rush, you speak little, never smile and never really look at another person, you project an image of being angry, impatient or in a hurry.

If you stroll along lazily, smile at people, stop to chat with anyone who looks interested, laugh and talk with your hands, your image projection is someone who is friendly, relaxed and easy-going.

There is no wrong answer. As long as you understand what image you are projecting, all of them may, at some point, suit your needs. You may choose to come across as brusque or impatient when you wish to be left alone, or you may want to come across as relaxed and friendly if you want to be approachable.

Did you know that your feet alone can tell a trained observer about your next move and about your level of comfort? A person's feet usually point in the direction they want to go. If you stand and face someone squarely when you talk to them and your feet are pointed right at them, you are very open and comfortable with the person and the encounter. If your feet are pointed away from the person, you are not as comfortable and wish to depart as soon as you can politely go. When your feet begin to shuffle, this signals you are bored, impatient or just plain uncomfortable.

Crossing your arms is a form of blocking the other person out and of keeping yourself safe. This conveys that you feel threatened at some level and need to erect a barrier between you and them. It conveys unapproachability.

Adding a physical item between you and the other person is another way of erecting a barrier. When you sit down across a table from someone, if you clear

away all the items on the table and lean forward, you are conveying your level of comfort and trust in that person. If you put your bag, backpack, briefcase, or purse on the table between you, that projects an image of being guarded and not entirely at ease.

Eye contact is very telling. When you are unwilling or are unable to make eye contact with someone, that projects the image that you have something to hide. Making and maintaining eye contact invites the other person in and conveys that you are both open and truthful.

Keeping your hands in your pockets can project different meanings. It can project a superior and arrogant attitude, discomfort or even confidence. People keep their hands in their pockets for multiple reasons: feeling cold, hiding something, confidence or discomfort. When it comes to reading someone whose hands are in their pockets, you must look for other context clues to help you figure out their motivation.

BODY LANGUAGE

A person can say a lot with their posture alone.

FEET: A person's feet will usually point in the direction they want to go, or directly at you if they feel comfortable.

EYES: Note whether or not they make eye contact with you, or where they choose to look instead.

ARMS: Are they loose and open (relaxed) or crossed (closed-off or guarded)?

Large arm movements project an image of extreme comfort. Whether the person is relaxed or agitated, they feel completely comfortable expressing themselves.

On the other hand, keeping your arms tucked close to you projects an image of discomfort, fear, anxiety and lack of confidence. People's arm movements become restricted as they become increasingly uncomfortable until their arms are practically pinned at their sides.

Leaning toward the other person, looking them in the eye, pointing your feet at them and removing all physical barriers projects an image that you are truly interested in what they have to say and that they have all of your attention. Be aware that this can be mistaken for romantic interest, however, so use with care.

Leaning away from the other person, looking away, pointing your feet away and placing a barrier item between you and them projects an image of discomfort and distrust.

You can become aware of how you are being subliminally read by others, and you can also begin to read the people around you. Reading the people around you is an early warning detection system that something is wrong and you need to get off the X. Deciding which image you want to project can move you out of the category of soft target and into the category of hard target.

THE SURVIVAL IMPLICATIONS OF ADDICTION

There is a wise, old saying that "an ounce of prevention is worth a pound of cure." That is absolutely true. There are so many things we can predict, for which we can plan and prepare, because we have seen them occur somewhere in history. The reason you are reading this is because you recognize the folly of thinking that adversity will never come to you. You know it will. What you may not know, however, is the type of adversity you will face. It is best to prepare yourself on every level you possibly can to maximize your own ability to weather that storm.

One of the things that will put you at an immediate disadvantage during adversity is having an addiction. Addictions take many forms: alcohol, television, tobacco, gambling, sex, sugar, video games, caffeine, illegal drugs, prescriptions, over-the-counter medications, routines, food, entertainment, achievement, clubs, sports, social interactions, books, stories, podcasts, YouTube, social media, web surfing, shopping, cosmetics, grades, accolades, music, movies, success, power, work, money, etc. The list is as long or as short as you want it to be. Human beings can become addicted to anything at all. We love patterns. We easily develop habits. We like ritual and routine and we can put up quite the fight when it comes to resisting change. That is the perfect recipe for developing an addiction or an unhealthy dependency on something.

While life is normal, this may seem like a manageable situation. However, the moment adversity arrives, addictions are as helpful as weights chained to your ankles. An addiction will slow down your progress, interfere with your decision making and cloud your judgment. Instead of starting your fight for survival with an advantage, you will be starting at a deficit.

Say I am addicted to coffee. I cannot start my day without it. I keep going back for more all day long. I get headaches if I go without it for too long and I get grumpy when I cannot have it soon enough. In fact, I will drag myself around all day unless I can get that regularly-scheduled dose of caffeine. But one day, disaster strikes. There is an epidemic. I am in a shelter-in-place situation. Suddenly, I cannot get to the store to replenish my precious supply of coffee, which means I have to start metering my intake and rationing myself to make it last. I am grumpy because I want more than I can have. My energy level is almost non-existent as I try to go from six cups a day to two. I am battling constant headaches. My morale is terrible and I am making everyone around me miserable. The addiction is so ingrained in me that I am actively considering going out anyway, risking my health and breaking into a closed market so that I can satisfy my withdrawal craving.

Do you see what happened there? I entered an adverse situation at a deficit because of an addiction. Coffee had mastery over me—it colored how I felt, what I did and all of my decisions. I became a drain on the morale of my companions and was even willing to do something unsafe and illegal to satisfy my cravings. I was unable to keep up physically and whatever stamina I had came out of a coffee cup. Is that how I want to tackle a survival situation? Is that any way to set myself up for success?

There is a difference between enjoying a pleasure and being a slave to it. Anything you are compelled to serve has enslaved you. Addictions are a

MASTER TACTIC

What do you use to function at your peak? Coffee? Tea? Cigarettes? Test yourself. Eliminate one of your necessary vices for two weeks and see if you can push yourself to do without.

perfect example. We have touched on advanced preparation of the battle space (pg. 13) repeatedly. If you are willing to take a hard look at yourself, you may find you have a dependency that you have never recognized. Take a moment to imagine yourself in an adverse situation, then ask yourself how you would do without access to your addiction. That information may inspire you to change your habits now so that you can set yourself up for success in the event of an emergency.

Years ago, I was in a terrible car accident. My leg was crushed into the dashboard and my patella was driven up into my femur. I had a series of surgeries to reconstruct my knee. It was so bad the doctor told me that the surgery was essentially a salvage operation and that he could not restore all that was lost. He did, however, tell me I would regain anywhere between 10 and 90 percent back and that the gain would largely be dependent on my level of physical fitness at the moment of the accident. Fortunately, I was young and I was an athlete. I was in the best shape of my life at the moment I got hit. As a result, I gained the maximum 90 percent of my capabilities back after the surgery by following a grueling physical therapy regimen. If I had been an out-of-shape couch potato at the moment when adversity struck, my prognosis would have looked far more grim.

I did not know that I was going to be hit by a car that day, or any day, for that matter. I never expected to experience that. However, it can happen to anyone and did to me. I was not an athlete because I was trying to set myself up to recuperate well from an accident. However, my lifestyle of physical fitness came to my rescue and helped me to overcome. One year, two surgeries, a wheelchair, a pair of crutches, many physical therapy sessions and a cane later, I emerged as a conqueror. I entered those adverse conditions at an advantage, not a deficit.

Do you have a dependency in your life that could soon become a liability when trouble strikes? Consider what decisions you can make today to gain the upper hand. Do not settle for a setback. Choose to live in a state of readiness and set yourself up in such a way that you will survive adversity, conquer it and thrive.

PRECONCEIVED IDEAS

Let me start by saying I am not going to tell you preconceived ideas are always a bad thing. On the contrary, preconceived ideas come from some amount of data and can even work to your advantage. It takes unclouded judgment to decide whether your preconceived ideas about a person, place, thing or idea are founded on sound data or rumor. Are they the result of facts or an emotional response based on a prior experience?

Preconceived ideas are sometimes completely accurate. When that happens, they serve to give you a warning of what to expect with regard to conditions, climate or known problems. If you plan to travel to Ukraine, you must first do your homework to understand the social and political climate of the region, the key players, the risk/threat level and the culture. You may want to visit the U.S. State Department's website (*www.state.gov*) and read about the country's current status. You should look for any U.S. travel advisories and you should also do a bit of independent research on Russia/Ukraine relations, Neo-nazism, the Orange Revolution, Victor Yanukovych, Yulia Tymoshenko, President Petro Poroshenko and the Euromaidan revolution of 2013–14. Read a bit about the culture and the current pro- or anti-U.S. sentiment. Study the baseline and decide how to pack and what to wear to stay in the gray. By the time you finish your research, you will have a preconceived idea of what Ukraine is like and what you will experience when you get there. Your preconceived ideas will be founded on research and data, while your in-country experiences will correct any misimpressions you may have had.

However, if you plan to travel to Ukraine and decide not to do any research, your preconceived ideas will be based upon vague recollections of news stories over the past five years and ill-founded emotional impressions. You will develop a nebulous standard by which you gauge your perceived threat/risk level. You will also likely discount the fact that they are a country at war and you will certainly not understand the reasons why. Looking through the lens of your isolated, uninformed understanding, your preconceived ideas of them might be limited to what you remember of *Dr. Zhivago* or *Fiddler on the Roof.* You may even regard them as quaint and you will not feel the need to take any notice of the standard recommended security measures. Frankly, your guard will be down and you will be a very soft target.

It may come as a surprise but the same principle works in the opposite direction as well. If your preconceived ideas about a place or a group of people are based on negative emotions like fear or hatred, you are likely to arrive with your shields up in condition orange. All it will take is a sideways glance or a frown from a stranger to take you from orange to red. You will not be able to make friends or to enjoy yourself. You will not have an easy time de-escalating your perceived threat level from condition orange to yellow so that you can relax. Your senses will be on alert, your system will be producing unneeded levels of adrenaline and cortisol, you will have trouble concentrating and trouble sleeping. Whether you are there for business or pleasure, your trip will be muted under a draining black cloud of unfounded emotion.

Ask yourself: Are my feelings the result of rumor? Someone else's story? An unpleasant encounter with just one person from that region or culture? Bigotry? News articles? Common social sentiment? Political leanings? Religious bias? First-hand experience? Second- or third-hand knowledge?

If you have had repeated first-hand unpleasant encounters in a region of the world or among a particular people, then your preconceived notions are founded. If that is the case, you must make two decisions: You must treat every new person you meet there as an individual who is innocent unless they do something to breach your trust, and you must brush up on your situational awareness and personal security measures to make yourself a hardened target.

The data at your fingertips these days is more than enough to allow you to gather information on any people, place, thing or idea you can imagine. Use it to research facts in order to develop a preconceived idea that is as close to the truth as possible. Do not allow yourself to fall prey to negative emotions based on rumors and hearsay. By all means, listen to your instincts, but back up your gut feelings with data. Gather all the information you can so that you will know what to expect. Situational awareness begins with advance planning. Make sure your preconceived ideas are grounded in reality and not fear.

BOUNDARIES AND PRINCIPLE-BASED LIVING

Boundaries are a relatively simple concept, right? A line between two zones, designed to keep out any unauthorized access. Easy to say. Easy to understand. But incredibly difficult to enforce.

Physical boundaries are found all over the place. Customers are not authorized to go behind the cash register. You need a passport to cross borders between countries. The demilitarized zone between North and South Korea in particular is a pretty contentious boundary that comes to mind.

Ethical boundaries keep us from doing the wrong thing. They are the lines we are not willing to cross because of our principles. Refusing to lie because lying is against your principles is a boundary.

Psychological boundaries keep us from all kinds of things. When we believe something is impossible, we do not bother to attempt it. For example, we would not jump off of a tower and expect to fly with no parachute because we do not believe that it can be done. Of course, this is a good boundary to have as it keeps us from potentially harming ourselves.

Meanwhile, emotional boundaries are the walls we erect to keep us from becoming hurt on an emotional level. When we try to resist falling in love, for instance, we may keep that person at arm's length and refuse to let them in. These boundaries are a mixed bag, as some can backfire and cause us even more pain.

Political boundaries are set by the party affiliation. Public opinion is king and people generally stay within their boundaries in order to avoid criticism.

Scientific boundaries are things that have yet to be explained, proven or accomplished.

Where are your personal boundaries? Do you make them known? Do you enforce your words with actions? People give lip service to all kinds of things: priorities, morals, etc. However, believing in something and wanting it to be does not make it so. For example, you can tell a person or an organization that they are your number one priority in the entire world, but if they consistently rank last in your thinking and planning, clearly they are not your true priority. The distance between what a person wants and what they actually have is the measure of their unhappiness. In order for something to be a true priority, it has to be treated that way. This is what defines a priority. It is what you actually protect, provide for and favor before everything else.

A boundary is not a boundary if it is not enforced. If I draw a line on the ground and tell you not to cross it "or else," then do nothing when you step across it, that is not truly a boundary. That is simply a line on the ground. On a personal security note, say someone has a personal boundary that they will not go to bed with the person they are dating because they insist on waiting for marriage. In order to enforce that, they need to make the decisions to uphold that boundary—namely, they need to make that boundary known to all parties involved. They need to guard against taking things too far. They need to avoid situations which would make crossing that boundary too easy, to say no if their date tries to push, guilt or charm their way across that line. If they are serious about maintaining that boundary, they are the one who will need to enforce it. No one else will care as much about keeping it intact as they will. Boundaries that go unenforced are nothing more than preferences.

It is not easy to enforce personal boundaries, but this harkens back to the Fulcrum Principle (pg. 31). No one can do it for you. Only you can decide where your boundary lines are and only you can protect them from unauthorized incursion.

Likewise, principles are like the boundary lines on a soccer field: if you stay in between them, they will help you get to your goals. Our principles guide us through life. The truly beautiful thing about them is that they become a beacon of light in the darkness. They are a trusty compass under a thick jungle canopy. They are our instruments in a zero-zero landing (when the pilot has zero forward visibility and zero cloud clearance at the touchdown point; in other words, the clouds come all the way down to the ground and touch the runway). Adhering to your principles when you cannot see the path laid out before you is the only way to stay on course. It is easy to navigate to something you can see, but it is much more difficult to navigate blind. However, it is not impossible. All you need is a little instrumentation. The instrument we have in adversity is our principles.

People do not stay static. They move constantly. When adversity strikes, it will produce movement in one way or another. People will either cling more tightly to their principles and make every decision accordingly, or they will move away from their principles and begin to make their decisions based upon expediency, convenience or fear.

Which way will you move when the moment comes?

PRE-MADE DECISIONS

"An experienced Navy carrier pilot got a bad cat shot [launch off the runway] and had to decide whether to eject out of a perfectly good airplane before the end of the catapult stroke. He had about two seconds to eject. If he waited too long he would be outside the safe ejection envelope and would likely hit the water with the aircraft and die. The decision had to be split second and once made, there was no turning back. He ended up safely ejecting. After they pulled him from the water, the squadron commander met him in the medical bay and asked, 'When did you decide you had to eject?' The pilot's reply was, 'Seven years ago during training. I was just waiting for the right time to act on the decision.'" (Author Unknown)

We need to consider what our options are long before adversity comes calling. Having a plan and sticking to it will inevitably increase your odds of survival. I am a big fan of the concept of "when, not if." Allowing yourself to say "if" gives you permission not to accomplish your goals, e.g. "If I get out of here alive, I will find my family." Does that sound even remotely like something a conqueror would say?

How about when instead? "When I get out of here alive, I will find my family." The word choice helps us sort out our pre-made decisions. When adversity comes. When I take action. When I move. When I fight. When I survive. When I conquer.

This simple but powerful wording is a major component of advance preparation of the battle space (pg. 13). Taking the time now to decide how you will act and what you will do takes much of the chaos and pandemonium out of the equation and replaces it with action and reason. Now is the time to plan because you are thinking logically rather than emotionally. There is nothing causing you fear or demanding immediate action on your part. You can take the time you need to consider how you really want things to be. Play the "what if" game and see what happens. Allow yourself to imagine all the possibilities, then decide what actions you would take in each situation. You will be amazed how quickly those pre-made decisions come to you in that moment of adversity.

INCREMENTAL DECISION MAKING

Goals and destinations are reached through incremental decisions. Every decision we inwardly label as small or unimportant takes us further down a path in one direction or another. If we pay attention to each decision and how it will affect the outcome, we will wind up where we desire to be. If we lose sight of the small decision's impact on the whole picture, we might wind up somewhere less than desirable.

How can we best help ourselves? If I develop a set of core convictions and values to which I hold myself at all times, they will guide me down the right path and toward the goal of my choosing. It should be said that stopping to compare a pending decision against my ethics every time can make for slow progress. It consumes time, brain power and energy. I will soon come to find that developing values and convictions is not enough, that I must adopt them and graft them into my very personality as well. If I can do that, my instinctive reaction in a given situation will be one which sets me up for future success.

For example, I would submit that no one sets out to become an alcoholic or drug addict from the beginning. Rather, they end up in that unenviable position when they lose sight of how their little decisions are moving them along toward a negative destination. By the time they arrive, they might be surprised to find out where they are and how they got there.

I was once diagnosed with anorexia and malnutrition due to starvation. I have long had a food aversion and an unhealthy perspective on it. In my quest to drop the weight I had gained slowly over time, I became frustrated with my inability to get any traction and elected to diet and exercise. It started out very well. I ate a baseline of a certain number of calories per day plus whatever I earned in exercise. I used a fitness heart rate monitor to help me figure out what my calorie burn rate was. I lost 20 pounds and then plateaued. I waited there for eight weeks, eating X calories a day and exercising and adding those back in. So, to give my metabolism a nudge, I added time to my workouts. I went from 60 to 90 minutes a day. I gave that four weeks. Nothing changed. So, I pulled back to less calories, plus calories burned. I gave it four weeks. Still no change. I increased my exercise routine to 120 minutes a day. No change. Even less calories, plus calories burned. No change. I pushed it up again to 150 minutes of exercise a day. No change. Finally, I stopped adding my exercise calories back in at all.

Between each of the changes, I waited a month to see results before pushing it to the next level. I ended up at two-and-a-half-hours of exercise and a total consumption of 900 calories per day.

I have a constant battle going on inside me about calories. I really hate them. I do not want to eat, then I pay the price. I know I should eat and I lecture myself about the damage I am doing. I fix a nice, appetizing plate of something, anything, eat three bites of it and push it away. I feel guilty for eating those calories when I am so unhappy with my weight and shape. Then, I feel physically bad for not eating. Friends, this is a no-win scenario.

By the time I went to see the endocrinologist, I had developed rapid onset migraines. I also developed an unpredictable tachycardia (spiked heart rate) while working out vigorously. I would start to shake, turn white, break out in a cold sweat and be overcome by a nausea so fierce that I would fly into the nearest restroom to vomit. It was sometimes accompanied by diarrhea and once caused internal bleeding. The endocrinologist explained to me that when the body does not have all it needs, it begins to prioritize systems and the ones that do not make the priority list get shut down. She warned me that if this went on, my systems would begin to shut down. The body cannot run all its systems on so little fuel, no vitamins, electrolytes or minerals.

I was shocked to learn I was an anorexic because I never paid attention to every little decision that contributed to the end result. I have since taken every step I can think of to correct the situation and change my path. I now take vitamins every day. I stay hydrated, eat a healthy calorie count every day, limit my exercise to 60 minutes per day and I no longer consume caffeine or sugar. These are the little decisions that have established me on the path of my choosing.

MASTER TACTIC

Take a step back and consider all the goals you have not yet reached. Have you tried taking a different approach? Getting a second opinion might help you see things more clearly.

If you were hiking through the woods on a trail you had never taken before, you would need to pay attention to your course, direction, the distance you had covered and your speed. You would need to stop every once in a while and compare your actual progress with your intended progress.

Every "little" decision we make has some impact on the big picture. What about your decisions to be situationally aware? Are you paying attention to the trend and overall trajectory? Are you capable of acting in a crisis, or are you becoming paranoid and afraid to go out in public? It is wise to stop and assess your current position and heading every once in a while as you track your progress toward success.

Where are your decisions taking you?

THINK DIFFERENTLY

I am a hostage negotiator and this is a recounting of an exercise in which I once participated...

I arrived at the Army base at 0530 and was immediately put to work as the only moulage artist (i.e., the artist who creates fake blood, wounds and injuries as a visual aid for training emergency response personnel) present. I was asked to create five wounded people, including myself. Sergeant (Sgt.) Jefferson was the target of the shooter's wrath. I was assigned the character of Sgt. Jefferson's family member. I was placed in the room of the initial breach by shooter, Sgt. Washington, and was the only eyewitness to his first kill. I managed to run out ahead of him and fled to an office in an adjacent building where I hid under a desk. After going on a shooting spree, Sgt. Washington grabbed one male and one female hostage before barricading himself in the office next to the one wherein I was hiding. More specifically, the female hostage was Sgt. Jefferson's daughter, Leona. He had shot her in the shoulder/collarbone and the bullet had exited her body via her back. She was coughing up blood.

The MP SWAT team came through and cleared the entry room, hallway and the office where I was hiding without looking under the desk. Sgt. Washington loudly cursed them and told them to get out of the building, threatening to kill Leona Jefferson if they did not comply. He further stated that, if he heard anyone in the building after that, he would kill her. Aware of the mounting threat but not wanting to provoke the shooter's wrath, the SWAT team pulled out and surrounded the building, calling in aerial support. Four helicopters arrived, relaying the situation as seen from the air to the teams on the ground. From my position in the office next door, I could hear everything. Neither the shooter, nor the hostages, nor the police knew of my presence in the building. I could hear Leona coughing. I could hear the exchange between the shooter on the inside and the hostage negotiator with the bullhorn on the outside. I stayed in place for an hour. During this time, the shooter demanded medical supplies for Leona. The negotiator ordered a phone to be included in the supplies, all of which were delivered carefully and left for the shooter to retrieve. The shooter refused to use the phone they provided, believing it to be a bomb or a trap. He took the medical supplies and ordered his male hostage to attend to Leona. Sgt. Washington insisted that if he had anything to say, he would shout through the window.

The hostage negotiator spent an hour trying to pry some concessions from the shooter. Unfortunately, Sgt. Washington was belligerent and completely uncooperative. There were windows in the office where I was hiding and the closest window was open and had no screen. After an hour under the desk, I quietly came out from under the desk, staying below the window frame. I made my way to the open window and raised a hand to allow SWAT to see me. All guns swiveled in my direction. I raised both hands above the window frame, indicating I was unarmed. I heard them exclaim there was an unknown hostage inside. I had been given a cell phone for the exercise, so I held it up for them to see and then placed it in the open window and backed away. No one came close. I looked through the drawers in the desk that was functioning as my concealment, and found paper and a pen. I wrote this note. "The shooter does NOT know that I am in here. He says if he hears anyone in this building, he will kill Leona. Please help us. Leona is hurt. I can hear her coughing. Where is Sgt. Jefferson? Please get me out." I made a paper airplane out of the note and flew it out the window as far as I could. It landed halfway to the SWAT team. All guns swiveled toward the paper airplane as the teams tried to identify what it was. After a few minutes, they were able to retrieve it.

Two SWAT team members approached my window from the opposite end of the building to the room where the shooter and hostages were barricaded. They asked me if I could get out and I told them that I was afraid to because if Sgt. Washington heard or saw me, he would kill Leona. The door to the office where I was hiding was wide open. They asked me if I could get out through the window. I said yes. They asked me to do that. I climbed halfway out and they grabbed me, pulled me out and got me away to safety. They took me to the incident command post where they handed me over to an EMT and a Criminal Investigation Department (CID) agent. The EMT worked on the laceration on my hand while the CID agent began interviewing me. I stayed at the incident command post for the remainder of the exercise. The building with the shooter and hostages was to my back and I continued to hear the entire exchange; meanwhile, since the incident command team was right in front of me, I had the chance to observe them, too. In other words, it was the perfect position for me specifically as a hostage negotiator and as a multi-disciplined member of Incident Command Teams. I spent an hour with CID, answering all their questions and drawing diagrams of the two buildings and rooms. The information they gathered from me was streamlined and given to the incident commander, who began to formulate a more comprehensive picture. All the while I continued to play my part, asking for Sgt. Jefferson and begging them to help Leona. Eventually, the hostage negotiator began to appeal for Leona to be released so she could be taken to the hospital.

After CID got everything they needed from me, they told me they would be contacting Sgt. Jefferson to come get me. Suddenly, Mrs. Washington arrived on scene and barricaded herself in her car, whereupon she pulled out a gun and held it to her own head. All non-essential personnel evacuated the incident command post and fled to Mrs. Washington's car. Meanwhile, I was told Sgt. Jefferson had been found and that he would be picking me up. I waited for two hours, watching the command post work. When my CID agent came back, I pulled him aside and called an academic situational time out. Knowing CID had failed to uncover the identity of the murdered man, I explained that Sgt. Jefferson was dead. He had been the target of Sgt. Washington's fury and was killed at the very beginning of the exercise. He would not be picking me up after all. Then I got back into character. He reported that to the incident commander and I was interviewed again, whereupon they were able to learn more pertinent information. I continued to watch the command post at work, while listening to the ongoing negotiations and working with CID.

After hours of trying, the hostage negotiator finally managed to secure Leona's release. Sgt. Washington realized there was no reason to allow her to die, so he released her and she was taken to the hospital. Now he was down to one hostage. He had no terms. He admitted loudly he knew he had ended his career, his freedom and perhaps even his life when he shot and killed Sgt. Jefferson, and that he was stalling out of fear. He began talking about a series of false allegations leveled against him regarding his daughter, how he had bravely served his country through multiple deployments, how he had been treated unfairly by Sgt. Jefferson and how he deserved so much better than that. He began to talk about ending it all by suicide, unaware his wife was outside in her car, threatening the same.

After another hour or two of ongoing negotiations, Sgt. Washington agreed to give up and come out. He was arrested and his remaining hostage was freed. The incident command post had been working for hours to secure a warrant to seize Mrs. Washington's car, disable it and download phone and GPS data from the vehicle's systems. When the authorization finally came through, they disabled her ability to get away, remotely accessing the data they needed. Two of the pieces of data they were trying to obtain were the location and contact information of Sgt. Washington's parents.

At this point, the exercise transitioned from critical incident management to a crime scene investigation and I was released for the day. The CID battalion commander thanked me and told me he looked forward to working with me again in future exercises.

Lessons learned:

- **Never declare a room clear until you have looked in every space big enough for a human to hide.**
- **Never give up hallway security once it is yours.**
- **Aerial support provides critical real-time information.**
- **All of the deceased must be positively identified before making any claims or promises to family members.**

- When a hostage-taker has no demands, it is nearly impossible to negotiate with them.
- The amount of information from just one interview can radically alter the course of the investigation and the flow of information at the incident command post.
- Hostage situations can rapidly escalate and secondary situations can arise.
- It is possible to have someone friendly on the inside and not know it.
- Ingenuity and clarity of thought are imperative for self-rescue.
- The psychiatrist and chaplain were needed much earlier than they were called.
- Psychological and spiritual triage would have been warranted.
- There needs to be one central person at the incident command post responsible for collecting incoming data and getting it up on the board.
- One eyewitness's report can make or break the case.
- The hostage negotiator can require backup if the negotiations are intense and protracted.
- It is still possible to appeal to the sympathy and humanity of a person, even after they have just killed an innocent man.
- Incident command posts are chaotic and incoming information needs to be streamlined. There needs to be processes in place for utilizing all pertinent data in one centralized way, instead of allowing it to become stove-piped by the incident command staff.

No matter your skill set, you must be willing to use unconventional plans to solve problems. Who would have thought a paper airplane could help rescue a hostage? Learn to make the most of the resouces around you and do what you can to think outside of the box. Remember this key takeaway:

Ingenuity and clarity of thought are imperative for self-rescue.

SMALL VICTORIES

In Survival, Evasion, Resistance and Escape (SERE) School, we are taught an incredibly valuable tool for resisting. On the surface, we are resisting our captors. We are resisting their questions, the cooperation they are trying to force, capitulation, aiding and abetting the enemy. In fact, we are resisting giving them any information at all. However, if we go a little deeper, we find an undeniable truth: What we are truly resisting is our propensity to give up. Remember that the true battleground is in the mind, right? No matter what is going on around you, focus on the strength within—that is where victory is won or lost.

We are not fighting the people around us. We are not fighting threats or abuse or manipulation or coercion or torture or toxicity or bullying or attempts to elicit information. We are fighting against our desire to succumb to defeat, depression, hopelessness, helplessness, victimhood, anger, a desire for revenge, fear, anxiety and despair. Instead, we are fighting to maintain hope, motivation, humanity, dignity, kindness, charity, gentleness, strength, character, peace, intelligence, ingenuity, calm, leadership, trustworthiness, an indomitable spirit, perseverance, loyalty, honor and pride.

In order to resist the lengthy list of negatives and the desire to give up, and in order to retain and maintain the lengthy list of positive attributes and a desire to survive, we are taught to look for small victories every day. You will move in the direction in which you are focused; if you can only see the negatives surrounding you, you will become negative, too. This is step one of giving up. However, if you allow yourself to truly look for a positive, no matter how small, and focus on that, that is step one in resisting, surviving and returning with honor.

In my life right now, I have a significant amount of difficult, weighty and sizable problems staring me in the face and I genuinely feel surrounded. To combat this, I decided to look for five small victories every day and tell one of my two best friends about them. The first day, I intended to write five things. I wrote 32. The second day, I intended to write five things and I wound up with 19. Each day I have taken inventory of my life, I have found more small victories than I expected. Because I am spending time looking for them, I am focused on them, and because I am focused on them, I cannot help but feel grateful. Now my attitude is one of gratitude. I am content. I feel more peace and I am actively looking for ways I can add small victories to my daily list.

When I recognize all of my many victories, I simply cannot feel helpless. Instead, it fuels my motivation. It moves me in a positive direction. It makes me more enjoyable to be around. It takes my focus off what I do not have and places it on what I do have. Doing this reminds me of the many things within my control. For me, practicing this simple habit imparts life and hope. It is the best antidote against despair I have ever encountered, and I do not say that lightly. It even helped me survive SERE school but the lesson was so much broader than that. Looking for small victories has translated into my daily life and has become my defense against the urge to succumb, the small voice urging me to give in.

This can be a life-saving tool when adversity strikes. If you ever find yourself weathering a natural or man-made disaster, you will need to remember how to count your blessings and keep your eyes trained on what lies ahead. It will save your morale, your life and that of those around you. It will mean the difference between victory and defeat. As always, remember advanced preparation of the battle space (pg. 13). Do not wait until disaster strikes to experiment with this for the first time. Begin to look for small victories today and shift your focus off of your problems and onto your wins. It will be of enormous benefit to you today and it will already be in place when you encounter adversity.

DON'T COMPARE YOURSELF TO OTHERS

My right-hand man, Kris, pulled out of specialized combat training for a couple of reasons. One of them was that our instructor talked a lot about the fact that not everyone who tests passes. He made that crystal clear, and we all showed up to the test knowing what to expect. However, there was one man who never seemed to do his best in class. He was an "energy conservationist" and seemed to exert as little effort as possible in order to do the bare minimum required of him. He would step out of training to grab food or check his text messages and emails. Kris and I thought he might not pass the test because we had never seen him demonstrate the stamina we were all repeatedly told we would need to have. As it happened, he took the test much like he trained and passed anyway. But Kris was very upset. We had worked ourselves sick to prepare for the test, and I exerted so much of myself during the test that I got a migraine. He, on the other hand, practically skated by, yet we all achieved the same outcome. This made Kris feel like our own accomplishments had been cheapened or, perhaps, were never worth much in the first place. However, I learned a few important things that apply to life and especially to adversity.

1) It is not about what anyone else does. It is about what I do and how I conduct myself. It was never about my instructor's decisions nor besting my fellow students. Instead, it was about me living up to my convictions and doing my best. As the saying goes, "Whatever your hand finds to do, do it with

all your might." This is another way of saying "do everything with excellence." Our fellow student's lack of effort or the instructor's lack of willingness to fail him in no way changed what I got out of applying myself, working hard, learning the curriculum and perfecting my technique. My knowledge base and skill set were earned through hard work and could not be taken away from me, nor could they be given to me had I not put in the work in the first place.

2) I never told this particular student about my own physiological difficulties. He had no way of knowing what I battle every day. What made me think there were no extenuating circumstances on his part? How did I know beyond a shadow of a doubt whether or not he was battling something that would prevent him from going all-out? The fact is I did not know. I could not rush to judgment when I clearly did not have all the facts.

3) Although we all took the test and passed, Kris and I emerged with a strength, stamina and balance that the other man did not have because he did not cultivate those attributes. Sure, he had the curriculum knowledge and the new position, but those are only two facets of many which go into making a person truly great. In fact, those are the only two things the instructors can provide. Everything else—balance, flexibility, power, stamina, attitude, reflexes, split-second decision making, etc.—can only be earned on an individual level through hard work and discipline.

4) Having finished my training, I must ask myself: What can I do for others with my newfound knowledge and skills? Perhaps I am here not only to receive training but to also give back in some way. I must look for ways to give of myself and help others. I also find that when I am in a position where all of my needs are not being met, I change my mission. Instead of asking, "Am I getting everything I want or need here?" I ask, "What can I contribute here?" Invariably, it changes my own attitude time and time again and shifts my mindset from stagnating to thriving.

In a survival or security situation, these takeaways are incredibly valuable. Adhering to your convictions, putting everything you have into preparing, conducting yourself with excellence and taking responsibility for yourself will make you and your group much stronger. These are the tools that set you up for success, establish you as a strong and trustworthy leader and safeguard morale as you get your people to safety.

PERSONAL RESPONSIBILITY

In this world of ever-changing values, personal responsibility often gets left behind or left out. People are quick to take offense and to assign blame, but they are not nearly so quick to accept responsibility for why things are the way they are. Personal responsibility begins with prior planning and advance preparation of the battle space (pg. 13). In order to do it right, we must determine how our own decisions factor into the outcome of our situations.

If disaster strikes, you must decide whether to shelter in place or bug out. If you shelter in place, that decision will come with a set of pros and a set of cons. The same happens if you decide to bug out. In either case, taking the time to plan your two options in advance in as much detail as you can will significantly reduce your risks and improve your chances of survival. Taking the time to walk through what-if scenarios, answer all the questions and solve all the problems that arise with your planning will arm you with a significant advantage when you need it most.

This is the key to assuming personal responsibility. When we can clearly see the role our own decisions played in the outcome of any situation, we can identify the cause-effect relationship between our decisions and our present circumstances. This works to our advantage in two ways: First, we can evaluate the outcome of our decisions and make better ones when we are unsatisfied with the outcome, and second, we can maximize the value of the good decisions by creating templates and applying them broadly.

I can make decisions alone just as much as you can. Ideally, we can make them and learn from them collectively. Making bad decisions and taking personal responsibility for the negative outcome allows us to learn from our mistakes. It makes us better leaders because we remain trustworthy and accountable throughout. It gives us the information and the authority to correct mistakes, sometimes even before they happen. Similarly, making good decisions allows us to learn what works and to take credit for positive outcomes. It allows us to replicate successes and to teach others what works in the long term. It also makes us trustworthy leaders with sound judgment. In an adverse situation, this is the kind of person that I would want to follow hands down.

I told you about a decision-making failure on my part while diving a rebreather (pg. 52) and how it almost cost me my life. Fortunately, I also took credit for a successful self-rescue that day. I learned a lot from that incident because I took personal responsibility for both my good and my bad decisions. I deconstructed how each careless decision got me into trouble and how each informed decision saved my life. Having identified my mistakes and having ruminated on what could have happened, I am certain I will never make those errors again. I identified what I did right and those are the tools I now carry with me on a daily basis.

What can you learn from your mistakes?

DECLINING OPTIONAL STRESS

We have all been told countless times to pick our battles, have we not? But how well do we do that? One way of picking your battles is something I like to refer to as declining optional stress. This means deciding which things are truly worth stressing over and which are not. It involves refusing to stress over the unimportant things and to instead focus on the things that will make a significant difference.

When we consider packing a bug-out bag (pg. 22), we are limited by space and weight. We must choose which things are valuable enough to carry. Which items are so critical in a true survival situation that they are worth taking up valuable space in your pack? Which things are so important to you that you would be willing to carry their weight around when you are hungry, tired, weak and possibly sick or wounded?

This same thinking should apply to stress. In a crisis, which predicament or information is worth your attention and your upset, and which can be filtered out? You cannot place everything at the top of your priority list. Only one thing can occupy the top slot. In a crisis, you cannot afford to ignore incoming information. However, once you receive it and process it, you must assign it a value. Not everything is worth becoming anxious, fearful or angry. Those feelings can sap you of your precious energy, stamina and morale. Think of it this way: The fact that the building is collapsing must take precedence over the fact that you are hungry. Deal with the collapsing building and do not allow yourself to stress over being hungry. You are far better off putting it out of your mind until you reach safety. Believe it or not, you can survive weeks without food if you need to. Decline to stress over minutiae that will clutter your thinking and prevent you from taking positive action on your own behalf.

PROJECTION

It should go without saying that we will all experience crises of one kind or another at some point in our lives. It is not a matter of if, but when. Accepting that, there are things we can do in order to maintain some level of control over ourselves and, in a larger sense, the outcome. We may not have any control of the situation as it unravels, but we will have control over our own actions and even, for those of us who know how, of our feelings.

As you know, the difference between a victim and a survivor is that a survivor has choices. A victim believes they have none. So, even in a crisis, we have choices to make. Projection is the ability to see beyond the crisis at hand to the desired (or at least the most likely) outcome. You will make it through this crisis. When you come out on the other side, what do you want life to be like? Having a clear understanding of what you want on the other side of the crisis, coupled with a belief that you have choices, is incredibly empowering. While the crisis is still unfolding and during the aftermath, you must make the choices that will contribute to the outcome of your heart's desire. That is the key to projection.

The ability to execute such a simple concept is profoundly effective. It imparts hope, the antidote to depression. It empowers the survivor with responsibility, the antidote to victimhood and learned helplessness. It gives the survivor a task and direction, the antidote to confusion. It brings order which brings peace, the antidote to panic. The key to all of this is what you believe now. You must believe that you will survive, that you have choices to make, that your choices will affect the outcome, and you must know which outcome you desire. For example, I lost the right engine in my Twin Comanche while in flight and needed to handle the emergency and save the lives of myself and my passenger. I immediately envisioned a safe landing back at our airport of origin. Every decision I made while handling the emergency, the weather and air traffic control was predicated on making the real outcome match the desired outcome. I wanted a routine and safe landing on the runway of my choosing and that is precisely what I got. Prepare that battle space in advance.

RELENTLESS

The only way to live is relentlessly. There are times when it would be so much easier to give up, give in and succumb. There are situations that are so overwhelming that dying seems preferable to continuing the fight. If your moral compass, pre-made decisions and convictions are already in place, they will provide the motivation you need to stay in the game.

I was in the fight of my life. While on a mission I am not at liberty to discuss in greater detail, I was trying to save my own life and that of a hostage. I was bloody and wounded. My uniform was torn. I was panting, hungry, thirsty and in pain. Weak and disoriented, I was carrying the heaviest load I have ever carried. I shivered in the cold, unable to see through the thick fog. It was so dark outside, the only way I could tell which direction to go was to note the simple fact that one way went uphill and took more effort while the downhill route took less effort. Heartbroken and sad, my tears obscured my vision. There were no humans in sight, friend or foe, but bullets were slamming into the trees around me on all sides, and I had been grazed by a couple already. With my heart rate maxed out, I sat in a defensive crouch. Out of ammo, all I could do was keep forcing myself along the uphill slope to safety. Had my radio not been broken, I would have requested an extraction immediately. For now, though, I was on my own.

Struggling my way up the hill, clawing my way higher under cover of darkness on my hands and knees, I reminded myself that nothing would stop me or force me to turn back. My code of conduct and pre-made decisions told me to keep going. Survive. Thrive. Live. Never give up. Do not succumb to despair. I had choices. The battle space is in your mind. Fight!

KEEP YOUR EYES ON THE GOAL

There is a concept in the military known as target fixation. When a person has a target in their sights, they lose sight of everything else, and when that happens, there is a phenomenon that occurs at the same time. If the person is in motion, they will move in the direction in which they are looking. For example, if my sights are set on something to my right and I am in motion, I will move to my right. The only way to alter my course is to allow myself to look elsewhere.

I am a cyclist. There is a long and beautiful bike trail near my house, which I use whenever I can. I learned a long time ago that if I see a rock ahead on the path, I cannot allow myself to fixate on the rock. When I devote all of my concentration to avoiding the rock, I look at the rock, I begin to steer toward it and before I know it—BAM—I hit the rock. My intense focus backfired because I fixated on the wrong thing. Instead, I need to focus on the space in between the rock and the edge of the path. When I concentrate on where I do want to go, I steer in that direction and pass easily through the open space next to the rock.

The same concept works for everything else in life. Whatever has my attention will set my direction. I have two choices here: I can allow myself to fixate on all that I do not want and all that I do not like. I can clutter my mind by telling myself over and over to avoid this or steer clear of that. I can obsess about things I do not like and make a concerted effort to stay away from them. Or I can ruminate on all the things I do like, want, approve of and admire. I can dwell on the positive rather than the negative, set a direction that is healthy and wise and I can set my sights on a good and noble goal.

I learned some profound lessons while taking my first off-roading class at North East Off-Road Adventures in Ellenville, New York, in the summer of 2018. Off-roading entails moving a large vehicle over rough, steep, rocky, sandy, wet, snowy or any other challenging terrain. It requires patience, trust, courage and skill.

My instructor, Scott, who is also the owner of the company, got out of the Jeep and stood next to my open window. He taught me the hand signals and told me to trust him, as he would be looking at the terrain and the vehicle for me. He pointed to a respectably steep and rocky descent and said he was going to get me down from that point. He asked me if I was ready and walked down the grade ahead of me, holding up the hand signal for STOP until he reached the bottom. I waited on the promontory and watched him make his way down. At last, he stopped and turned around. He gave the signal to move toward him slowly. I locked eyes on him and began my descent. I was not even nervous. Why? I never once looked at the terrain and instead looked only at him. I was amazed at how easy it was. I thought that trying to get down the side of a mountain in a Jeep would be very difficult. But it wasn't. I spent the rest of the day thinking about that first experience and asking myself why something so potentially dangerous and scary had turned out to be so easy and peaceful.

Here is what I learned: I did not so much as glance at the rocks or the steep grade because I chose to look only at Scott. He exuded calm confidence and I knew I could trust him to see everything I could not see. I trusted his superior experience and capabilities as well as his care for my safety and that of the vehicle. Throughout the exercise, I obeyed every signal as if my life depended on it. I refused to look at the problem. Instead, I kept my eyes obsessively fixed on the solution. I moved in the direction I was looking and I trusted. Where I chose to focus and where I put my trust determined the outcome of a potentially dangerous situation.

UNDERSTANDING THE MENTAL ARTS

As you have probably guessed by now, I am a huge fan of looking for the lesson in every situation. These are the things I believe and/or do to overcome adversity whenever it strikes. Crises do happen and I have weathered plenty of them in my life. These are my convictions, things that apply to seeing your way through times of war, peace, love, loss, strength, weakness, sickness, health, injury, disaster, terrorist attacks, routine life, travel and life at home. Surprisingly, it has been in the aftermath of my life's crisis moments that they have been my most valuable companions, my constant compass.

Service before self. Turning outward and serving others takes our focus off of ourselves, our personal problems and, the most detrimental of all to morale, our pain. It channels our energy in positive directions and leads to a feeling of pride when we make a positive difference in someone else's life.

- **Accomplishments boost morale like nothing else.**
- **The secret to contentment is gratitude.**
- **One's feelings are the caboose, not the engine of life.**
- **A person can direct their own feelings by acting as though they already feel the way they want to feel.**
- **The future is far more important than the past.**
- **Take responsibility for your own attitudes and actions.**
- **Actions precede attitudes.**
- **Attitudes precede actions.**
- **Be solid in your convictions and flexible in your interactions.**

- Strength is the ability to do great harm and, instead, to choose to do great good.
- Pain leads to strength.
- What spills out of a person when they get bumped is what they are really made of.
- Out of the abundance of the heart, the mouth speaks.
- The ability to bridle the tongue is the ultimate mastery of oneself.
- Worry is the abuse of the imagination.
- Respect cannot be demanded. It must be earned.
- Offense cannot be given. It can only be taken.
- Joy transcends situations.
- Peace transcends situations.
- One cannot cultivate grit without failure and pain.
- Forgiveness and mercy are the greatest of all strengths.
- As a man thinks, so is he. Positivity colors everything. Likewise, negativity colors everything.
- Negative thinking robs one of strength and the motivation to change.
- No one can imprison you but you.
- Truth sets people free.
- A secret only hurts while it remains a secret. Sharing a secret robs it of its power and ability to cause pain.
- Trust is the antidote to anxiety.
- Give what you need.
- Only perfect practice makes perfect.
- You will become what you focus on, whether that focus is positive or negative.
- You are the product of the inputs you allow into your life, be they good or bad.
- Nothing alienates others like selfishness.
- The measure of one's unhappiness is the distance between what they have and what they want.
- Desperation does not look good on anyone.
- Humility looks good on everyone.
- The only way to win then is to prepare now.
- The first and most important battle space is in the mind.
- Calm is contagious.
- Panic kills.
- Small victories lead to large victories.
- You will live up or down to your own expectations.

- **Work is a privilege.**
- **No one will cooperate with you if you want to make life all about yourself. However, if you want to make life all about others, they will move mountains to help you.**

These lessons did not come free to me, nor did they come cheap. They are the result of some monumental struggles, pain, fear and failures. However, they are my treasures and I offer them to you in the hopes that they also steer you toward peace and fulfillment.

THE FOUR KINDS OF PEOPLE YOU MEET IN A CRISIS

WILLING BUT UNABLE

In a survival situation, a willing but unable person is still a tremendous asset. Attitude and worldview are far more important than individual capabilities. Willingness covers absolutely everything. Ability only covers some things. A person who is willing to be of help and service, or do what it takes to keep themselves and others alive, can be invaluable even if they are unable to help in the way they wish they could.

Say you are in a firefight and someone who wants to keep fighting gets seriously wounded. They are bleeding from an artery and will die in minutes without emergency help. This person wants to be whole and strong and stay on their feet in the fight, but they currently cannot. You rush to their side and drag them behind cover that is not really enough cover for two of you. They are still awake and coherent. What do you do? Do you tell them to lie back and relax and close their eyes? No! You put their weapon (or yours) in their hand and tell them to cover you while you apply a tourniquet and a pressure bandage. As you save their life, you ask them to guard yours, which allows you to turn your attention from the fight to the casualty while the bullets keep flying. While they may be unable to stay on their feet, at least they can stay in the fight.

A person who is willing but unable can still do something to contribute in almost every situation. A bedridden patient in the hospital can still contribute to the morale of the other patients, medical staff and visitors by offering encouragement, a good attitude and a smile. Willingness is an attribute we need to cultivate in ourselves and in others. The act of being willing can overcome the inability that stares you in the face.

ABLE BUT UNWILLING

This is a very difficult person to work with in a crisis. In an emergency, there is nothing as maddening as having someone who is able to do what needs to be done but is unwilling to do it. It all comes down to motivation. If you find yourself in this situation, you may have to be creative or perhaps even a bit devious in order to get this person to do what you need them to do. Some people freeze. Some people run away. Some people lapse into a selfishness that causes them to totally disregard the needs of others.

Years ago, I was babysitting my 3-year-old nephew for a few days while his mother was at the hospital giving birth. Later, when his mom, dad and baby brother headed home, I initiated some clean-up of the guest room in which he had been staying so that I could take him home. I put his bedding in the laundry and, when it was dry, I had him go with me to put the bed back together. This, I thought, was only fair, since he had been the one using it. Handing him a pillow and a pillowcase, I asked him if he would like to help me by putting the pillow into the pillow case. He simply said, "No," as he stood there, holding them. I was surprised and asked him why. In an innocent, 3-year-old kind of way, he looked me straight in the eye and said, "I don't want to do the work." I had to smile at how unapologetically he said something like that. I nodded and took them out of his hands and said, "Well, I appreciate your honesty, if not your intentions."

That encounter made a deep impression on me. Adults will rarely be so direct and will most likely not admit to being lazy, selfish or scared. However, that may be what you are confronting when a person is able but unwilling. In a crisis situation, when lives are on the line, you may have to begin barking out strongly-worded orders to get their cooperation. I am sure we all agree that, in routine life when nothing is facing imminent destruction, we should be patient, kind and gentle as we try to motivate an unwilling person. In a crisis, you will not have that luxury. As you prepare your battle space in advance, you will need to figure out if you have it within you to take charge and offer that kind of strong leadership.

UNWILLING AND UNABLE

You do not work with these people. In a crisis, you simply protect them. The unwilling and unable person is simply going to be dead weight. And no, it is not a matter of motivation. When the fight for survival is at hand, when you are in the thick of the chaos, I promise you that is not the time to try to figure out what to do with them and how to make them care. All you can do is try to protect them, no matter how galling it may be. You can sort it out when the battle is won. This is one of the most profound examples of unfairness there is; if you spend time trying to convince or coerce them into helping you, you will lose valuable time and resources as you fight on two fronts: one against the situation and one against them. Let them be and focus on handling the situation. Let your own worldview motivate you to act according to your convictions, and do the best you can with what you have.

WILLING AND ABLE

This is the person I want to be. I want to have a good attitude and a healthy worldview, along with the ability to act where and how I want to act. These are the easiest people with whom you can work. They are a blessing and a half in a crisis or survival situation and make all the difference to the mission and the morale of all involved. These folks need little to no external motivation because their own internal worldview motivates them, as well as little to no coaching or oversight because of their capabilities. Just tell them what you need and let them do it without micromanagement.

As you prepare the battle space in advance (pg. 13), first evaluate which kind of person you are. If you are not who you want to be, now would be the time to change that, if possible. Next, start identifying the different types of people in your existing circles: home, work, faith community, sports team, hobbies, etc. If a crisis occurs, there is a very high likelihood you will be with one of these groups when it happens. Start sorting out who your willing-but-unables are, who your able-but-unwillings are, who your unwilling-and-unables are, and who your willing-and-ables are. Play out war game scenarios in your head and practice how you would deal with each type now, while you have time and space to do so.

DEFEATING THE AMYGDALA

Controlling how we respond to the world around us starts with controlling our own amygdalae—the two almond-shaped masses of gray matter deep within our temporal lobes. The amygdala allows us to process memories, make decisions and manage emotional responses. In terms of survival, it is the part of you tackling the raw fear, anxiety or primal aggression that washes over you when you find yourself going head-to-head with a clear and present threat.

This tiny place in the human body can control the entire person. All of us, at one time or another, have been at the mercy of our emotions. We have all been in situations where we act rashly, lash out, cry, say things we wish we had not said, tremble, freeze, panic, run away or any combination of such things. In these times, we are allowing the amygdala to control us with fear or anger. We are succumbing to chemicals. According to Ben Best, "Responses can be evoked by amygdala stimulation. The bed nucleus of the stria terminalis mediates the release of pituitary-adrenal stress hormone (Corticotropin-Releasing Hormone, CRH) in response to fear. CRH causes the adrenal gland to release epinephrine & cortisol." What we commonly call adrenaline is actually epinephrine. This is the hormone responsible for making you feel fear: sweaty palms, tachycardic heart rate, narrowed or tunnel vision, trembling, unsteady voice, dilated pupils, a decreased sensitivity to pain, increased sweating, an urge to run, etc.

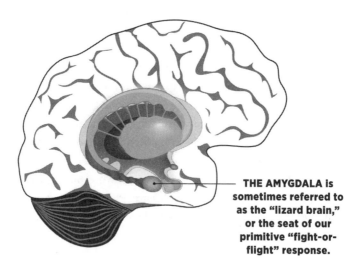

THE AMYGDALA is sometimes referred to as the "lizard brain," or the seat of our primitive "fight-or-flight" response.

Why do we need to know this? Because, we cannot hope to overcome what is happening to us until we know what it is and how it works. Once we know both, we can develop some countermeasures to calm ourselves down and stay in control. Here are some measures that you can employ in real time to counter what your brain is doing in a crisis situation.

HOW TO KEEP CALM AND STAY IN CONTROL

- Take a deep breath and pause.

- S. T. O. P. (Stop. Think. Observe. Plan.)

- Begin combat breathing (pg. 44).

- Focus on the very next thing you need to do.

- Calm the people around you with soft and reassuring words.

- Pray.

- Think of something funny.

- Laugh.

- Think of one muscle group at a time and make a conscious effort to relax it.

- "Listen" to a calming song in your own mind.

- Maintain logic and act, based upon that logic.

- Recite reassuring scriptures or holy texts from your faith.

- Develop and recite your own calming mantra over and over.

- Visualize a beautiful and serene place.

- Recall the smell that you like best in all the world.

- Visualize and recall the taste of the most scrumptious meal ever.

- Rub your thumb and forefinger together softly.

- Recall your own name and identity, age, location and time of day.

- Consciously feel the clothes on your own body.

- Stretch.

All of these things can help you take back control and stay ahead of your biology in a crisis situation. Remember that panicking is abandoning logic for instinct. Maintain a tenacious hold on logic and do not give it up without a fight.

F.LA.P.S

How do we protect ourselves from biases? How do we ensure that we are meeting a situation with as much objectivity as we can, especially when that situation is a crisis? Giving in to subjective and fear-based thinking can cost your safety, freedom or even your life.

THIS IS A SIMPLE THOUGHT PATTERN TO FOLLOW WHEN YOU NEED TO FIGURE THINGS OUT

F - Facts

   List the facts of the situation. Do not interpret those facts. Just compile a list.

LA - Likely Assumptions

   List the likely assumptions you can make based solely on those facts. Make sure you are not basing your assumptions on any extrapolations, but solely on direct data.

P - Problems

   List the problems you can identify from either the facts or the assumptions.

S - Solutions

   Based on those three lists, decide upon solutions to those problems.

When all else fails, this exercise can lead you to productive conclusions when emotion is clouding your judgment.

Engaging in active listening is crucial when it comes to stabilizing a person in crisis. It is also necessary when eliciting information (pg. 71). How do you know if you are a good listener? Have someone read the following fictional story to you and ask you the questions below without allowing you to look back over the story. Essentially, this is a closed-book test. Listen carefully, try to recall then answer the questions without looking. Learn how well you listen.

Rose lived in England During World War II. Henry, the man she loved, was in Germany behind enemy lines. Rose was desperate to get to Henry but there was no way for her to reach her one true love. She felt hopeless and miserable.

One day, when she was at work at a London newspaper, her boss, Mr. Evans, invited her to a meeting in his office. When she arrived, he introduced her to a man named Mike. Mike was an international political journalist for the same newspaper. He routinely traveled into enemy territory to cover the political happenings of the war, and his position as a journalist gave him access to many restricted areas. Mr. Evans knew that even though Rose could not get to

Henry, Mike could. He thought she might like to send him a message.

After making the introduction, Mr. Evans left Rose and Mike alone to talk. In Rose's desperation, she surprised Mike by begging him to take her with him. She was not content to merely send a letter. She had to see her true love. Mike was not keen on taking responsibility for a civilian in a war zone and said no. Rose cried, pleaded and begged Mike to change his mind. He began to wonder what he could get out of this situation. An idea struck him. Mike knew Rose had lots of inside knowledge about the war effort in London due to her trusted position at the newspaper. He suggested a deal: he would take her with him on the condition that she would share classified information with him. Rose recoiled. How could she betray Mr. Evans and the king that way? While she believed Mike was a loyal British subject, he had no right to the information she knew. But, if she did as he asked, she could see her beloved Henry again.

Rose asked Mike if she could take the night to think about it and give him an answer the next morning. Mike agreed. Rose went home and called her best friend, Alex. She explained the entire situation and asked what to do. Alex assured Rose their friendship was solid and that they would still be friends no matter what Rose chose to do. After a fitful, restless night, Rose met with Mike again and agreed to his terms.

Mike took Rose with him and escorted her safely to Henry's location. At long last, Rose flung her arms around a very surprised Henry. He asked her what on Earth she was doing there! She explained she had come at great cost and great peril, braving enemy soldiers and betraying her country just to get to him. Henry was very angry and told her she should not have done that and she should not have come. Hurt, confused and angry, Rose returned to Mike and asked him if she could return with him to London. He escorted her back.

Rose was so dejected when she returned she did not know what to do. She could not go back to the newspaper and she did not want to go home, so she decided to sit down in a coffee shop to think about her life. A man named James noticed her heartbroken appearance and asked if he could sit down. Rose was grateful for the company and, in no time, had poured out her heart and told James the whole story. James listened sympathetically and patted her hand. When she was done, James told her he might have a job for her, if she would also share with him the same level of classified information she had *given to Mike. Rose knew she needed a job to pay the rent on her flat. She knew she would never see Henry again. With a sad heart, Rose accepted James's offer and went with him to her new company.*

1. What was the name of the main character?
2. What were the names of all the other characters? Rate them from your favorite person to your least favorite person in the story.
3. Who was Rose's best friend?
4. Is Alex male or female? (Are you sure?)
5. Why did you rate the characters the way you did?
6. Were your ratings based on facts, or on assumptions and extrapolations?
7. Did you make moral judgments?
8. What were the assumptions you made based upon the facts you heard?
9. What were the problems you identified?
10. What would you have done if you were Rose?
11. What would you have done if you were Henry?

We learned how to think through problems critically by doing the F.LA.P.S. exercise. However, the most difficult and dangerous part to navigate is the Likely Assumptions phase that comes right after the Facts phase. If your assumptions are wrong, then the problems you identified and the solutions to those problems could be wrong as well.

SURVIVAL REACTIONS

» REACTIONS TO ABNORMAL EVENTS

As human beings, when we are subjected to traumatic events, there are several categories of possible reactions we may see in ourselves. These reactions can be normal or abnormal, and what determines that is largely based on how much they interfere with our level of functionality.

Above all, what I want you to remember is that many of the things you may experience during or after a crisis event are completely normal. They are your body and mind trying to process and come to terms with what has happened.

I cannot stress how beneficial it is to know these things in advance of experiencing them. If you have an understanding of what you might encounter before something actually happens, you will be prepared to allow yourself to process the event fully and without worry or self-condemnation. While I realize I keep hammering away at advance preparation of the battle space (pg. 13), nothing else I have taught you is as important as that. Everything you do, anything you endeavor to accomplish, goes back to your own willingness to prepare. Preparation may make the difference between success and failure, life and death.

Since the actual battle space is in the mind, this will be an especially important tool to have. Knowing what you may encounter during and after a crisis will be like having a map to see you through. I have walked many people through this information when they were experiencing grief or trying to deal with a recent trauma. They were hearing the information for the first time, right when they needed it, and I could not help but wonder how much better they would have felt if they had known these things in advance. That is why I am giving them to you now. My hope is you will learn some important information now and later, when you need it, it will already be in place.

In some cases, abnormal symptoms, feelings or other signs may require immediate medical attention. Pay close attention whenever evaluating yourself or others—you might save a life.

≫ PHYSICAL REACTIONS

NORMAL SIGNS	ABNORMAL SIGNS
• Fatigue	• Tachycardia
• Nausea	• Hypertension
• Elevated heart rate	• Headaches
• Hyperventilation	• Muscle spasms
• Adrenaline release	• Psychogenic sweating
• Cortisol release	• Fatigue/exhaustion
• Shakiness	• Indigestion
• Headache	• Nausea
• Sweating	• Vomiting
• Dilated pupils	• Blood in stool, urine, vomit or sputum
• Muscle tension	• Chest pain
• Hypertension	• Loss of consciousness

» COGNITIVE REACTIONS

NORMAL SIGNS

- Confusion
- Brain fog
- Difficulty concentrating
- Unusually clear focus
- Getting stuck between the steps "Observe" and "Orient" in the OODA loop
- Revisiting the images generated by the event
- Sensory distortion

ABNORMAL SIGNS

- Ongoing inability to concentrate
- Difficulty in decision making
- Guilt
- Preoccupation with the event
- The inability to understand the consequences of our/their behavior
- Becoming suicidal
- Becoming homicidal
- Psychosis
- Ongoing sensory distortion

» BEHAVIORAL REACTIONS

NORMAL SIGNS

- Running
- Hiding
- Fighting
- Freezing
- Crying
- Short-term hyper-vigilance
- Enacting new safety/security measures
- Short-term troubling dreams
- Becoming introspective
- Taking up new hobbies
- Having a fresh enjoyment of life and living

ABNORMAL SIGNS

- Impulsiveness
- Risk-taking
- Excessive eating/drinking/sleeping
- Substance abuse
- A hyper-startle response
- Compensatory sexual activity or spending
- Compulsivity
- Sleep problems
- Withdrawal
- Relational discord
- Crying spells
- Ongoing hyper-vigilance
- Staring off into space
- Violence
- Antisocial behavior
- Decrease in appetite/energy/sleep/libido
- Barricading

➤➤ EMOTIONAL REACTIONS

NORMAL SIGNS

- Fear
- Panic
- Anger
- Rage
- Desire for revenge
- Anxiety
- Worry
- Sadness
- Grief
- Depression
- Relief at surviving
- Happiness–glad to be alive

ABNORMAL SIGNS

- Anxiety
- Fear
- Vegetative depression
- Nightmares
- Irritability
- Irrationality
- Anger
- Panic attacks
- Development of a phobia
- Post-traumatic stress
- Guilt
- Pathologic grief/guilt
- Impaired ability to function
- Survivor's guilt

➤➤ SPIRITUAL REACTIONS

NORMAL SIGNS

- Spiritual shock
- Disbelief
- Questioning God
- Anger at God
- Studying the tenets of your faith more closely
- Becoming more involved in your spiritual community
- Increasing the frequency of participation in spiritual practices
- Reading your scriptures more often/ deeply/seriously than before
- Making sure that you are ready for the after-life, according to your faith
- Talking to other people about your beliefs

ABNORMAL SIGNS

- Inability to resolve anger at God
- Crisis of faith
- Withdrawal from your spiritual community
- Refusal to participate in spiritual practices
- Rituals and traditions losing their meaning
- Imposing your faith onto others
- Going on a crusade
- Abandoning your faith
- Anger at clergy
- A feeling of having been lied to by your religion
- Resentment of holy days and festivals

COPING MECHANISMS

While I do not recommend asking some of these questions to a troubled person directly (please leave that to a trained mental health professional), consider the following questions to help gauge progress in processing a traumatic event. There may not be answers just yet, but posing these questions is the first step in finding solutions.

- **Do you feel like the coping mechanisms are working?**
- **Have the behaviors changed?**
- **Are the adaptive behaviors working and are they appropriate?**
- **Is there a future focus?**
- **Are there any suicidal or homicidal ideations?**
- **How has "meaning" been made of the event?**
- **Is the processing and adjustment taking a very long time?**
- **Are there ongoing triggers? (sights, smells, sounds, tastes, touches, time of day)**

For all the categories in which we may identify reactions in ourselves (and others), there are both positive and negative coping mechanisms available to us. In order to process, heal, grow and reintegrate fully into our lives, it is paramount that we make a conscious choice to use the positive ones. These are the specific suggestions made by the National Center For Post-Traumatic Stress Disorder:

PHYSICAL SELF-CARE
- **Eat breakfast, lunch and dinner**
- **Choose healthy foods**
- **Exercise**
- **Get regular medical care for prevention**
- **Get regular medical care when needed**
- **Take time off when sick**
- **Engage in some kind of fun or pleasant physical activity**
- **Get enough sleep**
- **Wear clothes you like**
- **Take vacations**

- Take day trips or mini-vacations
- Make time away from telephones

PSYCHOLOGICAL SELF-CARE

- Make time for self-reflection
- Have your own personal psychotherapy
- Write in a journal
- Read literature that is unrelated to work
- Do something at which you are not expert or in charge
- Decrease stress in your life
- Decline optional stress
- Notice your inner experiences—listen to your thoughts, judgments, beliefs, attitudes and feelings
- Let others know different aspects of you
- Engage your intelligence in a new area, e.g., go to an art museum, history exhibit, sports event, auction, theatrical performance
- Practice receiving from others
- Be curious
- Say no to extra responsibilities sometimes

EMOTIONAL SELF-CARE

- Spend time with others whose company you enjoy
- Stay in contact with important people in your life
- Give yourself affirmations, praise yourself
- Find ways to increase your sense of self-esteem
- Reread favorite books or rewatch favorite movies
- Identify comforting activities, objects, people, relationships, places and seek them out
- Allow yourself to cry
- Find things to make you laugh
- Express your outrage in social action, letters, donations, marches, protests
- Play with children
- Look for small victories

SPIRITUAL SELF-CARE

- Make time for reflection
- Spend time with nature
- Find a spiritual connection or community
- Be open to inspiration
- Cherish your optimism and hope
- Be aware of nonmaterial aspects of life
- Try at times not to be in charge or the expert
- Be open to not knowing
- Identify what is meaningful to you and notice its place in your life
- Meditate
- Pray
- Sing
- Spend time with children
- Make time to be awed
- Contribute to causes in which you believe
- Read inspirational literature (talks, music, etc.)

For more information and resources on managing PTSD, visit *ptsd.va.gov*.

THE STEWARDSHIP OF PAIN

Pain, failure, loss and death are part of every person's life. Sadly, we do not get to pick when or how or who. The part within our control is how well we steward the pain. Yes, it is OK to experience pain. Please do not waste pain or merely run from it, as unpleasant as it might be. Use it to grow. We must steward the pain wisely, keeping in mind that we should not try to forget this experience but use it for the benefit of the world around us.

If I plan a complicated trip overseas and pour my efforts into perfecting the logistics, and something goes wrong, I will be disappointed. I may be angry, frustrated, anxious or even scared. However, there is no need for me to linger in that negative mindset, to dwell on what I do not have or did not accomplish. In order to steward that failure correctly, I need to assess what went wrong and why, then I need to factor that information into future logistical planning and execution. I can share my story and the lessons learned with others on a similar mission to maximize its usefulness. In so doing, I have turned a failure into a success, not just for me, but for everyone.

The same applies to loss. I can learn many lessons from loss and I can use those lessons to grow. I can teach others who come after me effective ways to deal with those feelings and heal. I can impart hope to others and use the lessons I learn to light the way for those who are struggling against the confusion and the overwhelming desire to give up. This is the way to turn loss into gain.

Pain is no different. We all experience many kinds of pain: physical, emotional, mental, spiritual, financial, relational, professional, etc. Like it or not, pain is a regular component in every facet of our being. If we choose to look for the lessons and learn, we can grow and teach others to do the same. As we turn our attentions outward and seek ways to serve the world around us, we will experience a catharsis and healing of our own. We can turn pain into protection.

Stewarding the pain means choosing to allow it to move us closer to perfection instead of farther away. The pain is an opportunity. We can use it as a catalyst to draw closer to health or we can get upset and pull away. That is a stewardship decision.

Not dwelling there means not throwing in the towel and choosing to drown, but to keep fighting. Keep swimming. Keep climbing. Move. Press in. What good is failure or loss unless we learn from it, grow and teach others to do the same?

Decide to learn. Decide to heal. Decide to grow. Decide to teach. Decide to serve.

PRACTICAL THEISM

Feel free to take this with a grain of salt, but hear me out: For all those who do not believe in God and for all those who are unsure but seriously doubt the existence of God, this one is for you. There is a concept I call practical theism. If you cannot decide or cannot tell whether or not there is a God, is there any sense in choosing to believe or acting as though there is? I say yes, and if you have ever heard of Pascal's wager, you will know I am not alone in this reasoning.

We have all heard that there are no atheists in foxholes. When adversity strikes, people's knee-jerk reaction is to cry out to God. Even if it is simply to say, "Oh, God!" That is an appeal for God's attention. When the dust settles, every person everywhere begins to ascribe meaning and purpose to what happened. They look for a place to cast the blame and often choose to put it squarely on God's shoulders. Later, during the rebuilding process, they encourage others who are in despair by reminding them of God's love, goodness and sovereignty as they advocate for prayer and moral living.

Whether or not you believe God exists, what harm will invoking His Name bring in a crisis? If you wish to emerge as a trustworthy and respected leader when adversity comes, you must see to all the needs of your followers. Lifting their morale includes tending to spiritual needs by providing comfort and encouragement in the midst of disaster, pain and loss. As they search for understanding and meaning, it will be up to you to point them to something or someone greater than themselves. If you are unable to impart hope, you are unable to lead.

What do you have to lose? If you are right and there is no God, you will act in the best interests of those around you and build morale. You will prove how much you care about human suffering and do all you could think of to impart hope and prevent despair. You will save lives, engender trust and build unity. If you are wrong and there is a God, you will use the most powerful of all tools on behalf of your people: prayer. You will point them in God's direction and appeal for God's protection, provision and favor. You will bring hope to a seemingly hopeless situation as you involve the only One whose power surpasses that of the disaster.

THE POWER OF SUBMISSION

Have you ever used a Chinese finger trap? You put one of your forefingers into each open end, pull and then you are stuck. Tugging will not pull them apart. The harder you pull, the tighter the trap clamps down on your fingers. The solution? One of your fingers has to concede. Your hands need to stop pulling in opposite directions and come together. Once one hand moves in the direction of the other, the trap loosens and both are freed. Decide to cooperate. It takes using your intellect to choose the gentle and peaceful option instead of using your pride and brute force to overpower it. One solution resolves the problem and leaves everyone intact. The other brings destruction.

Submission is a taboo word and subject in our culture. It is largely regarded as a show of weakness on the part of the one who demonstrates it, and domination or bullying on the part of the recipient. This one word can anger more people faster than any other concept. It is viewed as a synonym for slavery and a race-orchestrated tenet, designed to keep a particular people in power.

I am not here to meet that argument with an argument. My goal is to present an alternate perspective. What if, in the midst of chaos and disaster, we found another way to affect change and improve the situation? What if, in the midst of true adversity, we could navigate a peaceful course from animosity and distrust to cooperation and rebuilding?

Have you ever considered how powerful the place of submission can be? That sounds like an oxymoron, I know. How can submission and power have anything to do with each other? Have we not all been taught that submission is weakness and accepting it is bullying?

Years ago, I went to work for a Korean Grandmaster who owned his own Taekwondo school. When he interviewed me, I was an assistant master (third degree black belt) and I had just come from owning and operating a school of my own. I was an established instructor and an international-level competition coach. In the interview, Master Lee told me plainly that I would not be allowed to teach his classes nor have any authority in his school, since I was not Korean. Ouch.

This was a non-changeable fact he would not overlook and he made it clear to me that I could run the office, handle contracts, be a liaison to the parents, and warm up and stretch out the classes, but that I should never expect to do any more than that. Very well then, I thought. I accepted his terms and went to work for him.

You may be surprised to know that I never once tried to talk him out of his views. Why? Well, I knew even attempting to do so would have been counterproductive. Instead, I sought to win his confidence by my conduct under his authority. I did my job to the best of my ability for a couple of years and then, one day, something remarkable happened. Master Lee was hosting two young men from Yong-In University in Seoul, Korea. These men were stateside on a six-month internship to learn how to teach and to run a school. When I arrived to work that day, Master Lee introduced me to these young instructors and we talked briefly. I excused myself to change into my uniform and came back out to the mat to stretch before the students arrived.

When the time came, Master Lee called the class into formation. Everyone stood in rows, facing the mirror and the flags, in descending order of rank. Given what he had told me upon hiring me, I took my place behind these two Korean men. Master Lee gave the command to come to attention but, before he proceeded, he noticed my position in the mirror. What he did next shocked me as much as anything I had ever seen. He turned around and, in Korean, told the two instructors to move down by one space each because I outranked them and should be in the highest position. He then told me to relocate myself to the proper place, turned back around and, satisfied, proceeded with the opening salute.

About six months later, Master Lee needed to travel to Korea, and he did not want to close his school during his absence. When I arrived at work one day, he gave me a set of keys and told me that not only would I be running the whole school in his absence, I would be teaching all his classes while he was gone. Wow! He had only given me one stipulation when he hired me and I had agreed to it. By this second act of trust, he had just rescinded his own terms of my employment.

I knew I would never endear myself to him by going toe-to-toe with him or threatening an equal opportunity lawsuit or by belligerence. That entire situation caused me to think deeply about human interactions and identify a lesson. I saw that I would never have any influence over this man by rank, age, position or life experience. If I hoped to influence him in any way, it would have to be from a position of submission. From that place alone, if I did it with excellence, he would see someone he could respect. He would begin, through that respect, to value my opinions and convictions. It turns out I actually had a much greater chance to influence him from a subordinate position than I ever would have by assuming an equal or superior position.

Years later, upon his retirement, Master Lee completed his change of heart. He called me and asked me to come in and meet with him. What he asked me at that meeting was to take over his school when he retired. He wanted me to have it. We had worked together for seven years and in that time he had come to trust and respect me. He told me it would only go one of two ways: either I would be the one to take over his school, or he would close it down. He was unwilling to turn it over to anyone else.

But there is one thing you should know: This path takes time. Establishing yourself as a subordinate of excellence and integrity does not happen overnight. Gaining a person's trust and respect takes patience. Once those are in place, relying on your submission with excellence as a vehicle for change takes even more time. I have found that it is worth it and there is nothing else like it in life.

You may be surprised to learn I used to berate myself inside for "wimping out" or "giving in" to the desires of others instead of holding out for what I wanted. I was not proud of this, and I used to call myself a pansy, a marshmallow and a spineless coward for not standing up for myself. Thankfully, I have come to realize just how wrong I was. Choosing to hold my tongue when I would rather argue back, choosing to prefer someone else's desires over my own and obeying when I want to go my own way are not always weaknesses. In fact, I would submit to you that these are strengths. If I can hold my tongue in check when I am hurt and not lash out, that is strength. If I can sacrifice what I want for what others want, that is also strength. If I can obey when that is the last thing I would rather do, that is strength too. As the saying goes, "Whoever guards his mouth and tongue keeps his soul from troubles." By no means is that easy to accomplish, and I have had my share of troubles. But if I can hold myself to that standard, and truly humble myself when the situation calls for it, I have found that submission can be one of the greatest strengths and vehicles of change we will ever know.

ACT, DON'T REACT

There is a difference between responding and reacting. A response is a thoughtful and considered approach, whereas reacting is more or less instinctive. Of course, the only way to respond rather than react is to prepare for things in advance.

This works in interpersonal interactions as well as personal security situations. If a person says something that makes me angry, I have two choices: I can respond or I can react. If I react, I could lose my temper. I might yell, swear, call them names or otherwise insult them. I will certainly go on the attack. If I respond, however, I will choose not to say or do anything until I have calmed down and thought things through. I can then choose a productive path to facilitate understanding. If I react, I harm the relationship and I will need to go back later and apologize before working to rebuild trust. On the other hand, if I respond, I will save the relationship and will have done nothing for which I need to go back and apologize. That sounds like a win to me.

In a self-defense or personal security situation, you might think that the goal is to react, not respond. Is that true? I would ask myself: What about all the combat training that has been poured into me for almost three decades? What about all the scenarios I have run, the techniques I have honed? What about all of my pre-made decisions? All of that has been advanced preparation of the battle space. The point of all of this training is that I have already decided what I am going to do in various kinds of situations and spent years building the tools to be able to do so. I have locked it away in my mind and built it into my programming. With all this careful thought and hard work, I would say that even a self-defense situation becomes a matter of responding, not reacting.

What about a natural disaster resulting in a survival situation? Having a plan in place, food, water and equipment means you will have the luxury of responding instead of reacting. While everyone around you is scrambling and panicking to find what they need, you can calmly enact your plan based on your training, provisions and gear.

The key to being able to respond is preparedness.

KEEP IT UP

Sure, endurance is necessary, but why do all coaches and cheerleaders everywhere make such a big deal out of it? Why are the first few weeks of every new game season dedicated to conditioning? It seems only natural that if a person is pursuing a lofty goal, they will need to stick it out when the going gets tough. We all know the going will absolutely, positively, inevitably get quite tough. Why isn't that fact alone enough to keep us motivated to endure?

Human nature is a funny thing. We often know exactly what we need to do in order to win, to change circumstances we do not like or to succeed. But we are simply not always willing to put in the kind of time and hard work it requires. So, what will it take to inspire and motivate a person to develop endurance and stamina? That, unfortunately, is not a question which can be answered in one blanket statement. Different people find inspiration and motivation in different places.

For me, I often develop endurance when I honestly have no say in the matter. When I find myself in a tough circumstance outside of my control, I have two options: I can throw in the towel and give up on life, or I can fight to keep living.

A few years ago, I was diagnosed with malaria and Lyme disease. The next five years were a very tough time for me, physically, financially, emotionally, relationally, professionally and mentally. What were my options? If I was going to keep breathing, paying the mortgage and waking up each day, I had to endure. I made myself a promise based on some horror stories I had heard. I promised myself that, no matter what, every single day I would get up, get dressed and leave the house. It did not matter if I was going to work, to the store or out for a walk. I was determined to not be one of those people who became bedridden due to the slippery slope of not feeling like getting up today.

I learned more during that season of my life than I did at any other point along the way. I had to humble myself and accept that my new baseline was much slower than it had ever been before. I had to plan and do things deliberately. My schedule revolved around my daily IV infusions. My joints hurt. I was tired and depressed. However, what was the alternative? For me, the alternative was death, so I developed a stamina and a resiliency I had never even hoped to have. It is still growing. Happily, I am now back to full health and vigor, and thank goodness I am no longer on the PICC line. I have returned to martial arts and cycling, flying, skiing and scuba diving. I have lost 22 of the 30 pounds I gained while I was sick. I am traveling, working hard and catching up financially.

If I had it to do all over again, I would not change anything. That which did not kill me definitely made me stronger than I ever could have dreamed, and it motivated my endurance. It was a pretty extreme way to go but it was maximally effective.

ABSORBERS, REFLECTORS AND PROJECTORS

From my own experience, people can be broken down into three different personality types: Emotional Absorbers, Emotional Reflectors and Emotional Projectors.

Absorbers do exactly as you would think: They absorb the emotions of the people around them. They are emotional chameleons. Why do they do this? If the emotions of the people around them are high, they can ride the wave and feel good along with everyone else. If the emotions around them are low or tense, their absorption is an attempt to diffuse the tension by taking the negative emotions upon themselves, thereby freeing those around them from carrying the burden.

Reflectors are the exact opposite of absorbers, anti-chameleons. They do not change their mood to match that of their setting but reflect what people are already projecting right back at them. In fact, the positive people around them will appreciate it and the negative people around them will resent it. If you are interacting positively with a reflector, you will have all of that positivity bounced right back at you. They will not absorb it. They will give it back. If you are interacting negatively with a reflector, you will feel the negativity bounced right back at you too, and it does not feel very good. The reflector will not adopt the mood of those around them.

Projectors, on the other hand, feel what they feel based on their own circumstances and personality. Their feelings are not determined by the feelings of those around them. Projectors will strongly exude what they feel, be it positive or negative. Those around them will feel it too and be impacted. For projectors, personality is a huge factor. Their baseline, their default emotional state, will be what they project. Whether they are peaceful, angry, anxious, joyful or sad, those around them will always feel it radiating from them. It will come not only through words but through body language, facial expressions, tone of voice, decisions, actions and a general aura. You know it when you feel it.

What does any of this have to do with travel, security or survival? Well, if you find yourself in a crisis situation, there are two immediate questions you will need answered. Which type of person are you, and what are the types of people around you? If you can answer those two questions, you can begin to understand the dynamics of your interactions, especially those under pressure. Once you see the patterns develop, you can use your inside knowledge to lead people in a positive direction because you will know what they need from a leader.

Not to beat a dead horse, but you really need to know your own type in advance of the crisis situation. Advance preparation (pg. 13), remember?

COMPLACENCY

I have said it before and I will say it again: panic kills. Now, however, we need to address the problem at the opposite end of the spectrum: complacency.

Complacency is the polar opposite of panic and yet it is just as deadly. Where panic is stark and impossible to ignore, complacency is insidious. It comes on so gradually we usually fail to recognize it until it has taken hold. Complacency is what causes us to think the things we already know or already have are good enough; that bad things will never happen to us; that we can relax now, we have done enough, and we can knock off the hard work. It causes us to think we can let down our guard, stop taking security measures and lower our shields. It whispers in our ear that nothing bad has happened before—why should it happen now? Suddenly, all those security measures start to feel dreadfully inconvenient and expensive, and so far, it seems they have all been a waste of money, effort and time.

No! Snap out of it! When that begins to happen, we are on a slippery slope. We risk ignoring all our training has to offer. There is only one cure for complacency: vigilance. No matter what, we must keep training, preparing, fighting and taking preemptive measures on our own behalf. We have talked and talked about advanced preparation of the battle space (pg. 13). The war between complacency and vigilance is in our minds. That is where we must win it before it bests us in real time.

If you are being targeted, you will be watched over a period of time so the bad guys can figure out an ideal time to attack. Will they attack on your most vigilant day when all your security measures are firmly in place? Not if they can help it. They will watch and wait to see how and where you allow those measures to slip up. They will lull you into a false sense of security, and when you seem to believe nothing bad could possibly happen, that is when they will strike. Worse, through your carelessness, you opened the door. Do not give them that advantage. It could make for quite the costly mistake.

Stay vigilant. Stay focused. Prepare. Do not be paranoid, just be aware.

BOREDOM

Nothing affects morale quite like boredom. It is insidious. It creeps in and steals our peace while we are not looking. It lends itself to formulating all kinds of negative thoughts of hopelessness and helplessness. It squashes our motivation and the will to change our reality. Ultimately, it leaves us feeling depressed, irritable and listless.

You can combat this phenomenon with, you guessed it, prior planning. If you are about to launch out into the great outdoors, pack a bug-out bag (pg. 22), or plan to shelter in place (pg. 24), take some precautions against morale-squashing boredom.

- **Pack a deck of cards.**
- **Pack a book.**
- **Pack a puzzle or game of some kind.**
- **Pack resistance bands.**
- **Look for enough space to do some push-ups, sit-ups and jumping jacks.**
- **Have a few good stories to tell (even to yourself).**
- **Pray.**
- **Meditate.**
- **Take time to appreciate nature in its all macro and micro forms.**
- **Tackle a project like building a bigger fire or a better shelter.**

Use your imagination. Take time to imagine what you would want to have with you if you had no electronics and, perhaps, no people. Then be sure to factor that into your emergency planning.

LAZINESS PAYS

In a summertime or a desert survival situation, often the best course of action is to stay put and do as little work as possible in order to conserve your energy. Once you have seen to your immediate needs—first aid, shelter and water— utilize your shelter and rest. If the day is hot, take advantage of the shade. Ventilate your shelter and enjoy the breeze. Sleep while the sun is up and prepare to move at night.

Continuing to work hard in the heat once your needs are met is counterproductive. Rest. Save your energy and reduce your perspiration. Remember that this is the point at which boredom can set in. Be prepared to occupy your mind to ensure your morale stays as high as possible. Low morale leads to learned helplessness which means giving up on the problem. Instead, allow your body to recover and keep your mind occupied as you tackle the many challenges of survival.

CONTINUAL IMPROVEMENT

There is a secret to every great hero and leader across all times and cultures: These are the people who continually seek to improve themselves, the people who are never satisfied. They are focused on what they can become, what they can accomplish and perfect. They always read; hone their skills or learn new ones; sign up for the next course; and take on the next challenge. They shudder at the thought of resting on the laurels of their past achievements and maintain the attitude that what they will become is better and far more exciting than what they were.

These are the people who achieve. These are the people who lead and govern. These are the people who change the world. These are the heroes who save lives. Do you want to be such a person—a conqueror? Imagine what you could do in a survival, security or crisis situation if you were expertly studied and well-trained. We all like to think we would fare well enough, but why settle for just enough? When the chips are down, do you want to be an asset or a liability? Would you like to emerge as a competent, trained and experienced leader in a crisis situation, or would you rather be the one who requires rescuing?

Choose to lead. Choose to remain vigilant. Never be satisfied.

COGNITIVE DISSONANCE

A friend of mine once told me the measure of a person's unhappiness is the distance between what they want and what they have. Very astute, if I do say so myself. In a similar way, cognitive dissonance is when a person's beliefs and actions do not align. When a person gives lip service to their beliefs or convictions but acts in a manner contrary to their words, they live with a constant dissonance they cannot rectify. The only solution to this problem is to either modify the belief set or the actions to bring everything into alignment.

How does this help in the survival or security realm? Determining a person's cognitive dissonance is one means of taking control of a situation or setting, either to prevent a crisis or respond to one. If you are dealing with a bad guy (robber, burglar, rapist, kidnapper, extortionist, murderer, gang, cartel, syndicate, you name it) and you can determine their belief set versus their actions, you can expose and exploit those beliefs to take control back from them and save your own life. However, before you do so, make sure you know your own cognitive dissonance. Think about that for a minute. We all have them. Not one of us lives true to our convictions 100 percent of the time. You are just as vulnerable as the person you seek to exploit if you do not recognize your own cognitive dissonance.

The battle space is the mind. Prepare that space for battle and victory by discovering where your own cognitive dissonance lies and changing either your beliefs to match your actions, or your actions to match your beliefs. If you can manage to do this, you will always have the upper hand when dealing with bad guys.

CONFRONTING BIASES

❯❯ CONFIRMATION BIAS

When we believe something, are we willing to be talked out of that belief? What would it take to convince you something you believe is not true? Would facts alone be enough to change your mind?

These are very tough questions to answer, and the answers may be different for different people. When we research a topic to find answers, do we only look at data that supports our preexisting viewpoint? Do we talk about things only with the people who agree with us? Do we live in an echo chamber of opinions that match our own? Are we willing to be wrong? Are we willing to hear out the opposition with patience and attention, trying to understand their perspective?

If you see yourself in any of these questions, there are three concrete suggestions I can make:

- **Do not answer a question before you ask it.**

- **Be willing to truly listen to the opposite perspective with a closed mouth and an open mind.**

- **When conducting research, look equally at both sides of an opinion and the supporting data for each perspective.**

Why do we need to know this in survival or security? Assuming you already know the answers to the questions and refusing to be proven wrong can get you killed. A person who is traveling and/or lives and operates in or near a dangerous area (whether known or unknown to them) needs to assimilate as much data as possible all the time. They need to be willing to learn new things. They need to have preconceptions challenged. They need to have their information updated. They need to believe verifiable reports of friends, neighbors, witnesses and news media. They need to be willing to change their opinion if the facts support the other view.

It is natural to believe that your own neighborhood is a safe community. That is why you live there. It might be where you grew up. It might be where your most cherished memories were formed. It certainly has a strong sentimental place in your heart. So, you want (even need) to go about your days feeling safe in your own home and surroundings. You need to be able to sleep well at night and not worry about your children.

But what if the facts do not support your sentimental and nostalgic opinion? What if they actually suggest a growing problem with crime? Allowing your views to be challenged and adapting your beliefs to fit the facts can save your life if it causes you to enact more security measures or move to a different neighborhood. Remaining intractable in your opinions could cost you your safety, security, freedom or even your life.

≫ RECENCY BIAS

Who do you like more: the people who are currently in your life or the ones who used to be? Sympathizing more with the current people in your life is called recency bias. There can, however, be another explanation. It is possible your life migrates away from the people with whom you disagree and toward the people with whom you agree. That is natural. Disagreeing with people does not usually evoke a pleasant feeling. However, if the reason you agree more with current friends is only because they are current, that is recency bias.

How do we get around this proclivity? All of us are influenceable creatures. We were designed to influence or otherwise affect one another. Properly applied, this can lead to all kinds of positive things. Improperly applied, this leads to abuse and manipulation. In order to avoid recency bias, we need to hold fast to our own firm set of convictions. Not our parent's convictions, mind you. Not our religion's teachings. Not even our friends' opinions. We need to decide what our own unique convictions are and whether or not they are negotiable. A strong person with immoveable core convictions will be constant in their regard for others, regardless of whether those include past or present relationships.

How exactly does this factor into security? The world is at odds with itself. If you travel, you know that wherever you go, you will be crossing back and forth between differing opinions, cultures and beliefs. There will be social, political, religious and cultural differences between any two places. This is even true between two different states. If you are not grounded in your own worldview and convictions, you will be pulled back and forth between some very volatile views. Your own security can be easily compromised if you lose track of which cause has your sympathy right now.

Decide now what you believe and why you believe it. And stick to it!

≫ AVAILABILITY HEURISTIC BIAS

Simply put, availability heuristic bias is the inflated importance of the information we already have. Suppose you are staying in an unfamiliar part of an unfamiliar city. You chose the exact location of your hotel based on a briefing you obtained from the U.S. Department of State prior to making your plans, which was an informed choice. The briefing alerted you to dangerous places on the opposite side of the city and recommended you stay away. However, everything else was quiet with no known criminal or terrorist activity. So, you chose a hotel in the safe section of the city. Believing that there is no good reason to update your information because you implicitly trust the data you already obtained, is availability heuristic bias. If you find yourself in that situation you can combat this bias by obtaining data from local sources. Local knowledge is king. Make sure the data you collect is up-to-date and the sources are trustworthy, inasmuch as you are able.

» THE BANDWAGON EFFECT

I know every one of us can remember a time when our parents asked, "If everyone else jumped off a cliff, would you jump, too?" That is the bandwagon effect in a nutshell: going along with the crowd without using independent or critical thought.

I love the saying, "None of us is as dumb as all of us." Groupthink and social/peer pressure can push people to do a plethora of potentially awful or detrimental things they would not otherwise do.

Long ago, my grandmother and her niece traveled with a group to Israel. On the first day, the hotel staff and other affiliated locals asked them to surrender their passports for the duration of their stay. Everyone in the group handed them over without question, surrendering their passports without so much as a word. Unlike the others, my grandmother flatly refused and recommended her niece do the same. Instead of going toe-to-toe with anyone, my grandmother made up an excuse each day for why she did not have it on her or could not provide it when asked. She did that every day until they left the country because she knew that no one should ever willingly surrender their passport. My grandmother knew full well her security was in her own hands, not the hands of the hotel staff or liaisons. For the sake of her security, she refused to succumb to the bandwagon effect. Neither should you.

» ANCHORING BIAS

Anchoring bias is a lot like availability heuristic bias. It is the inflated importance of the first information you hear. The first thing to which a person is exposed in a given area often becomes the foundation of their beliefs about that subject. They tend to anchor to that information and build upon it, even if it is incorrect.

If you were told the most important thing to consider in a survival situation is food, and that was the very first information you ever heard on the subject, that would stick with you and color your perception about survival priorities. You might pack your bug-out bag with food first and sacrifice signaling devices or first aid equipment or fire-building items for the sake of space and weight. In a true survival situation, you might then spend all your energy, intellect and daylight trying to secure food and forget about building shelter and fire. Why? Because you are anchored to the bias you inherited as a result of the very first information you heard.

A bit of critical thinking would combat this effect nicely. Have you heard from multiple sources? Have you talked with experts? If you have done your own research, how recent is the data you have collected? Is the source of the data trying to sell you a product? What are your likely needs in the field and have you provided for all of them? What are the Facts, Likely Assumptions, Problems and Solutions (pg. 132)?

›› CHOICE SUPPORTIVE BIAS

Choice supportive bias is defending a choice I made because I already made it. I may or may not think it was the best thing I could have done. However, because it was my choice, I defend it. It is that simple and that frustrating.

You must be willing to be proven wrong if you find that you have been presented with sufficient evidence or sound information contrary to your point. Choice supportive bias makes this very difficult. If I have the trip of a lifetime planned and, before I depart, there is an eruption of a volcano at my destination, choice supportive bias causes me to defend my choice and go anyway, even if people are questioning the wisdom of my trip. Yes, there may be lava, I might think to myself, and ash, and diminished air quality, and maybe even panic, but perhaps it will not affect the areas I plan to visit? And at any rate, I already bought the flights and hotel. No! How foolish does this sound? Please do not fall prey to this thinking.

I need to be willing to evaluate my choices, even in hindsight, and learn from them. I need to be willing to realize that I made a poor choice so I can make better informed choices in the future. My safety and security may depend on it.

» OSTRICH BIAS

Ostrich bias, as you might surmise, is refusing to acknowledge or accept negative information. You might as well be sticking your head in the sand. It is not hard to see the security tie-in here.

If there is someone you have known for a while who begins to exhibit concerning behaviors, and you choose to look the other way because you want to believe the best about them, this is classic ostrich bias behavior. Do not do this. It is good to want to see the best in everyone. I genuinely believe that is a decent trait to have. It is good to render the benefit of the doubt and be forgiving. However, it is decidedly not good to ignore your gut when it tells you something is wrong.

I once knew someone for 20 years. A friend of mine cautioned me about him because my friend did not like some of his behaviors. He was socially awkward, but he was manifesting symptoms my friend found concerning. Far more than simple awkwardness, this person began to act and talk in such a way that slowly revealed he was not entirely mentally balanced. Eventually, he came to think of himself as God's mouthpiece. He sent me a letter and signed it, "Your Father and your Savior, God." Huge red flag. Well, that was enough for me. I cut off our friendship and asked, under threat of a restraining order, that he never contact me again.

For 12 out of 20 years, a faithful friend had tried to caution me about this guy. I wanted to believe the best, so I ignored any negative information. In doing so, I made a great ostrich. It could have become a true security situation, all because I would not acknowledge anything bad. As the saying goes, "When you see something, say something." Do not expect a problem to resolve itself. Do the uncomfortable thing and call out strange behavior. You might be the only one who does.

» OUTCOME BIAS

Outcome bias is judging the efficacy of a decision solely by the outcome. The ends justify the means.

We have talked a bit about taking the lead in crisis situations. Suppose you were the leader of a group and were responsible for keeping them alive after a crisis. Say you had a decision to make and everyone around you was recommending a particular course of action, but your gut was telling you to do the opposite. In this case, you listen to your gut and choose to ignore your trusted counselors. You achieve the outcome of your heart's desire by trusting your gut, but your people are understandably mad at you for going against everyone's best advice and acting alone, contrary to popular opinion. You defend your decision by saying that your gut was right after all and you made the right decision because of the outcome. That is outcome bias.

There is a time and a place to ignore the group and trust your gut. There is also a time and a place to trust your advisors. Be judicious and choose wisely.

▶▶ OVERCONFIDENCE

Outcome bias leads to overconfidence. Overconfidence is trusting your gut more than you trust the facts. Occasionally, that might work out well. However, left to go on unchecked, it can lead to dangerous overconfidence.

Why dangerous? Overconfidence tricks us into thinking we are invincible. It can cause us to take inappropriate or disproportionate risks because of how much we believe in ourselves. If you are spending time in or near crisis or high crime areas, overconfidence will lead you to believe you can operate with impunity and never get captured by the bad guys because your gut will tell you when to go out and where to go. Since you believe your gut will never let you down, you may take unnecessary risks with a false sense of security.

An unchecked ego can lead to disaster. The solution? Stay humble and learn to anticipate the unexpected.

▶▶ PLACEBO BIAS

When you believe something will have a certain effect upon you, it more often than not does, simply because you believe it. How profound is that?

Of course, this can be used for good or for bad. If you are in a lost hiker situation and your buddy breaks his ankle, you might be able to relieve his pain by convincing him you have a guaranteed remedy for any level of pain. You tell him that if he will just take this magic pill (perhaps an aspirin), it will relieve ALL his pain within 20 minutes, 100 percent guaranteed. You have never seen it fail to work. If he truly believes you, his own brain will relieve him of the pain, because that is what he fully expects. He has put his whole faith in what you have said.

Be aware, however, that the opposite is also true. Hypochondriacs can manifest the symptoms of the diseases they believe they have, just because they believe they have it. The power of suggestion is a powerful force, both positive and negative.

It is a handy psychological tool to have in your pocket but one you must absolutely use with care.

➤ SURVIVORSHIP BIAS

They say hindsight is 20/20. Survivorship bias is judging a situation solely by the information which persists until the end.

Imagine a news story that unfolds slowly and is in the media for months. Often, the early facts of the story will be forgotten and replaced by more recent or sensational breaking developments. By the time it all comes to a conclusion, a great deal of early data will have been lost or forgotten and its bearing upon the story minimized or marginalized. Imagine forming your opinion about the entire story based solely on the very last article written. That is survivorship bias.

In a survival or security situation, it is important to keep all the data in front of you, inasmuch as you possibly can. Go back and revisit the early data. If it has been truly superseded, OK. Facts are facts, and this can go by the wayside. However, if your data is still accurate, keep it in the mix as you make decisions about your life and safety. Never discount that which has been proven true.

➤ SELECTIVE PERCEPTION

Selective perception is perceiving messages and actions according to your own frame of reference. Most of us would ask, what else can we do? Good question.

My uncle married a woman of a completely different culture than that of my family. His wife really hurt him and wound up divorcing him. It was a terrible divorce, as nasty as any I have ever seen. It involved kidnapping and all kinds of trauma. As a result, my family looked with concern upon the culture from which she had come. Years later, I fell in love with someone from that same race and wanted to get married. My grandparents, aunts, uncles and parents were hard sells on backing this new union. Their own frame of reference was not good and they were concerned about this happening again (and I do not blame them). I did obtain their cautious approval but, when my own marriage fell apart, that unfortunately cemented everyone's feelings. Their only experiences had now twice proven to be negative and they developed the selective perception that this particular culture produces bad spouses.

As we move around in a world that is in crisis, we need to be careful about our selective perceptions. Are we ascribing more malice aforethought to a particular group and allowing it to fester into real prejudice? Conversely, are we placing undue trust in a group that we have not vetted? As always, keep the security implications in mind when judging a person or group of people.

» BLIND SPOT BIAS

Blind spot bias is the belief that I am either not biased at all, or that I am less biased than everybody else. The irony of blind spot bias is that if you think you have no biases, you are exhibiting a bias.

In a security situation, having a blind spot can cost your life. That is exactly the angle from which the danger will approach. Evaluate yourself. You have read about many types of biases now. Do you see any of them in yourself? Only an honest evaluation will help you prepare the battle space in advance.

» THE G.I. JOE FALLACY

The G.I. Joe Fallacy says that merely knowing you have a bias is all you need to overcome it. After all, "knowing is half the battle." This dovetails nicely with the blind spot bias. Knowing your biases is not all you need to overcome them. People who know they have a particular bias will still exhibit that bias until and unless they put safety measures in place to prevent them from doing so.

If you know you have an overconfidence bias, you may want to tell the people you trust about it and ask them to act as your loyal opposition when they see you acting on that bias. For instance, if you and a group of friends decide to go rappelling and you have made them aware of your overconfidence bias, they can be your checks and balances against you doing anything truly stupid and unnecessarily risky.

» MENTAL ACCOUNTING BIAS

We tend to put things into different accounts in our heads as a way of organizing our lives. For example, you may have a checking account and a savings account.

You may choose to live month-to-month, solely out of your checking account and use those funds to cover routine expenses. You may also choose to allow yourself to access your savings account only when you have an extraordinary expenditure.

We do that with decisions and behaviors, too. When we say something grumpy or ill-tempered, we ascribe that to the "account" of being tired or under too much stress. However, when we do something kind or heroic, we ascribe that to the "account" of our true selves and our base personality. It may sound valid to others, but you will know whether or not it comes from a place of truth.

Be careful. This can be a slippery slope, and you can begin to allow rationalizations for the things you know you ought not do. One way to prepare your battle space in advance is to decide early on what your convictions are and which ones are non-negotiable. That makes it very easy for you to act wisely in times of crisis. Having already laid down the rules of engagement for yourself, you can take action much more quickly and effectively when the proverbial or physical bullets are flying.

» PRICING BIAS

As consumers, we all prefer higher-priced goods, even when we know pricing is arbitrary. Why? We confuse price with value. I am guilty of this too. I have certain brands of gear and weaponry that I trust and like more than others because they are more expensive, so I presume they are of a higher quality. Of course, that may or may not be true.

When it comes to purchasing survival and tactical gear, I do have some suggestions to offer, in order to help you overcome this bias:

- **Read market reviews.**
- **Read customer feedback.**
- **If you can, try it out before you buy it.**
- **Talk to people who use the gear and ask for their opinions on user friendliness, reliability, durability, availability of parts, manufacturer helpfulness, defects or design flaws and safety rating.**
- **Talk to salesmen at outdoor or tactical stores and ask for their opinions on a variety of brands.**
- **Attend a demo day or a field test of a product to see it in action.**

Do not be quick to assume the highest price denotes the best quality. It might not, so do your research before committing to any item.

RASCLS + SOCIAL ENGINEERING

You might think the title today has a typo in it. Actually, it is an acronym that refers to the finer points of social engineering.

▶▶ R IS FOR RECIPROCITY

Have you ever seen the show *Chicago* or listened to the music? If you have, there is a song called "When You're Good To Mama" and it is all about this concept: If you want something, you must first give something.

There are many reasons for social engineering. If you know you want or need something from someone now, or in the future, begin by investing in them. This is called Enlightened Self-Interest, meaning you can see the value in giving something away now because you know you will reap the benefit of that sacrifice later.

In a crisis, wouldn't it be nice if you had made such good investments into the people around you that they wanted to reciprocate? You cannot wait until you have a request to make before you offer something up. To truly practice social engineering, you must begin your relationships by doing something for the other person. It could be picking up the tab for a meal. It could mean making an introduction that is important to them, doing them a favor or giving them a ride. You are only limited by your own imagination. Just remember that when you do something for someone, they will feel personally motivated to return the favor.

In a time of adversity, this could save your life.

▶▶ A IS FOR AUTHORITY

If you want to socially engineer something, you must present yourself as an authority, someone to whom other people will listen. It can be based on net worth, position, education, title, experience, subject matter expertise, connections, status, affiliation, accomplishments, career, political clout and many other things. Sorry, but you cannot begin to shout your agenda on a street corner. You will be ignored (or probably thought of as crazy) at best. You must give people a reason to listen to you. The hook that will capture their interest in what you have to say is who you are. What is your claim to authority in this situation?

» S IS FOR SCARCITY

People are drawn to that which is not easily attainable. It is impressive to have something scarce. It makes you the envy of others and elevates your status. If you want to socially engineer, offer something scarce to the person or people you are trying to reach. Elevate their status on their behalf. Make them feel special and important and singled out for good things. Make them feel like they deserve the royal treatment. They will be yours.

» C IS FOR CONSISTENT ACTION OVER TIME

If you are trying to socially engineer a situation, you will naturally arise as a leader. Whether you are the public leader or a king-maker, you will be in a position of influence over those who can change the world. What they need to see from you is consistent action over time. They cannot doubt your motives, reliability, punctuality, capabilities, dependability or anything else about you. They need to trust you implicitly. They need to know exactly what to expect from you and have every confidence that you are a person of your word and that you can deliver everything you promise.

» L IS FOR LIKABILITY

You cannot socially engineer anything without this critical component. You must be likable. It does not matter whether or not you care for the situation or the person or people with whom you are dealing. You must be the likable one. You will start by influencing just one person. Eventually, he or she will introduce you around. Most likely, the initial person is not the one over whom you really wish to have influence. You will want to start with a person who has placement and access to the person/people whom you truly want to influence. Your likability factor will determine whether or not your new friend will care to give you more of their time, and certainly whether or not they intend to introduce to other people they know.

» S IS FOR SOCIAL PROOF

This can be the most difficult one of all. You have to be able to prove your claims socially. If you claim to be rich, you need a limousine, the best hotel suite, the best restaurants, whatever fits the bill. If you claim to be well educated, you need to have connections with tenured figures in academia. If you claimed to be a subject matter expert, you must have the knowledge base to back up that claim. People need to see the proof of who you are with their own eyes. You need to appear to be transparent, and the people with whom you are dealing need to believe what they see in you is what you really are. They need to be able to vet you and verify your claims.

» SOCIAL ENGINEERING

So, why social engineering? What is it for? When will you ever need to use it? Is it ethical?

Let's say you are traveling to a crisis area of the world where violence and crime are high. You need to be there, but you recognize it is not a safe place to be. When you get to where you will be staying, greet the people closest to you. They may be a host family, hotel staff, a vendor at a market, a driver or a translator. Talk and establish who you are. Establish your likability and give them something to start the cycle of reciprocity. What are you actually doing? You are social engineering. You are making friends in your immediate area so that you will have resources, protection, a place to hide, food to eat, information and whatever else you need in order to function in this high-threat environment.

It can be as simple and as small-scale as that. Social engineering can also change the world. It has started revolutions and toppled governments. It is a powerful tool in the right hands. Use it, but do not dare abuse it.

SELF-DEFENSE

IN FIGHT-OR-FLIGHT SCENARIOS, IT PAYS TO KNOW YOUR OPTIONS.

NO MATTER YOUR intentions, how diplomatic you may be or determined to let bygones be bygones, you may one day find yourself having to face off against someone who wishes to cause you harm. Worse still, this may occur at a theater, stadium, place of worship or any number of public venues, in which case you may have no choice but to outlast the enemy and make a run for it. From learning the four cardinal rules of shooting to the finer points of using random objects as weapons to training for the unknown, these tips will guide you when you are forced to fight for your life.

THE TIMELINE OF SELF-DEFENSE

In all situations where self-defense is or may be the outcome, there is a timeline of decisions and options. The timeline, as seen from the beginning all the way through to the end, begins with sensing the danger and ends with successfully stopping it.

The activation of the timeline begins when you sense or see that something is not right. Identifying it and catching it this early is dependent upon maintaining good situational awareness. You must be living in condition yellow (relaxed but aware), meaning you must notice the things going on around you and be able to read the signs.

Something is not right, you tell yourself. You might not know in this moment exactly how or why that is, but you can feel it in your gut. Get off the X.

THIS CAN HAPPEN IN ANY NUMBER OF WAYS.

• **SOMEONE IS MOVING IN YOUR DIRECTION.** They are not in your immediate vicinity but they will be shortly.
LEAVE. Do not be there when they arrive.

• **SOMEONE IS HEADING YOUR WAY** and you cannot move away in time or there are physical barriers blocking your swift exit.
ACTIVATE A "VERBAL DEFENSE." In a loud, no-nonsense voice, command them to stop and then go away.

• **SOMEONE IS ALREADY MUCH TOO CLOSE** and is now attempting to put their hands on you.
USE A SOFT OR "EDUCATIONAL" DEFENSE. Block their attempt to grab or strike you without counter attacking or harming them to ascertain their true motives. This works well in schools, churches and businesses where the person belongs there and might just need help.

• **SOMEONE BEGINS TO ACCOST YOU.**
DEFEND YOURSELF WITH MINIMAL FORCE AND "BAIL OUT" or run away as soon as you break free.

• **SOMEONE ATTACKS AND/OR CORNERS YOU.**

GO RABID CHIPMUNK (pg. 42) on them. Bite, scratch, claw, kick, punch, gouge, bludgeon, stomp, scream, hit, strike, stab or use any other option available to you. Keep fighting viciously until your attacker is completely subdued, then move away. Scan for any friends or accomplices the attacker might have close by. Get to safety. Check yourself for wounds or injuries. Call the police and/or an ambulance.

While you may not always see the danger coming, it can begin at any point on the timeline. Keeping the timeline in mind helps with personal security decision making. It allows you to be ahead of the curve and gives you the ability to plan for any contingency. Knowing what you will do in an emergency, having a solid plan, is halfway to success.

DRESSING DEFENSIVELY

We all love style, men and women alike. Fashion appeals to our nature. We like to look good and, when we feel attractive, we feel good. Rarely do we consider the role our clothing and accessory choices play in our security.

SCARVES

Scarves are a very popular fashion accessory and have been for years. I keep hoping this particular fashion will fall out of favor soon, but it seems like it might be here to stay. While scarves look lovely, wearing one is one of the worst personal security mistakes you can make. Whether you wear an open scarf, an infinity scarf, a winter scarf or a fashion scarf, scarves provide a handle for control and manipulation. If I were a bad guy, casing the street to select a target, I would choose someone with a scarf. There are so many ways to grab a scarf and turn it into an instant noose, controlling my target immediately.

NECKLACES

Thick or especially heavy necklaces can also be used for controlling a person, much like a scarf. If the necklace is sufficiently thin, it will simply break away when grabbed. If it is thick, it can be used to choke, strangle, manipulate or otherwise control the wearer. If you decide to wear a necklace, make sure it is weak enough to break away upon being grabbed and be prepared to sacrifice it.

HIGH-HEELED SHOES

Ladies, I realize I am treading on sacred ground here. Perhaps, if you are Lara Croft, you could use a stiletto to fight dirty and do serious damage to your attacker. For all others, high heels are a terrible idea. They prevent running away, are quite likely to result in a twisted, sprained or broken ankle while trying to flee and prevent you from fighting back. Consider shoes that will allow you to walk, run and fight if needed.

FLIP FLOPS, MULES AND SLIDES

These are almost as bad as high heels. They do have one, small advantage: all of these shoes can be kicked off or stepped out of quickly if you need to run. Should you have to fight, however, you will now have to do so barefoot. Shoes are an amazing weapon in a fight, one that should not be sacrificed lightly.

RESTRICTIVE SHIRTS, PANTS OR SKIRTS

Anything that keeps you from exercising your full range of motion becomes a liability in a moment of adversity. When you get dressed in the morning, ask yourself if you could walk, run and fight in the clothes you are about to don. Will they slow you down?

Immodest clothing is not only physically restrictive, it also makes you a target. This does not apply solely to women, either. Men who wear their pants down low, exposing half their boxers to the world, are prime targets because they cannot respond to threats fast enough. It could be something as simple as pickpocketing. A savvy thief will choose someone who will get tangled up in their own clothes and cannot execute an immediate chase.

HOODS

Hooded shirts and hooded jackets provide both a downside and an upside. While a hood can be used to manipulate a person, it is not nearly as dangerous as a scarf. Hoods do not encircle your neck but simply rest on your back. While they will absolutely be grabbed in a fight, there are many ways to counter attack if your hood is grabbed. Hoods also allow you to conceal your hair and part of your face in a hurry, aiding the wearer in a quick change of appearance if needed. If you do wear hoods, make sure that you are familiar

HOOD SELF-DEFENSE

1. If your hood or hair is grabbed from behind, that does not automatically put the attacker in the driver's seat. You have two hands free, they have one.

2. In one movement, turn toward your attacker and bow down at the waist to stay under the hand that has you caught.

3. Now that you are facing them, strike strike strike strike strike until they no longer want to play.

Conjure up your inner rabid chipmunk and turn the tables on them.

with hood and hair grab self-defense techniques.

It is not just a matter of what you wear but also how you wear it. When it is cold, do you stand with your hands in your pockets? Do you cross your arms or lace your fingers? These things will also slow down your reaction time as you first need to untangle yourself before you can even respond. If your pants are down way too low, you have to take the time to hike them up before you can give chase, then you have to hold them up while you run in order to prevent them from falling down to your ankles. As confident as she might appear, a woman in a miniskirt will unfailingly tug the hem down all day as it rides up. She will have to take the time to do that before, during and after responding to a robbery or an assault. It should go without saying, but untied shoes are an accident waiting to happen. The extra second or two you take to ensure your shoes are secured properly before going about your business is always worth it.

What should you wear, then? Pants, shorts, skirts, dresses, shirts, blouses and jackets should be loose enough to move around in but not flowing, dragging or trailing. Pockets are premium and preferred over bags and purses for Every Day Carry items (pg. 19). Shoes should be closed-toe and snugly fit. Socks should be snugly fit and made of a wicking material to minimize blisters and maximize control of your foot and shoe.

As you can see, our style choices directly impact our security. When in public give some thought to your own wardrobe. How are you setting yourself up? Run a few "what if" scenarios in your own head and see how you would do in your favorite outfits. Are you dressing for success?

CONCEALED CARRY DRAW TECHNIQUES

If you carry a firearm concealed, here are two techniques for drawing your weapon that minimize the likelihood of getting tangled up in your own clothing.

FROM UNDERNEATH AN UNTUCKED SHIRT

1. Using your dominant hand, the thumb hooks the shirt while the fingers sweep for the pistol. Keep your eyes on your target. Use your non-dominant hand to hold the shirt out of the way during the draw.

2. As soon as the pistol is clear of the holster, pop the wrist of the dominant hand toward the target while supporting it with the non-dominant hand. Keep your aim and move both hands to an ideal shooting position. KEEP YOUR EYES ON THE TARGET.

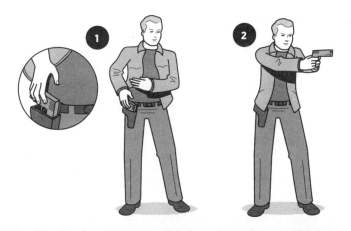

FROM UNDERNEATH A JACKET

1. Sweep the jacket back with your dominant hand while the fingers find and draw the pistol.

2. As soon as the pistol is clear of the holster, pop the wrist of the dominant hand toward the target while supporting it with the non-dominant hand. Keep your aim and move both hands to an ideal shooting position. **KEEP YOUR EYES ON THE TARGET.**

Remember to practice all competencies related to target shooting, like drawing your weapon from concealment. Trying it for the first time at the moment when you need it is likely to get you hurt or killed.

WHAT IS BEHIND YOUR TARGET?

These are the four cardinal rules of shooting:

1. **Never point the gun at anything you are unwilling to destroy.**
2. **Never put your finger on the trigger until you are ready to pull it.**
3. **Always keep the gun pointed down range.**
4. **Always know what is behind your target.**

Pretty straightforward stuff, right? Not by a long shot. How can you always know exactly what is behind your target? Furthermore, do you know what kind of damage your particular round will cause? Will your target stop the round? Will it go right through? Will it go through drywall, doors or furniture? Will it ricochet? Do you know who is on the other side of that drywall or door if it does go through? Is your target back-stopped by true cover or only by concealment? How many sectors of fire do you truly have in your own home when your children are in bed? Where are your pets? How effective is your lighting? Where will that bullet travel if it goes through your wall and out of your house?

Obviously I cannot answer these questions for you without knowing your weapon and your rounds, let alone seeing your home. However, the answers to these questions are critical to home defense. Walk around your house, inside and out, and make a point to answer all of these questions. Build a plan that factors in all of those answers, then memorize it. Rehearse it regularly. Run exercises. Practice, practice, practice. Know the firearms laws in your state and precinct. Once that round leaves your gun, it is yours. You own it, and all the damage it may cause.

My sidearm of choice is the Sig Sauer P320. I use the 9mm. My partner prefers the .45 and has a conversion kit to the 9mm, but we both carry P320's. We believe in them and they have never let us down. We train with them, test with them, teach with them and operate with them. Moreover, we take great pains to always know what lies behind our targets. The cost of not knowing is simply too high a price to pay.

FOUND OBJECT FIGHTING

Found object fighting means taking any object and using it as a weapon. This is a crucial skill for anyone with the drive to survive a precarious situation. There is a slight difference, however, between found object fighting and improvised weapons.

An improvised weapon is when you identify the potential usefulness of something like, say, a roll of quarters and a bandana, and have the time to make a weapon out of those things. One of the easiest improvised weapons to make is a lead umbrella. It is concealed by its nature. If you simply take a few wrenches from your household toolbox, you can slip them inside a folded and bound umbrella, reinforcing its strength and converting it into a lead pipe.

Found object fighting, on the other hand, is exactly what it sounds like: picking up a handy object and employing it as a weapon against an attacker. This is reserved for situations where the person defending themselves had no warning and therefore no time for prior planning. Time to make do with what you can find.

The concept is simple and only as limited as your own imagination. We have all seen old murder mysteries where an unplanned murder occurred and the murder weapon was a bookend or a candlestick, employed over the head, and this is not that far from reality. When a reaction to violence is spur-of-the-moment (which is to say, not premeditated), any object a person can grab becomes a means of self-defense.

Remember the difference between a reaction and a response? Reaction is quick and instinctive, with no time for thought or measure, whereas response

MASTER TACTIC

What are some of the things you carry on your person every day? Keys? A pen or two? A water bottle? Consider what you could use to defend yourself with if you were to find yourself face-to-face with an attacker.

is a measured, reasoned, thought-out answer to a stimulus. Both are necessary tools to keep in your survival toolbox and both have times and places of appropriate use. In order to avoid, evade, escape or de-escalate a situation, a thoughtful response is needed. In a found object, self-defense situation, reaction is the priority.

In light of their definitions, reaction might seem like the lesser of the two answers. It is not. Instincts are there for our protection in times of danger, when there is no time to thoughtfully catalogue our options. However, there is a way to bring response and reaction together to form a powerful multi-tool. For those of us who take their own survival seriously, we can train in some sort of self-defense style. We can work out, gaining strength and stamina as we learn the techniques and the strategies of defending ourselves. That is a pre-response. In a moment of unanticipated violence, the tool of response gets coupled with reaction. We might not have expected to be accosted today, but the time we spent in training will show. There will be no pausing to think or flipping through options. What comes out of us in that moment of adversity will be a lightning quick reaction, predicated on what we spent time pouring into ourselves in advance. My mother's wisdom is worth repeating: "What spills out of you when you get bumped, is what you are really made of."

They say that necessity is the mother of invention. When it comes to found objects, this can be as obvious as your keys. Placing your keys between your fingers as spikes prior to punching someone will exponentially increase the effectiveness of your punch. Paperweights, bookends and candlesticks are classic because of their weight. Backpacks and purses can be swung like an ancient slingshot. Any pen, even if it is not a tactical one, can stab and hurt. A water bottle can be opened and water flung into the attacker's face, causing them to close their eyes for a split second and ultimately giving you the advantage. A salt or pepper shaker in a restaurant can be gripped in your fist to add power to your punch, or opened and thrown into the eyes of your attacker. Dirt and gravel can also be flung at the attacker's face. Rocks can be thrown, as can canned goods and many other things. Sticks can stab. A scarf can strangle. Glass can cut. Think about it the next time you take a walk and see if you can spot things you could use to your advantage in a tricky situation. You are only limited by your own imagination.

OTHER FOUND OBJECT FIGHTING CONSIDERATIONS

- You can use an umbrella to extend your reach and to block incoming strikes.
- A hot drink thrown in the face of an attacker will scald.
- Charger cables and cords can be used to trip or choke.
- Any solid object like a book or a cell phone can be used as a bludgeoning weapon.
- Depending on how thick they are, solid objects may even work as a temporary shield. Use them in tandem with another found object to maximize your chances of survival.
- Glass beverage bottles can be broken and used to slash or stab an attacker.

KNOW YOUR ENEMY

The Army Ranger Handbook tells us to know our enemy. If something threatens your safety and puts your life in danger, analyze the situation by ascertaining these pertinent data points:

COMPOSITION

What forces and weapons can the enemy bring to the fight? What weapon systems are available and what additional weapons and personnel are supporting them?

DISPOSITION

What is the exact location and posture of the enemy against the backdrop and terrain?

STRENGTH

How strong are they?

RECENT ACTIVITIES

Recent attacks or activities, such as intelligence gathering, may indicate future intentions.

REINFORCEMENT CAPABILITIES

How many and from where might the attacker receive reinforcements?

POSSIBLE COURSES OF ACTION

Use these data points to determine possible courses of action. Remember F.LA.P.S. (pg. 132).

OFFENSIVE CONSIDERATIONS

How can the enemy use these approaches, which avenues are the most dangerous, and which would support a counter attack?

If you can answer these questions with verifiable data during an attack or even a crisis, you will have the information you need to run, hide, fight and survive.

TRAIN LIKE YOU FIGHT

In your hour of need, you cannot expect to be able to use the gear and weapons you have acquired correctly or at least efficiently unless you have taken the time to train with them. I am a huge advocate of trying every skill you possibly can. Once you have read about it or seen a video on it, go and try it. You will never know just what it actually takes until you do. People buy gear and then feel snug and secure because they have it. Obtaining the gear is only step one. Step two is to try it out. Step three is to learn from your experience. Step four is to become proficient. Then you have earned the right to feel smug. One of the things I carry on my non-dominant side is a Benchmade SOCP dagger or an Emerson Super Karambit. The SOCP dagger is housed in a Kydex sheath with a firm detent so that I can pull it straight out when I wish to deploy it, but—and this is key—it will never fall out accidentally. The Super Karambit is self-deploying when I pull it from my pocket in a particular way. When I go to the range, I carry dummy blades of those very knives in the same place I customarily carry the real one(s). Occasionally, I will act as if my firearm has jammed or been dropped or taken away from me and transition to my knife. I also practice pulling the knife out with the non-dominant hand and keeping it in my grip as I join both hands around my gun (in the

> # MASTER TACTIC
> **If you are going to acquire and carry weaponry, it becomes
> your responsibility to train to proficiency so that you and
> everyone else around you stay safe.**

normal position) and fire. The beauty of these two knives is the finger loop that makes this possible. I also practice my no light and low light techniques, drawing my flashlight and using it to illuminate the target at off angles and/or in short bursts before I fire. If I am carrying a firearm or a knife, I also carry multiple RATS Tourniquets at all times. I practice gaining cover and applying a tourniquet to myself and/or my partner as we stay in the fight.

RUN, FIGHT, RUN

We have all heard the expression "practice makes perfect." Is that true? What if you practice something incorrectly? When it comes time to perform that skill, will you execute it flawlessly? I would submit that only perfect practice makes perfect. You have to train right if you want to perform well.

We all need to train the way we fight. It does no good to cut yourself slack, stop when it gets hard, cut corners or take excessive time off. You are ultimately doing yourself a disservice in the long run, one that could prove quite costly. Those decisions will leave you vastly unprepared and land you in a world of hurt when the day of adversity strikes. If you want to set yourself up for success, you have to integrate perfect practice into your routine now, in advance of the problem.

The best method I have seen for training is something I refer to as Run, Fight, Run, which is exactly what it sounds like. To condition your body for fight, you must fight. To condition your body for flight, you must run. If you wish to have both fight and flight as options, you must train in both. If you wish to be able to use both in the same situation and move easily back and forth between them, you must train that way—in a circuit.

Start by running for a preset amount of time, say 10 minutes. Next, practice your combatives: kicking, punching, wrestling, holding, stomping, blocking and any kind of striking for 10 minutes. Then go back to running for another 10 minutes. Once you get used to the pattern, you can shorten the intervals. Run for 1 minute, fight for 1 minute, run for 1 minute. Eventually, you can add weights and/or resistance to your runs so that your workload is increased. If you can run with weights, running without them will practically feel like a piece of cake. Get yourself in the proper mindset ahead of time and your conditioning will more readily fall into place.

You may find, when the day of adversity strikes, that you cannot confront the threat at hand but merely do your best to escape it. That is OK. There is no shame in running when running is the best option for survival. Depending on the situation, it might be the wisest and most appropriate action you can take. A true warrior needs to have the ability to both fight and run, as well as the decision-making skills to choose correctly for each encounter. Prepare accordingly.

BUSHCRAFT BASICS

HOW TO MASTER THE ELEMENTS AND MAKE IT IN THE WILDERNESS.

YOU MAY KNOW how to build a fire, sure. But have you ever had to make your own compass? What about the finer points of creating ground-to-air symbols to communicate with air search-and-rescue teams? From determining what plants you can safely consume to building a highly effective shelter to knowing what gear to pack for any environment, these survival hacks will help you thrive when you find yourself in the middle of nowhere.

S.T.O.P.

If you become lost, there is a very simple checklist to follow to aid yourself and those trying to find you. It only has four items to remember: S.T.O.P.

S - STOP

A moving target is far more difficult to hit than a stationary target and in this case being targeted is a positive. I realize boredom sets in quickly and that adults want to take action on their own behalf, but you will vastly improve your chances of being found by simply staying put.

T - THINK

You may need a whole slew of things but rushing around in a blind panic will not improve your situation. Instead, if you have any gum, take a piece out and put it in your mouth. Savor the taste. When it is nice and soft and all the flavor is gone, then you can begin to give your situation some serious thought. Can you make or do you already have a visual or auditory signaling device?

O - OBSERVE

Assess your situation. What time of day is it? Is it likely to get dark soon? What will you need, and do you have access to it? Do you have survival skills and a knowledge base to take care of yourself? Are you injured? Do you need to treat yourself? Evaluate the situation. Leave no stone unturned.

P - PLAN

Decide what you will do. Begin to formulate a plan to construct a shelter, build a fire and procure water. Food can wait, even though it gets uncomfortable.

If you follow S.T.O.P., you will respond rather than react. You will maintain situational awareness and prioritize your needs. Best of all, you will be able to take care of yourself as you wait for help to arrive and you will aid their search by staying still.

GROUND-TO-AIR SYMBOLS

Have you ever been snowmobiling? It is an exhilarating feeling zooming through vast expanses of stark winter beauty and untracked snow. You can go and go and go for hours and never stop enjoying yourself. Or perhaps you have been 4-wheeling in the desert. It is the same feeling. Freedom. Exhilaration. Wide open spaces. Untouched nature. The rush of the wind. The lonely expanse of earth. The neverending sky. If you have ever ridden a motorcycle across vast stretches of highway, you already know what I mean. One hundred miles of road between towns and nothing but serenity.

But accidents happen. What if your snowmobile runs out of gas when you are at the farthest point away from home? What if you crash the quad in the middle of the desert? What if you get a flat tire on the highway, 50 miles from anything or anyone in every direction?

Fortunately, there are internationally recognized ground-to-air signals that you can create so that a passing aircraft can read and interpret them. Of course, to accomplish this, you must obtain and move materials big enough to make symbols that can be read from the air. This can usually be done with rocks, logs, branches or by writing in the dirt, sand or snow.

Using these symbols will not only help aircraft locate you but also communicate to the crew what condition you are in, what direction you are moving and what you need.

Message	Code Symbol
You require assistance	V
You require medical assistance	X
No or Negative	N
Yes or Affirmative	Y
Direction in which you want the aircraft to proceed	(arrow)

HOW TO MAKE A COMPASS

Did you know you can make your own compass?

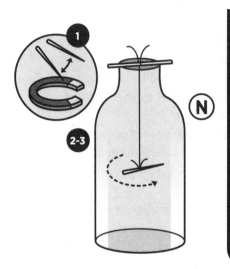

D.I.Y. COMPASS

1. Take a needle and stroke the end of it on a magnet or on silk. Lacking either of those, you can use your hair or a piece of leather.

2. Suspend the magnetized needle from a piece of string or hair.

3. Hang the suspended needle inside a clear plastic or glass bottle to avoid it being disturbed by air currents.

The free-hanging magnetized needle will point north/south.

You also can use a paperclip, bobby pin, safety pin or any other thin piece of metal that can be magnetized. If you do not have the means to suspend it, you can float the needle on a leaf in the water. You will know that you did it correctly if, after you suspend or float it, it automatically corrects its own orientation.

PACE COUNTING

How can you measure distance without any tools? By using your own two feet, of course! Measure out 100 yards and mark it.

At a normal stride, walk the entire 100 yards, counting your paces. Note: Only measure your left footfall. Every time your left foot hits the ground, that counts as one pace. Record how many paces it takes you to cover 100 yards.

Do this three times to ensure you are consistent. You will also need to do this on level ground as well as uphill and downhill, as there will be a difference between the two terrains.

Remember, though, that not all paces are the same. Everyone's pace varies according to their height and other measurements.

If you are worried about losing your place as you count multiple hundreds of yards, there are many systems you can use to keep track. For example, some people use a rosary. Every time you count to 100, move to the next bead in your hand. When you stop, count the beads you have passed and multiply by 100.

You can use the fringes from a prayer shawl the same way. For anything up to 1,000 yards, I use my own fingers. Every time I pass another hundred yards, I put one finger out. That gives me 1,000 yards before I have to transition to another system.

No beads or fringe on you? Use the buttons on a button-down shirt (button or unbutton one with every 100 yards). Or pick up a blade of grass every 100 yards. Or make marks on your skin or gear. Use your imagination. I think you will find that being able to measure distance without using tools makes for a very freeing and empowering experience.

RESPONSIBLE DRINKING

No, this skill is not about alcohol (although the "responsible" part still applies). Should you ever find yourself in an unintentional survival situation, there is one thing you should know which is completely counter intuitive: drink your water.

Most people who find themselves in a true live-or-die survival situation get there by being lost or injured. In those situations, they will quite often have water with them at the time of their separation from the rest of mankind. These people are hikers, campers, backpackers, runners, fisherman, hunters and all kinds of outdoorsmen. Considering the fact that they have planned to be outdoors in a controlled environment anyway, most of them already have basic provisions like food and water.

When we realize we are on our own and it is a matter of survival, most of us begin to instinctively hoard and ration. It makes sense. We have no idea when we will be able to resupply, so we want our provisions to last. This might work to a point with food but it certainly does not work with water. If you find yourself surviving on your own and you have any amount of water with you, drink it. It is far better to have the water in you than in your canteen or pack. Dehydration is no joke and its effects can become life-threatening in no time. Go ahead and drink the water you have on hand. Then you will be hydrated enough to find water and find or build shelter. Stay as strong as you can for as long as you can. That means rest, hydrate, eat and stay warm or cool. Use the calories and the hydration to your benefit as you tackle the demanding tasks of finding water and building shelter and fire. Rationing your water will only hamper your efforts to make it home in one piece.

HOW TO TEST IF A PLANT IS EDIBLE

If you are stranded far from civilization with no food, how will you determine what is or is not edible? It takes time and patience to learn this skill, but it will last you a lifetime.

HERE ARE THE GROUND RULES:

- Do not eat anything for at least eight hours prior to the test, so that you can establish an accurate baseline.
- Do not try more than one plant at a time.
- Do not choose any type of fungus or anything with sap or milk.
- Begin by selecting a plant you believe will actually have some nutritional value.
- Examine different parts of said plant. Some parts may be edible and others may be poisonous, so you must test them separately.
- Test the plant by rubbing each part of it on your skin, then watch for any kind of reaction.
- Wait 15 minutes before proceeding. If there is any kind of reaction, discontinue the test of that plant.
- Rub a small piece of the plant gently on your lips and wait for five minutes, watching and feeling for a reaction.
- Place a small piece of the plant in between your lower lip and your gum and hold it there for five minutes.
- Chew the plant and hold it in your mouth without swallowing for 15 minutes.
- Swallow the piece and wait for eight hours.
- Eat half a cup of the plant and wait for an additional eight hours.
- If there are no reactions at any stage of the test, the plant is safe to eat.

Each person present can be assured the plant is not poisonous after only one person conducts the test. However, this will not tell you if any person present is allergic to the plant. If a reaction happens at any point during the test, try to make yourself vomit, then drink plenty of water. Discontinue the test. Clear your system for eight hours, choose a different plant and start again. Make sure you choose a plant that is abundant in the area to assure yourself an ongoing food source as you make your way back to civilization. It may be a laborious test, but when it comes to staying alive, these things are worth the wait.

HOW TO JUMP INTO WATER SAFELY

There may come a time when, in order to save your life, you need to drop from a great height into water. It can be scary but it does not have to be painful or harmful. Keep in mind a few simple things before you go:

WATER JUMP

1. Drop feet first.

2. Look straight ahead.

3. Keep your body (spine) as straight as possible.

4. Hold you gear in one arm and leave the other arm free to swim.

5. Keep anything you are carrying, tucked in tightly against you on one side or the other, at waist/rib level.

6. Relax when you hit the water, hold onto your gear and swim back to the surface. Since you entered the water feet down, the surface should be above your head.

7. Upon surfacing, swim your way to safety. If evading detection is most important, you need to stay under the surface as much as possible, so be sure to take deep breaths when you can.

CARING FOR YOUR FEET

If you are going to be out in nature or launching into a survival situation, one of the most critical decisions you will make is how to take care of your feet. Believe it or not, this can be a life or death decision. If you fail to take proper care of your feet and become incapacitated as a result, your ability to move, fend for yourself or get help will be extremely limited, if not altogether impossible.

You should always have a bare minimum of two pairs of socks with you, but I recommend at least three. You will always want to have at least one clean and dry (or drying) pair on standby.

CLEAN FEET

You must keep your feet, your socks and even your shoes as clean as possible. Nothing breeds infection like bacteria. Bacteria hides in sweat and dirt. Wash your feet well. Inspect them for any cuts, scrapes or scratches. Make sure to tend any open wounds. Change the dressing often, especially after getting it wet or sweating. Pay attention to your nails. Be fastidious about cleanliness and wound care. Stay ahead of problems with good hygiene.

WARM FEET

Survival situations come in all shapes and sizes. Frostbite hits digits (fingers and toes) first and extremities next, and your feet are at significant risk in a winter survival situation. Prioritize the warmth of your feet. Frostbite to your feet can kill you if it prevents you from finding shelter or help.

Make sure to wear appropriate socks in terms of material and thickness. Wool or a synthetic blend are the best choices for warmth. Wrap the outsides of your shoes in plastic from a garbage bag to trap the heat in. Stop and build a fire to keep them warm. If they are simply cold and do not have frostbite, rub them to increase circulation. If you have a companion, put your feet between their legs or under their arms to warm up. Wrap yourself in a blanket. Immerse them in warm water. Use a water bottle. Do whatever it takes to prevent frostbite.

If you already have frostbite, DO NOT RUB YOUR FEET! You will damage the tissues by cutting into them with the icicles that have formed. Use cool or lukewarm water to bring the temperature back up. Seek medical attention as soon as possible.

LAYERED FEET

Yes, even your feet can benefit from a good layering. Gentlemen, I know that this is traditionally the ladies' domain. However, wearing a layer of nylon knee-highs against your skin and adding your socks on top of that can actually save you from painful blisters. Blisters not only slow you down but can also lead to infections. Out in the field and without proper treatment, infections can result in gangrene or sepsis. Either one of these can prove fatal.

When you add a thin layer like nylon against your skin, the nylon and skin stay together as one. The rubbing occurs between the nylon and the sock rather than between your skin and the sock. Trust me, this makes for a much more comfortable walk over the long haul.

DRY FEET

Perhaps the most important part of foot care is making sure your feet stay dry. Trench foot, as many soldiers learned firsthand during World War I, is a condition that sets in after allowing your feet to stay wet for too long. Bacteria abounds. Carrying extra pairs of socks allows you to stop and change into a clean, dry pair at regular intervals. Wash the dirty pair, then hang it on your gear to dry as you keep moving. As I said earlier, the best material for socks is wool. Believe it or not, wool stays warm whether it is dry or wet. Wool also acts as a natural deodorant, and because it allows air movement, wool will help you thermoregulate and keep your body temperature under control. That said, if you are allergic to wool or lanolin you will want to find a synthetic equivalent. DO NOT use cotton, as cotton will exacerbate any problem you encounter.

Take care of your feet and they will take care of you. They are your transportation to safety and freedom.

WHAT TO WEAR BY ENVIRONMENT

» C.O.L.D.

When it comes to dressing for chilly locales, think C.O.L.D.: Clean, (avoid) Overheating, Layered and Dry.

C - CLEAN

The clothing must be clean and fresh when you put it on. This gives you the longest possible wear, prevents the spread of infection, ensures that the material does its job and contributes to morale.

O - OVERHEATING

Avoid it. It will do more damage in the long run than being a little bit cold. It will cause sweating and that sweat will freeze and can cause a cold weather injury. When you are about to move and/or do work in the cold, take your outer layer off and stow it somewhere. You will be chilled at first but work and movement will quickly warm you up and give you the capacity to work without overheating. Your sweat will evaporate. Put the outer layer back on when you stop and it will remain clean and dry.

L - LAYERS

Choose to dress in layers. They can be configured to your specific needs. If you do not wear layers, you might be too hot or too cold. Layering allows you to find the combination that keeps you comfortable.

D - DRY

This one is critical. If you get wet in the cold, your life could be in danger from hypothermia and your limbs and digits could be in danger from frostbite. If you get wet, change immediately. Dry out the clothing that got wet. Do not use them again until they are dry and preferably clean.

These common sense rules will help you plan for and function in cold environments as safely as possible.

» MOUNTAIN CLOTHING

NOTE: Temperatures fall about 1 degree Fahrenheit every 300 feet of altitude.

- Protect your skin and eyes
- Minimize your loss of fluids
- Wear layers
- Wear a head covering
- Use eye protection
- Have gloves on or with you

- Wear a long-sleeved shirt
- Wear long pants
- Keep a jacket with you
- Keep your feet dry
- Do as the locals do

» ARCTIC CLOTHING

NOTE: Temperature can be as low as -58 degrees Fahrenheit or -50 degrees Celsius.

- Protect your skin and eyes from wind burn and snow blindness
- Minimize your loss of fluids
- Wear layers: wicking, thermal and waterproof
- Wear a thermal head covering

- Use eye protection
- Keep your head, face, body, arms, legs, hands and feet covered
- Keep your body and feet dry
- Do as the locals do

» DESERT CLOTHING

NOTE: Temperature spectrum between day and night can range from 30-130 degrees Fahrenheit or 0-50 degrees Celsius.

- Protect your skin and eyes from burns and glare
- Minimize your loss of fluids
- Wear loose fitting, light color layers
- Wear a headscarf
- Use eye protection
- Keep your face covered to minimize inhalation of dust and sand

- Keep arms and legs covered
- Wrap a piece of material around your neck for sunblock and wicking sweat
- Blouse pant legs or wrap legs in strips of cloth (gators) to keep sand out of your boots
- Keep your feet dry
- Do as the locals do

» JUNGLE CLOTHING

NOTE: Temperature averages 50-80 degrees Fahrenheit or 10-25 degrees Celsius with 90 percent humidity.

- Protect your skin from bites, stings and punctures
- Maximize evaporative cooling
- Wear layers of light, wicking, quick-dry fabric
- Wear wide-brimmed headgear to protect against falling insects and/or snakes
- Use eye protection against branches and vines
- Wear quick drying boots with drain holes
- Keep your arms and legs covered
- Carry a poncho for multiple uses
- Blouse your pant legs or wrap your legs in strips of cloth (gators) to keep bugs out of boots
- Keep your feet dry in breathable footwear and change your socks often
- Do as the locals do

» URBAN CLOTHING

NOTE: Temperatures vary by destination and season.

- Wear layers for maximum flexibility and utility
- Wear clothing with lots of pockets so that you can survive out of your pockets
- Match the styles of the local baseline
- Wear comfortable shoes for walking and running
- Do not wear restrictive clothing
- Wear or carry a hat and glasses/sunglasses for quick changes of appearance
- Wear or carry a jacket
- Do as the locals do...and then some.

» WATER CLOTHING

NOTE: Temperature spectrum between tropical and freezing, depending on the latitude and time of year.

- Protect your skin and eyes from burns and glare
- Minimize your loss of fluids
- Wear loose fitting, light color layers
- Wear a head covering
- Use eye protection
- Keep your face covered to minimize sunburn
- Keep your arms and legs covered
- Wrap a piece of material around your neck for sunblock and wicking sweat

EVERY DAY CARRY (EDC) FOR EVERY ENVIRONMENT

Here is a useful inventory of items based on what you will need in any given environment. Familiarize yourself with these lists before embarking on your next trip to maximize your efficiency and prepare for the unknown. For specific gear recommendations, see pg. 50.

» URBAN EDC

CLOTHING

- Bandana
- Jacket
- Layered clothing

GEAR

- Alternate form of payment
- Barrette
- Bobby pin
- Carabiners
- Cash
- Cell phone
- Compass
- Firearm
- Kevlar shoelaces or paracord
- Knife
- Lighter
- Map
- Tactical pen
- Watch
- Whistle

» MOUNTAIN EDC

CLOTHING

- Eye protection
- Footwear
- Hat
- Jacket
- Long pants
- Long-sleeved shirts
- Socks
- Underwear

GEAR

- Beacon
- Carabiners
- Compass
- Fire starter
- Firearm
- Flashlight
- Food
- GPS
- Knife
- Map
- Mirror
- Paracord
- Rope
- Leather gloves
- Salt
- Satellite phone
- Sunblock
- Water
- Wedges and cams
- Tubular webbing

» ARCTIC EDC

CLOTHING

- Balaclava
- Coat
- Eye protection
- Mittens
- Thermal footwear
- Thermal hat
- Thermal socks
- Thermal base layer pants
- Thermal base layer shirt
- Underwear

GEAR

- Beacon
- Boot blousers
- Compass
- Fire starter
- Firearm
- Flashlight
- Food
- GPS
- Knife
- Lip balm
- Hand/foot heat packs
- Map
- Mirror
- Paracord
- Salt
- Satellite phone
- Water

» DESERT EDC

CLOTHING

- Breathable footwear
- Eye protection
- Hat
- Head scarf
- Jacket
- Loose, long pants
- Loose, long-sleeved shirts
- Socks
- Underwear

GEAR

- Beacon
- Blister kit
- Boot blousers
- Compass
- Fire starter
- Firearm
- Flashlight
- Food
- GPS
- Knife
- Map
- Mirror
- Paracord
- Salt
- Satellite phone
- Sunblock
- Water

» JUNGLE EDC

CLOTHING

- Drainable footwear
- Eye protection
- Hat
- Quick-dry long pants
- Quick-dry shirts
- Socks
- Underwear
- Waterproof jacket

GEAR

- Beacon
- Blister kit
- Boot blousers
- Compass
- Fire starter
- Firearm
- Flashlight
- Food
- GPS
- Hammock and
  mosquito netting
- Knife
- Machete
- Mirror
- Paracord
- Rope
- Salt
- Satellite phone
- Water
- Stormproof matches

» WATER EDC

CLOTHING

- Eye protection
- Loose, long pants
- Loose, long-sleeved
  shirts
- Poncho
- Socks
- Underwear
- Wide-brimmed hat

GEAR

- Beacon in a waterproof
  housing
- Chemical lights
- Compass
- Energy bars
- Firearm
- Fishing gear
- Flare
- Flashlight
- GPS
- Knife
- Lip balm
- Mirror
- Paracord
- Satellite phone
- Sunblock
- Vitamins
- Water

SHELTER TIPS AND OTHER CONSIDERATIONS

THERE ARE MANY THINGS YOU SHOULD CONSIDER BEFORE CONSTRUCTING A SHELTER.

- How much time and effort will be required?
- Do I have the time and energy?
- Will it adequately protect me?
- Do I have the tools I need or can I make them myself?
- Do I have enough materials?
- Can I modify an existing structure or natural shelter?

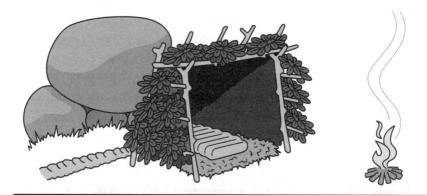

CONSTRUCTING A SHELTER

AFTER EVALUATING YOUR CIRCUMSTANCES AND ENVIRONMENT, KEEP THESE TIPS IN MIND WHEN CONSTRUCTING YOUR SHELTER.

- Only make your shelter as large as it needs to be. Your body will warm a small space.
- Digging a runoff channel will help keep you dry.
- A lean-to is the best choice of natural shelter.
- Maintain a fire 5-6 feet from the opening, close enough to keep you warm and dry, but far enough away not to catch your shelter on fire.
- Choose a natural windbreak or create one.
- Cold ground conducts heat away from your body. Pad your sleeping space with leaves, boughs, pine needles, moss or any other material you can collect. The rule of thumb is to build it up about 18 inches high.
- When creating shingling for your shelter, lay the "tiles" in an overlapping fashion that causes rainwater to run off of (rather than into) the shelter.

WHEN IT COMES TO SELECTING A SHELTER SITE, YOU WILL NEED TO ASK YOURSELF:

- Is the space big enough for me to lie down?
- Is the ground level?
- Is it close to a signaling site?
- Is it close to a water source?
- Is it free from bugs and snakes?
- Is there protection from wild animals, falling rocks, trees and limbs?
- Can this site flood?
- Is there any danger from rising water, running water or avalanches?
- Can I make a fire close enough to keep me dry and warm?

FIRE-STARTING TECHNIQUES

What happens if you get caught in a situation where you need to build a fire but you have no matches, lighter or flint? Keep in mind these simple ground rules when starting fires:

You will need tinder. This can be wood shavings, paper, hair, dryer lint, dry pine needles, certain kinds of dried moss, dry leaves, etc. It can be a combination of these things. It needs to be dry, fine and easily ignited.

You will also always need to clear the area of combustibles and make sure you have a sufficient perimeter around your fire for containment.

Once your tinder begins to smoke and you see it start to glow, gently blow across it to encourage it to light by the addition of the extra airflow.

» THE BATTERY METHOD

You will need a 9-volt battery and a steel wool pad, the finer the better.

- Rub both of the battery's contacts back and forth on the steel wool. It will begin to spark and glow immediately. Be ready to light tinder and then kindling rapidly.

NOTE: Do not store your battery and steel wool together. Wrap them individually in a non-combustible material and store them separately.

» THE MAGNIFYING GLASS METHOD

If you have sunlight, tinder and a magnifying glass, you can start a fire.

1. Place the tinder in a place that is safe for building a fire.

2. Hold the magnifying glass so that the sunlight shines through it in a focused dot, right onto the tinder. Manipulate the distance and the angle until you have as intense and round a dot of light as possible.

3. Focus the dot on a dark and flat area of the tinder. The magnifying glass will intensify the heat. When you have the distance and position just right, you will begin to see smoke and the tinder will catch on fire. Make sure to have kindling and wood ready to burn. (In terms of how to arrange your setup, my favorite method is the teepee formation. While it is marginally important with the kindling, it is imperative when you finally add the real fuel which is the large logs.)

» THE PARABOLIC MIRROR METHOD

If you have a flashlight that can be dismantled, or a soda can, you have a parabolic mirror.

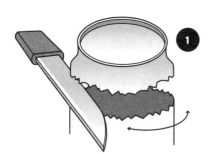

1. If you are using a flashlight, unscrew the end and pull out the curved lens behind the light bulb. If you are using a soda can, cut the bottom (curved) end off of the can.

2. Place your parabolic mirror in the sun until a white spot of concentrated light forms in the center. Make sure it is positioned as a bowl, not a dome.

3. Place your tinder right on that spot and wait for the smoke and glow. Once those occur, blow to cause the fire to catch and begin to add your kindling.

NOTE: You may have to build your tinder up a few inches high. The deeper the bowl, the closer the focus point will be to the ground. The shallower the bowl, the higher the focus point will be above the parabolic dish. For the shallow soda can bowl, the focus point will be a few inches in the air.

» THE FLAT MIRROR METHOD

For this method, you will need around 10 to 15 mirrors, each of which must be 1-inch square or larger. There is a safety concern with this method of sustaining a burn, so please take the necessary precautions.

• Make sure your tinder is of the highest quality you can find (meaning the driest, darkest and most flammable).

• If the day is windy, stake your tinder to the ground but do not adjust it with your hands once the mirrors have been placed.

1. Position all the mirrors in a curved arc around the tinder to reflect direct sunlight onto the exact same spot.

2. Stay behind the mirrors. Keep yourself and your clothing away from the focused sunlight in order to avoid serious burns.

3. Wait for the smoke and tell-tale glow. Blow on the embers to ignite the fire.

4. Dismantle and remove the contraption once your fire is lit to avoid future unwanted fires.

❯❯ THE WATER BOTTLE METHOD

You will need a smooth, clear, plastic water bottle with a dome-shaped top, water...and lots of patience.

1. Fill the bottle with water and try to knock all the bubbles out of it.

2. With the cap securely fastened, turn it upside down.

3. Create a standing X with two sticks and use it as a stand for the bottom of the water bottle. Position the water bottle so that the top of the bottle is touching the ground.

4. Look to see where the sunlight is being concentrated and place your dark, high quality tinder there.

5. Make sure that the bottle is perfectly still.

6. Wait.
   Wait.
   Wait.
   Wait.

7. When you see smoke and a glow, blow on it and prepare to light your kindling.

❯❯ THE FRICTION METHOD

The old "rub two sticks together" method really does work, if you do it right! You will need a flat piece of wood into which you will carve a notch.

1. Place your tinder close by so you can be ready to make it catch fire.

2. Obtain a stick and place one end in the notch.

3. Hold the stick in between your palms and rub it briskly back and forth. The friction will create smoke.

4. When you see a glow, place your tinder all around it and blow across it to make the fire catch.

HOW TO MAKE A BOW

1. You can also fashion a bow out of a flexible stick and a shoelace.

2. Wrap the friction stick once in the taut shoelace.

3. Draw the bow, back and forth in a sawing motion. This will twist the stick as it sits in the notch of the flat piece of wood.

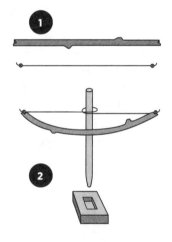

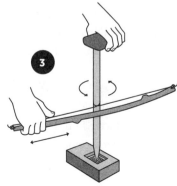

›› CHAR CLOTH

Finding good tinder can be the hardest part of building any fire. But did you know you can use your current fire to help you build the next one?

1. Take a small piece of cloth and put it into a sealed, metal container.

2. Put the entire container into the fire for a few minutes.

3. Withdraw the container and let it cool.

If done properly, when you open it, you should find the cloth has turned black but is not yet burnt. This is called a char cloth. It makes for perfect tinder because it will catch fire from a single spark and works perfectly in the more difficult fire-starting methods (like those using flat mirrors or water bottles).

›› PETROLEUM-SOAKED COTTON

A good homemade type of tinder is a cotton ball soaked in petroleum jelly. The combination packs easily into a plastic bag, travels well, catches fire quickly and burns for a long time. You just have to have it with you when you need it. One of the advantages of this method is that it gives you time to really get the kindling lit, and from there, the wood.

›› DRYER LINT

If you have the time to prepare it, my absolute favorite type of tinder is dryer lint. I collect it for a couple of months in a jar. When I have enough, I stuff some inside empty toilet paper rolls. I put each roll into a plastic bag and keep two of them in each of my bug-out bags. The lint and cardboard combination catches fire quickly and burns for a little while. They are light and easy to pack, and there is no fire hazard or greasy mess if they were to escape from their bag.

›› SHREDDER TINDER

If you have a shredder and some petroleum jelly at home, you have the makings of a great fire starter. Simply collect the confetti left by the shredder and mix it with a bit of petroleum jelly. Put the concoction in a small paper cup. If desired, insert a piece of cloth, twine or paracord into the center to act as a wick. You now have a homemade tinder block that will rival anything you can buy at the store. It will last a few minutes and enable you to build a good fire, even in the rain and wind.

HOW TO DISPOSE OF FOOD

Every hiker, camper and hunter knows you cannot allow the enticing scent of food to linger in your vicinity overnight without expecting a visit from foragers and predators. Sure, the foragers are merely a nuisance, but the predators can be downright dangerous.

Here are my tips for disposing of carcasses or other food-related items to help you keep a low profile in the wild.

» LAND DISPOSAL

1. Dig a cylindrical hole two feet deeper than the length of the carcass you need to bury. If you have already removed any organs, I recommend dropping those into the hole first.

2. Then—I hope you are not squeamish—lower the body into the hole headfirst to push the organs, which produce the strongest scent, deepest underground.

3. Exit the hole, then fill it in with all the dirt you dug up and pack it down as tightly as you can.

» THERMAL DISPOSAL

YOU WILL NEED:

- A 50-gallon metal drum
- Jet A fuel (you can buy Jet A at most municipal airports)

1. Check the weather for wind direction and speed. Select a site that is safe for fire building and does not risk starting a wildfire.

2. Place the carcass in the barrel and fill the barrel halfway with jet fuel.

3. Stand back, light the fuel and be prepared to tend the site for two hours.

In about two hours, even the bones and teeth will have turned to powder. This method produces a lot of smoke and smell, so be sure to protect yourself against smoke inhalation.

CAUTION: The heat produced in this method will be extreme, so use with great care.

» WATER DISPOSAL

YOU WILL NEED:

- Something to act as weight
- Cloth, a tarp, or plastic
- Chicken wire

1. Take the carcass and wrap it in perforated cloth, perforated tarp or perforated plastic along with the material you selected for weight. This can be rocks, metal, bricks, cement, cinder blocks or any other heavy object.

2. Spread the objects lengthwise along the carcass to ensure it will evenly stay underwater. The perforations will allow trapped air to escape.

3. After the carcass and weights are wrapped in the perforated material, wrap the outside in chicken wire to prevent parts of the carcass breaking off and returning to the surface.

4. Take your package away from shore and drop it into the water as gently and evenly as possible.

HELPING OTHERS IN CRISIS

HOW TO BE A LEADER (AND POSSIBLY SAVIOR) IN TIMES OF STRIFE.

THERE ARE MANY instances in which ensuring your survival will hinge on outlasting adversity as part of a group. Even if you are an outdoor expert, you might just find yourself needing to talk someone down off the ledge. Your best bet for a positive outcome is to anticipate those needs ahead of time so that you can better face challenges as they arise. From knowing how to speak to someone in a state of extreme distress to mirroring body language to looking for signs of human trafficking, these critical tips will help you lead others out of harm's way and show them how to be conquerors.

SLOW DOWN

If you are dealing with a person in a non-medical crisis (mental, emotional, spiritual, psychological, financial, relational, professional, etc.), speed begets stress for both of you. In the aftermath of a crisis situation like a natural disaster or an active shooter, many of these personal crises are happening concurrently. Bear in mind that if the crisis in question is medical, however, speed is critical and time may not be on your side. When dealing with the non-medical aftermath of a traumatic event, though, take heart and take the time you need. DO NOT rush through an encounter with a person in any of these non-medical crisis states. You need to exude calm and they need to feel unhurried.

There are multiple ways you can accomplish this:

• **SLOW YOUR SPEECH DOWN.** Not in a patronizing way, of course, but ease up just enough to deliver your words in an un-rushed way.

• **LOWER YOUR VOLUME.** Speak in a soft and soothing voice.

• **LOWER YOUR PITCH.** We naturally sound like sopranos when we are under acute stress. Instead, we want to sound like baritones. Try to keep an even tone. Ask yourself: How would you want someone to reassure you if you needed help? What do you think that person would sound like? Then mimic that as best as you can.

• **INSERT THOUGHTFUL PAUSES IN YOUR COMMUNICATION.** These brief breaks allow the person time to think about what is being said. This helps them process what you are saying and helps them feel as though they are gradually regaining a sense of control. A little goes a long way.

Be sure to keep your speed of communication in mind as you talk and listen. If you slow yourself down, the other person will follow suit. Try to subliminally communicate that you have all the time in the world and, because of that, you are relaxed, confident and ready to help. If you set the example, they will begin to relax as well.

80% LISTEN

When we are dealing with a person who is angry, scared, confused, depressed, shocked, grieving, hurting, etc., they are not likely to be thinking rationally. If they are not thinking rationally, they will most likely not communicate rationally, either. There is one thing they all have in common, though: They need to be heard. It can be quite difficult to understand what they mean and to let them vent but the way forward is to allow them to do 80 percent of the talking. That means you will need to do 80 percent of the listening. Make the person feel heard by you. Allow them to talk themselves out. Your part will be to listen and pay attention to what is being said.

"I" STATEMENTS

It is nearly impossible to help someone or overcome their fears and objections by going head-to-head with them. This is not the time for an argument, and good luck changing their minds by force. People do not appreciate being strong-armed. When you are the one thinking rationally and offering the help, you will need to approach the person in crisis with dignity, respect, gentleness and care. That is where "I" statements come in so handy.

Instead of saying "You are driving me crazy!" you might try this instead: "I do not feel very comfortable." It has a noticeably different tone, approach and overall feel because rather than pointing a finger at the source of your frustration, you have turned the focus on yourself in a constructive way. Rather than making an accusatory "you" statement, you assume the responsibility or blame for your own feelings and reactions by making an "I" statement. Rather than being confrontational, you offer an insight into your own concerns and encourage the other person to evaluate your feelings, too. If you launch into a "you" statement now, they will become defensive and intractable. Offering an "I" statement conveys your concern in a non-threatening way.

TRUTHFULNESS

Never lie to a person in crisis. If they should ever find out you are lying to them, your usefulness will have run out. They must be able to trust you are who you say you are and that you are there to help them. If they catch you in a lie, they will start to doubt your intentions or even question your identity. They will stop listening to what you have to say, stop working toward a solution with you and stop communicating. This helps no one.

You may have to think of creative ways to answer difficult questions. *Is my daughter going to make it? Am I going to die? What is going to happen to my marriage? Will I ever recover from this? How do I get my house back? Am I going to jail? When will I see my kids again?* You may elect not to answer certain questions at all, in which case you should gently deflect. Choosing to not answer a question is far preferable to lying. Trust is everything in a relationship. It is the foundation upon which all relationships are built. In order to help a person in crisis, stay truthful or stay quiet.

MINIMAL ENCOURAGERS

When you are actively listening to someone, you will need to encourage them to keep talking by inserting little things that they can either see or hear. If they are looking at you, look at them. Nod your head when you understand. Make sympathetic facial expressions. Lean in when they talk. Face them directly. If they are not looking at you, fold in a few well-timed interjections like, "I see," "Oh dear," "Interesting," "Wow," "Fascinating," "I understand," "Yikes," "Amazing" or any other word or phrase that shows you are listening to their story. It could be something like, "Yeah, I can see how that would be upsetting." It could even be as simple as "Mmhmm." Just keep it casual and make sure whatever you are saying encourages them to keep talking. After all, one too many "Mmhmm" moments sounds dismissive, as though you are bored or annoyed with the conversation. Pay attention.

That said, you also do not want to make the easy mistake of throwing in a phrase like "I understand exactly how you feel." Chances are, you do not and hearing this could put the speaker on the defensive, jeopardizing all your hard work to help them. It is enough to communicate that you understand what they are telling you, that the message has been received in full. Try not to finish their sentences for them. Just let them talk and occasionally insert a word, sound, phrase or physical gesture that encourages them to continue.

I know you are eager to help, but take a moment to commit this to memory as a life skill. It is enough to let someone know that they are heard and seen. You do not have to throw your own experience into the mix. Just listen.

LABEL EMOTIONS

It may seem counterintuitive but this is a very sound technique. When dealing with a person in crisis, it is OK to make statements like, "You seem upset," or "You sound angry," or "You look sad." If you have accurately identified their emotional state, they may admit you are right and even expound on why. If you inaccurately identified it, they will correct you. Either way, you have just conveyed that you care enough to notice how they seem to be doing and to comment on it in a concerned way. That goes far in establishing that they are worth your time and that you are there to help.

VALIDATE EMOTIONS

You may know from personal experience that a person in crisis is experiencing intense emotions. Part of navigating an encounter with them is going to be validating those feelings. How can you help? Normalize what they are struggling with, plain and simple. You can say things like:

- **"It is perfectly natural that you would feel angry when you just lost everything."**
- **"Of course you are afraid. That is very human."**
- **"I would feel confused, too, if I had gone through what you just went through. That is a lot to process for anyone."**

One of the best things you can do for a person in crisis is to reassure them that no, they are not crazy, unbalanced or overreacting. They will trust themselves more and they will trust you more if you believe their feelings are justified and normal.

PARAPHRASE

Every once in a while, take a few seconds to paraphrase what the person in crisis has been telling you. In other words, summarize their story a little. It may sound something like this:

"So, your house survived the earthquake, only to catch on fire when the gas line broke in the final aftershock."

That is quick, direct and accurately depicts the essence of what they told you. It proves you have been listening to the details of their story and not merely standing there politely waiting for them to finish. Sure, you already know the answer to the question because it is what they just said, but politely paraphrasing shows you want to get their story right, that what they say matters to you, that they matter to you. A person in crisis will often feel a great deal of relief just to be able to tell their story and know they have been heard.

MIRRORING AND PARROTING

If you are face-to-face with a person in crisis, one of the ways you can put them at ease is to do as they do. Mimic their movements, but be subtle. No one wants to feel mocked.

If the person is leaning back against a building with one foot one the ground and the other resting on the wall behind them, slowly adopt the same position. Just make sure to do it naturally. If you cannot do it, do not bother trying as it will definitely look awkward. Doing this conveys the subliminal message that you are more alike than different, that they are acting in a normal and acceptable way, and that you are comfortable with them.

You can do the same thing with words, a process called parroting. When you summarize their story to them, you can use the same phraseology and expressions they did. If you notice they are speaking in simple sentences with short words, for instance, now is decidedly not the time to wow them with your impressive verbal prowess. That will only throw them off and potentially aggravate them further.

Whether verbal or nonverbal, mirroring subconsciously puts them at ease and establishes common ground.

ESTABLISH AND BUILD RAPPORT

Rapport is the key to effective communication. People need to see the common ground they have with you before trust can start to form. Here's how:

ESTABLISH A COMMON "ENEMY"

In a crisis situation, it is not going to be a person, nor should it be. However, if they just lost their house in a fire, the fire itself can be a common enemy. I have been in two fires, a house fire and a hotel fire. I can relate to a common fear or anger directed at the destructive nature of flames.

MEET NEEDS

If they need something you can provide, provide it. According to psychologist Abraham Maslow's famed Hierarchy of Needs, people have physical needs like food, clothing and shelter. They have safety needs. They have social needs like love and acceptance. They have esteem needs like self-respect and recognition. They have self-realization needs like achieving goals and reaching their potential. In a crisis aftermath, the first needs you address will be physical and safety-related. Having achieved those, you will see social needs arise. To the extent that you can, meet their basic needs.

HOLD YOUR OWN EMOTIONS IN CHECK

Do not show impatience, irritation, worry, frustration or anger.

OTHER COMMUNICATION TIPS

- Express compassion for the person in crisis.
- Look for and highlight your common ground.
- Listen actively and without interrupting.
- Avoid strong statements like "always" and "never."
- Do not be defensive or argumentative.
- Do not make choices or decisions for the other person. Present them with options instead.
- Do not say or do anything that could be construed as judgmental. People want to feel understood, not judged.
- Use good judgment. Treat the person with kindness, patience, compassion and dignity.

THE SIGNS OF HUMAN TRAFFICKING

Human trafficking is a worldwide epidemic and it grows worse every day. There is a gradual shift occurring as cartels, gangs, criminal networks and terrorist organizations move away from narcotics and start to turn their attention to human beings as a commodity. As anti- and counter-narcotics agencies make headway in their war on drugs, the criminal elements are finding that the risk vs. reward for narcotics trafficking is becoming increasingly unprofitable. Criminals have since turned their attention to another illegal and immoral enterprise to make up for their declining drug revenues, and we must be on the lookout.

There are four main categories of signs that a person is being trafficked.

» WORKING AND LIVING CONDITIONS

THE INDIVIDUAL IN QUESTION:

- Is not free to leave or come and go at will
- Is under 18 and is providing commercial sex acts
- Is in the commercial sex industry and has a pimp/manager
- Is unpaid, paid very little or paid only through tips
- Works excessively long and/or unusual hours
- Is not allowed breaks or suffers under unusual restrictions at work
- Owes a large debt and is unable to pay it off
- Was recruited through false promises concerning the nature and conditions of their work
- High security measures exist in the work and/or living locations (e.g. opaque windows, boarded up windows, bars on windows, barbed wire, security cameras, etc.)
- Is living and working on-site
- Experiences verbal or physical abuse by their supervisor
- Is not given proper safety equipment
- Is not paid directly
- Is forced to meet a daily quota

» MENTAL HEALTH AND BEHAVIORS

A person who is being trafficked for sexual exploitation, domestic servitude or forced labor is under extreme duress. They are enslaved in the truest sense of the word. They will manifest behaviors and show symptoms of their duress. These include being:

- Fearful
- Anxious
- Depressed
- Submissive
- Tense
- Nervous
- Paranoid
- Confused
- Unfocused
- Disengaged
- "Checked out"
- Unresponsive
- Fatalistic
- Unusually fearful or anxious after hearing about law enforcement or immigration officials
- Addicted to alcohol, drugs and/or other controlled substances

▶▶ PHYSICAL HEALTH

A person who is being trafficked will not be provided with mental or physical healthcare. They will exhibit signs of having to do without sufficient levels of food, sleep, exercise and personal hygiene. Due to these factors, they may show signs of:

- Poor hygiene
- Malnourishment
- Fatigue
- Physical abuse (burns, cuts, broken bones, etc.)
- Sexual abuse (tears, bruises, welts, bleeding, etc.)
- Physical restraint
- Confinement
- Torture
- Dental problems
- Pain
- Injuries
- Abortion
- Miscarriage
- Illness (STDs and other)
- Poor muscle tone
- Jaundice

▶▶ CONTROL

One category of signs that should set off alarms for all of us are signs that someone is being controlled externally. I mean it when I say these people have been enslaved and their captors own them. They have no control over themselves or any aspect of their lives. All decisions are made for them and they are expected to obey. If they fail to obey, the consequences are usually severe. Some signs that they are under someone else's control are if the individual:

- Has few or no personal possessions
- Is frequently monitored
- Is not in control of their own money, financial records or bank account
- Is not in control of their own identification documents (ID or passport)
- Is not allowed or able to speak for themselves (a third party may insist on being present and/or translating)
- Has to ask permission before accepting an invitation or revealing information
- Will not speak in the presence of a particular person
- Looks to another person for permission to act or speak
- Has no independent movement (is always accompanied)
- Obeys someone else instantly and without question

» OTHER SIGNS OF HUMAN TRAFFICKING

There are signs that do not fall into one of the other categories. These are not found in people in healthy situations and they absolutely stand out as major red flags to anyone who is paying attention. At the very least, if a person is manifesting these signs, you will know something is seriously wrong.

- Claims of "just visiting"
- Inability to clarify where they are staying (address)
- Lack of knowledge of whereabouts (do not know what city they are in)
- Does not know the date
- Appears to have lost their sense of time
- Shares scripted, confusing or inconsistent stories
- Protects the person who may be hurting them or minimizes abuse
- Gives evasive answers
- Keeps long and/or abnormal hours
- Cannot predict their schedule

If there is a person in your life manifesting these signs and symptoms, question them directly and look for signs of deception. If you cannot get a satisfactory answer, or if the answer is, "Yes, I am being held against my will and used as a prostitute, maid, worker, etc." report it to the police and the FBI. Do not ignore it. We can only fight this abominable industry if we all do something about it.

MASTER TACTIC

If you suspect someone is in danger due to human trafficking, DO NOT attempt to confront or otherwise alert their captor(s). Maintain a low profile and go to the authorities.

URBAN SURVIVAL

A GUIDE TO MAKING IT OUT OF THE CONCRETE JUNGLE.

WITH SCHOOL SHOOTINGS and acts of domestic terror on the rise, we all need to know a thing or two about how to navigate an attack at the workplace, as well as stadiums, theaters, places of worship and more. Even when the turf is not our own, there are still ways we can gain an advantage over our assailants and ultimately make a successful escape. From learning how to barricade a door to finding your way in the dark, knowing these skills could mean the difference between life and death.

FACILITY SECURITY

Facility security can apply to your home, office building or any other man-made structure. Because of the amount of time we spend at home and the priceless nature of what is found there, this entry will focus on securing your home. That said, most of these concepts can be applied to any facility you wish to secure.

If you have a home with any amount of property, beyond building positive relationships with your neighbors, your first layer of security will be perimeter security. This is literally the edge of your property. Motion sensing lights are a great place to start. Ideally, you want to be able to illuminate everything on your property at will, and in an instant. You will also want a clear line of sight for a considerable distance from your house. If you have wooded property, your house should stand in a clearing. There should be no landscaping anywhere close to the house behind which a person can hide.

Alarm systems are also good deterrents. If you have an alarm system, ask the alarm company for a yard sign or two, telling visitors that your home is being monitored.

A good sized dog can also send the right message. If you do not have a dog, consider buying two large dog food bowls, fill one with water and put just a little dog food in the other. Leave them on your front porch or step. Perception is reality.

Cameras mounted on the house, surveilling your property have also become quite popular. Some home alarm companies have combined these systems together. Again, it does not take much to fake a mounted camera. Take an old, broken camera and mount it on your house, or take just the shell of the camera housing and mount it empty. A perfect solution would be a working and monitored camera but a decoy is better than nothing. It keeps honest people honest.

Having a firearm in your home is a personal choice and comes with a good deal of responsibility. This definitely adds to security. Make sure each person in the household is trained in its use and handling, and know your local and state laws.

Have a plan for all the members of your household for what to do in the event of a home intruder. Run drills twice a year to establish where each person will go, who will call the police, whether a firearm gets involved, where the family gathers, etc.

All of these security measures have been established to thwart humans with malicious intent. What about other facility security threats, though? Any facility is potentially at risk of a fire, for example. Your house should have one fire extinguisher on each floor. As you may recall from "Fires Grow Fast" (pg. 95), a fire can become debilitating and potentially deadly faster than the time it takes to go to another floor, grab a fire extinguisher and return.

No matter how many people live in your home, you should conduct fire drills twice a year. You need to establish a plan of action for what each person will do, how to clear the structure and where to rendezvous. Become familiar with basic fire protocol. In the event of a fire, you will need a clear plan of action for who will do what.

Snow can be a security matter if it begins to interfere in the normal operations of the home. It is never a good idea to leave too much standing snow on your roof. Most roofs are slanted for just that reason and the snow will slide right off. For those with too shallow a pitch, however, you may have to clear it off occasionally to prevent flooding and/or roof collapse. Remember to watch out for falling icicles.

In excessive cold or heat, losing your electricity can become a security matter. People need both heating and cooling, and letting the temperature go too far in either direction can endanger your safety, health or even life. The best solution is to have a gas-powered generator that can run your heating or air conditioning in the event of a power loss. Lacking that, make sure to have a plan to heat or cool yourself without power: blankets, coats, sleeping bags, ice, open windows, battery operated fans, food and fresh water that require no electricity to consume, etc.

MASTER TACTIC

Your home is only as safe as you make it. Take the time to evaluate its weak points or areas of improvement. If you have a home security system, be sure to test it regularly.

It is also a very good idea to have a substantial first aid kit and AED in your home.

Ultimately, facility security is about the people inside it. In the event of a disaster or an attack, frightened people are likely to get hurt. Stress can cause problems too in the form of cardiac arrest. For that reason, every member of your household should be certified in first aid, CPR and AED use. All things considered, the best way to manage these risks is to make a plan, rehearse the plan twice a year, and stick to the plan when something happens. Do so and you will find that what you were trained to do will kick in automatically in a moment of adversity.

ACTIVE SHOOTER RESPONSE

Run, hide, fight. Three simple words, one potentially life-saving plan. This is the most common teaching today for active shooter situations. It is being taught in office buildings, schools and every other place where the innocent gather on a regular basis. The order of prioritization is exactly as the title suggests.

RUN

Simply move yourself and your family, friends, coworkers, classmates and anyone else around you to a safe location. Do not spend too much time trying to convince an uncooperative person to run with you. Offer to take them with you, absolutely. Prompt them to respond and address their fear. However, doing this means you are losing valuable time, time that might save your life. There comes a moment when you have to decide to go anyway, even if someone will not leave with you.

HIDE

If running is not an option, you will have to make do where you are. Your escape route may be obstructed. If that is the case, hide and barricade the room where you take shelter. Know the difference between cover and concealment. Cover is any material that will stop bullets: concrete, marble, steel, thick wood, trees, granite, stone, brick, etc. Concealment offers to hide your location but does not stop bullets: drywall, foam-core doors, aluminum, glass, furniture, etc. Always choose cover whenever you can. If no cover is available, choose concealment. Do whatever it takes to make yourself as difficult to find as possible. Lock the doors. Pull desks and file cabinets in front of them. Put trip hazards in the way. Turn off the lights. Layer your security.

FIGHT

This is when you have no other recourse. If you cannot run and there is nowhere to hide, you must fight. Remember the rabid chipmunk (pg. 42)? Now is the time to be the chipmunk. Be aggressive. Go crazy. Use the objects around you as weapons. Enlist the help of all the other people around you and band together. Everyone should attack at once. Throw things at the shooter. Hit them with a chair. Shed all your inhibition and attack them with everything you have. Do not stop until it is clear they are completely subdued.

BARRICADING A DOOR

In a run, hide, fight scenario, you may find yourself hiding. One of the things you will want to do as you go is create as many barriers between you and the thing you're hiding from as you possibly can. Do everything you can think of to make it as difficult as possible to get to you.

Have you ever seen a door closer, mounted at the top of a door, which has an elbow joint? When the door is fully open, the mechanism is straight. When the door is fully closed, the mechanism is collapsed into a V. These are fairly popular mechanisms in larger buildings and commercial spaces. And they're incredibly easy to use to your advantage if you need to close off an entrance.

If this happens in a commercial space with the type of door closers referenced above, there is one quick way to create a barrier to entry.

Imagine bending your arm all the way until your elbow is in a V, and then wrapping an elastic bandage around your whole arm to prevent yourself from straightening it again. That is exactly what you are doing to the door closer. It will be much tougher to open.

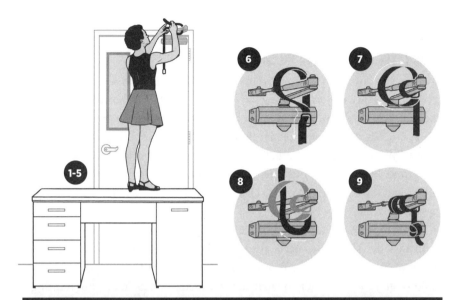

HOW TO DO IT

1. Close the door with yourself on the side of the door closing mechanism.

2. Lock the door.

3. Find something to stand on (chair, desk, file cabinet, etc.) and drag it in front of the door, positioning it right under the mechanism.

4. Obtain a leather belt, from yourself or anyone else.

5. Climb up onto the platform you created.

6. Wrap the belt around the metal V-shaped door closer. Insert the end of the belt into the buckle. Pull it tight.

7. Keeping pressure on it, wrap it back in the other direction, going all the way around the mechanism.

8. Leave enough belt to push the end back under the layers of belt already laid down. Keep it pulled taut.

9. If you can, make a knot in the end of the belt to help it resist being pulled loose.

HIDING IN PLAIN SIGHT

By now, you have certainly picked up on the theme of blending in and going gray. The concept of hiding in plain sight has two advantages over concealment. It allows you to 1) blend in quickly and 2) keep an eye on the situation. When you opt for concealment, taking the actions necessary to conceal yourself might, in and of themselves, give you away. They also take a little time. Please do not misunderstand: cover, concealment and hiding in plain sight are all good options. The situation alone will dictate which one is best at the time.

Here are some of the ways quick-thinking people can hide in plain sight:

In an active shooter scenario, drop to the ground as if you have fainted or are dead. Be warned: this may or may not work. Under this kind of stress, the shooter may move past all downed and stationary targets in favor of hunting down live, moving targets. However, there is a chance that they will shoot rounds into the dead or otherwise motionless bodies they pass. This is a risk you will have to weigh.

When your situational awareness perceives that someone is searching for a soft target, choose to walk directly toward them. Keep normal amounts of eye contact with them and pass them as you would any other person, appearing totally oblivious to who they are and what they want.

Do not hide, cower or show any sign that you understand who they are or, most importantly, that you fear them.

In a vehicle surveillance situation, make a stop. Go to a cafe and use the restroom. Order a drink. Sit down to enjoy it (or at least pretend to). Look out the window. Browse through your phone. Make a phone call. Keep it casual. Stay in that populated coffee shop until your surveillance team departs, acting oblivious to their presence.

If you are being followed on errands or while shopping, this tip is surprisingly simple: keep shopping. Discreetly send a text message to someone who can meet you there. Continue to browse and comport yourself as you normally would. When your person shows up, greet them as if you were expecting them and immediately leave together.

If someone is following you on foot in a populated area, make a scene. This part is key, though: DO NOT draw attention to the surveillance team. Instead, start an argument with a stranger. Have a major emotional meltdown about a fictitious event. Fake a medical emergency. Accuse someone of stealing from you. Get loud and draw as much attention to yourself as you can. Be obnoxious. Make a phone call where you speak too loudly and laugh in a loud and irritating manner. Keep it up until you see people's heads turn to find out what is going on. When you start to get looks of disapproval from the crowd, look to see if your tail is still around. Chances are, they will be gone. Make enough of a scene that someone will call the police or an ambulance because of you. It is far better to explain the real situation to police or EMS than to risk being kidnapped.

If someone seated at a nearby table at a restaurant has been showing up across time and distance, make eye contact with them. Smile. Wave. Send them a drink. Wink. Flirt with them. Let them know that you have noticed them, too.

In a situation where you are receiving unwanted attention or sexual advances, cuddle up to someone else nearby. Make the interested party think you are out with someone already. This works even better if the person you cuddle up to is of the opposite sexual orientation as the interested party. If the interested party is of the opposite sex to you, cuddle up to someone of the same sex as yourself. If they are of the same sex as you, cuddle up to someone of the opposite sex. This provides an additional barrier.

If you are being followed or watched, walk up to the person and ask them what time it is. Usually, having a direct encounter with the selected target will cause the criminal to break off and begin a new target search.

Pull out some sort of a note-taking device and conduct a man-on-the-street interview about anything. Walk directly up to the one surveilling you and ask

MASTER TACTIC

If you realize you are being followed, do everything to remain visibly calm. Fight that fear instinct to the best of your ability and focus on your options. When you cannot go gray, be bold.

them if you can interview them. You will likely scare them off when you ask for their demographic information.

This list is only a small sample of what an imaginative person can do to hide in plain sight. Your choice will depend on the setting, situation, your own acting ability and your poise in a nerve-wracking situation. However, in all likelihood, the criminal(s) will choose another target. Your willingness to make a scene or act oblivious in the face of a threat may save your life.

FIRE ALARMS

I have noticed over the years that the true concern in a fire alarm situation is not panic and chaos. In fact, it is exactly the opposite. Not long ago, I was sitting in a briefing at work and the fire alarm went off. The lights went dark, the alarm noise began to sound, an announcement was made to evacuate the building and each red box on the walls began to flash its strobe light. As I stood up to gather my things, I was astounded at how no one else around me moved. We had all received a safety briefing the day before about the procedures we would follow in the event that the fire alarm went off. We knew the route out and the rally point. We had been told to evacuate. Why, then, did no one take it seriously? Since we could not see fire, feel heat or smell smoke, people took their time to decide whether or not they wanted to leave. It was also raining outside and no one wanted to get wet.

Eventually, we all followed the procedure and evacuated the facility. We waited outside in the rain for the fire department to arrive and do their job. After conducting their investigation, they pronounced the all-clear and we were allowed to go back inside. This, of course, only made things worse for those who had originally been reluctant to believe there was any danger in the first place. Their suspicions were confirmed that it was a false alarm, which likely means that, next time, they will be twice as resistant to evacuating.

As someone who has been in two fires, a hotel fire and a house fire, I can say with full clarity that I would much rather evacuate a building 100 times for a false alarm than get caught once in a real fire. However, nowadays we have seen a rise in a disturbing trend regarding fire alarms and evacuation routes. During the 2018 shooting at Marjory Stoneman Douglas High School in Parkland, Florida, for example, the shooter used the fire alarm as a tool to funnel the students out to him. Because he knew the evacuation procedure, he knew exactly where people would go once the fire alarm was pulled, and he used that knowledge for mass murder.

If you find yourself in a building and the fire alarm goes off, get off the X. Move. Program it into your brain that a fire alarm is synonymous with a fire. Respond accordingly.

Of course, there is nothing wrong with playing it safe. If you remain concerned about a repeat of Parkland, exit by a side route. There are many ways to exit every building. Some routes are only to be used in the event of a fire. Use them. Leave by a back door. Leave by a delivery entrance. Leave by a garage exit. Leave by any means other than the front doors. But whatever you decide to do: leave.

STADIUMS AND AUDITORIUMS

This may seem to be too obvious to teach, but it is amazing how the human brain can short circuit right when we need it most. This accounts for the Freeze part of Fight, Flight or Freeze. People want to act but they often get stuck, bouncing back and forth between Observe and Orient in the OODA Loop (pg. 35). Fear and confusion cause them to freeze when a far better option is to fight or flee. The way to overcome this is to have a solid plan of action which you have rehearsed. It does not need to be a complicated plan. In fact, the simpler it is, the higher your chances are of successfully carrying it out.

In theaters, auditoriums, sanctuaries, chapels, stadiums or any place with rows of seats, benches or pews, the best plan for surviving a shooting is the same. Remember the difference between cover and concealment? The rows of seats will obscure you from view but they are not bulletproof. That makes them concealment, not cover. Concealment can save your life, however, because the shooter does not know where to aim.

• Memorize the location of all possible exits when you enter the room.

• Identify the shooter. Try to get a good look at them without exposing yourself. Listen for their voice, the sound of their movements. Are they male or female? How fast are they? Are they acting alone or do they have an accomplice? These details will come in handy when you need to recount what you have seen. Try to take in as much as you can.

• Drop to the floor between the rows and stay down.

• Be silent.

• Use hand signals to communicate.

• Crawl toward the exit, staying out of sight for as long as possible.

• Keep your eyes on the shooter as much as possible.

• Make your way, under concealment, to the best exit for the situation, opting to stay concealed as long as possible before breaking free and making a mad dash for the door. Concealment is key to prolonging or ensuring your survival.

• Run all the way out of the building and get to safety before calling 911.

• Tell emergency responders everything you can remember about the shooter: location, description, general type and number of guns, age, gender, clothing, etc.

I know this seems like such a simple concept, that anyone would naturally do these things without being taught. However, in a situation with stressors that high, where your life and the lives of the people around you are on the line, people often forget the simple and common sense things they know. Until you have been there, you do not know exactly how you will react.

Get ahead of the curve. Start preparing that battle space now. If you never take the time to ask yourself what you would do, and to answer that question before a crisis occurs, then you will not know how to respond. Give yourself a fighting chance.

URBAN CONCEAL

There are many places in most homes, businesses and hotel rooms to hide things. All it takes is some forethought and imagination. Bear in mind that the more time and effort it takes to conceal it, the more time it will take to get to whatever you have hidden. Yes, broadly speaking it will generally be more secure, but that extra time might result in you getting caught before you can access it.

When it comes to small things, hiding places abound:

- In the hems of drapes
- Behind light switches and outlets
- Inside the hollow rod of a shower curtain
- Inside the zippered cushions of a couch
- Inside the tank of a toilet
- Under a carpet or a rug
- Inside pipes
- Behind wall-mounted pictures
- Between a mattress and the box spring
- Inside air vents

Use your imagination, but keep in mind how much time or trouble will go into accessing it. Keep these spots in mind when you need to conceal something or, conversely, when you suspect something may have been hidden prior to your arrival.

FINDING YOUR WAY IN THE DARK

How do we train to move, fight and find our way in the dark? The same way therapists teach patients who have lost their sight. If you should ever find yourself needing to find your way in total darkness, here are some tips to keep in mind.

Your other senses are just as real as your sense of sight. They have simply not been utilized to the same extent. A seeing person relies on their vision for 80 percent of their data inputs. That also means their senses of hearing, smell, touch and taste are not as developed. However, like any skill, using your other senses can be practiced and honed. With time, you will come to place the same confidence in them that you do in your sight.

- Remember what things look like. Use your visual memory to recall how things are or where they are situated.

- Hallways actually sound different than rooms. If you were to walk down a hallway blindfolded, you would hear a difference when passing by an open doorway as opposed to continuing along a wall.

- Your sense of touch will allow you to find your way if you use the "maze trick." Place one hand on one wall and do not remove it as you move forward. You will eventually come across the way out.

- Pay attention to the surface underneath your feet. Is it carpeted or hard? Wood or tile? Concrete? Do your shoes make any noise?

- Your sense of touch and your sense of smell can detect air currents.

- Sound takes longer to bounce back to you in a larger place than in a smaller one. Large rooms sound different than small rooms.

- Your sense of smell can detect perfume or cologne long after the wearer has departed.

- You can "see" through your hands by touching objects around you and identifying them.

- If you feel closed in, you are probably in a smaller space. If that feeling goes away as you move, you have entered a larger space. Your brain is using all the other senses to gather data and process inputs, even when you are not aware of it.

Give it a try. Have someone blindfold you and accompany you as you find your way around a space that is already familiar to you. If you wear glasses, remove them and practice walking around in the dark. What you learn may surprise you. If you ever really need to use these skills, you will remember your practice and it will give you the confidence you need. You will make it out.

MASTER TACTIC

Make a point of developing your senses and incorporate them into your training routine. Be sure to train indoors and outdoors to accustom yourself to different environments.

FIELD MEDICINE

THESE BASIC FIRST-AID TIPS SAVE LIVES.

HEALTH IS EVERYTHING. More than advance preparation of the battle space, more than knowing how to build a fire or hide in plain sight, maintaining one's health is the first and foremost directive when facing a dire survival situation. Whether we need to tend to a spider bite or know how to fight off the wrath of the elements without causing ourselves further harm, keeping our bodies in fighting shape ensures we have, at the very least, the physical means to endure whatever might come our way. These tips will help you stack the deck in your favor when injuries are part of the deal.

RULE OF 3

When it comes to survival, here is a quick reference that will help you prioritize your needs.

- **You can survive for 3 minutes with a heavy bleed or without oxygen.**
- **You can survive for 3 hours in extreme cold or heat.**
- **You can survive for 3 days without water.**
- **You can survive for 3 weeks without food.**

IN PRIORITY ORDER, YOU NEED:

- **Air and medical care for serious bleeding**
- **Shelter and a source of heating or cooling**
- **Water**
- **Food**

If you can remember the Rule of 3, you can use it to help you make decisions and prioritize what you need. We do not always think clearly or logically when beset by fear, anxiety, panic, loss, disaster and pandemonium. Happily, when we practice these things in advance, we need not struggle to remember. Knowing this simple rule can help establish you on a productive and life-saving course.

AIRWAY, BLEEDING, SHOCK

There are three major things that can take a person's life so quickly that if they do not get medical intervention within a few minutes they will die. Full stop. According to the Rule of 3, these are the things that fall within 3 minutes.

A - AIRWAY

If a person cannot breathe, their life expectancy is measured in minutes. Restoring a person's air is of paramount importance.

B - BLEEDING

If a person has profuse bleeding, it is critical to get that under control right away. A person can bleed to death in seconds to minutes.

S-SHOCK

If a person goes into shock and does not receive treatment, they will die.

If someone around you goes unconscious, check for signs of breathing. Is their chest moving up and down? Can you hear their breath, feel it with your hand or see it on a mirror? If not, lay the person on their back. Tilt their head back and their chin upwards to open their airway. If you are trained in CPR and AED, begin administering that. If emergency services are available, call 911 immediately and continue to give assistance until help arrives.

If you see blood, you will need to determine the source. If appropriate, apply a tourniquet. Once you locate the wound, create a makeshift dressing and bandage out of whatever material is available to you: clothing, towels, sheets, etc. Take the dressing material and press it firmly against the wound to stop the bleeding. From that point on, do not release the pressure or remove the dressing. If the first dressing soaks through, add additional material on top of the blood-soaked material and continue to hold pressure. You may remove and replace the outer, bloody material with fresh, clean material as long as you do not remove the piece that is in contact with the skin as it is helping them to clot. If you have the capability and the know-how, you can create a pressure bandage out of more material to hold the dressing in place. Call emergency medical services and stay with the person until help arrives.

There is always a risk to you whenever you come in contact with someone else's blood. If you have the option to wear gloves or create a barrier between your skin and theirs, always do so.

If the person is in shock (unconscious and/or not processing commands), lay them flat on their back and control their body temperature to the best of your ability. If they are cold, wrap them in a blanket. If they are overheated, get them to shade, wet them with cold water and fan them. Call for emergency help.

In all three cases, DO NOT give the person food or drink. Stay with them and continue to render assistance until help arrives. Try to collect data to give to EMTs or paramedics when they arrive to help them decide on the right treatment. In all three cases, the person is going to need hospital care. Ensure that you help them to the best of your ability.

SPIDER BITES

In a survival situation, spider bites are a real possibility. However, even some of the more poisonous bites, like those of a brown recluse or black widow, can be treated in the field.

BEFORE DOING ANYTHING ELSE	AFTER CLEANING, ICING & ELEVATING
• Clean the wound with soap and water and keep it clean to avoid developing an infection at the site.	You only need to apply <u>one</u> thing on the list below, which should give you options to keep in mind as you pack a bug-out bag or a go kit, or scrounge for supplies.
• Ice the site of the actual bite to reduce swelling. (Use the coolest thing you have on hand. It may just be natural, running water.)	• Apply a baking soda paste of three parts baking soda and one part water to the wound.
• Elevate the bite to aid in the reduction of swelling.	• Apply an activated charcoal paste to the wound to draw out toxins.

MASTER TACTIC

DO NOT scratch the bite. It increases the chances of developing an infection.

• Using lavender essential oil can reduce swelling and redness and encourage healing.

• Apply shavings of raw potato to the wound to reduce swelling.

• Applying witch hazel as an astringent can reduce redness, swelling and itching.

• The sap from the aloe vera plant can also reduce swelling and calm the skin.

If the wound becomes infected, if you experience any difficulty breathing, if you develop a dangerously high fever or one that will not break, you will need to escalate your level of care. However, such serious reactions to spider bites are incredibly rare. Following these field care instructions will reduce the likelihood even further.

CIPRO

It should go without saying that I am not a doctor. I have, however, been a patient many times for many reasons. I have traveled all over the world and found myself needing antibiotics in the most remote and inconvenient places. And I have also learned a handy thing or two from the people I have taught in my survival courses.

One class in particular had a physician in the audience. I had been talking about the kinds of things to stock at home for sheltering in place and what to keep in a bug-out bag. At one point, the physician raised his hand and I invited him to address the class.

He advocated for carrying or stocking a broad spectrum antibiotic for survival situations, specifically Cipro (which is short for ciprofloxacin). He informed the class that he kept it on hand at home and it saved him a lot of time and expense. Apparently, Cipro is good for everything from ear infections to infected cuts. In the course of normal living, it can save you from having to go to urgent care on the weekend. But in a survival situation, it can save your life. Make sure to include your medicine cabinet in your advance preparation of the battle space. Have what you need before you need it and your future self (and anyone else) will thank you.

WEATHER-RELATED INJURIES

Weather-related injuries are serious and can be life threatening. There are multiple possible injuries for both cold and heat.

▶▶ HEAT EXHAUSTION

Heat exhaustion begins with dehydration and is characterized by overheating.

THE SYMPTOMS INCLUDE:

- Rapid heart rate
- Profuse sweating
- Red (flushed) skin
- Panting
- Cool, moist skin
- Goosebumps
- Dizziness
- Faintness
- Fatigue
- Weak pulse
- Muscle cramps
- Nausea
- Headache

THE TREATMENT IS SIMPLE AND STRAIGHTFORWARD:
- Stop all activity.
- Rest.
- Move to a cooler place.
- Rehydrate.

Always take weather related illnesses/injuries seriously. As soon as you identify symptoms, cease your activity and begin counter measures. It might save your life.

» HEAT CRAMPS

Heat cramps are usually the first indicator that a person is headed toward a heat injury. However, this is not always the case. Years ago, I was hospitalized for a heatstroke and had absolutely no symptoms of heat cramps or heat exhaustion leading up to it. Frightening, right? For most people in most places, however, heat cramps will precede the other problems.

Heat cramps come on painfully in conditions where physical work is being done in hot environments. This is triggered by the loss of electrolytes through sweat. Although these involuntary muscle spasms can occur in any muscle group, they are most often felt in the calves, arms, abdomen and back.

IF YOU ARE EXPERIENCING ANY OF THESE SPASMS:
- Stop the physical labor.
- Find a cool place.
- Sit down and rest.
- Rehydrate with electrolytes.
- Gently stretch the affected muscles.
- Do not resume the physical activity for several hours.

Although heat cramps are not dangerous unto themselves, they are a painful warning that you are approaching a bad place, headed toward heat exhaustion, and losing electrolytes faster than you are replacing them. If this happens to you, prioritize rehydrating, replenish your electrolytes and stop the progression toward a more serious heat injury.

>> HEAT STROKE

Heat stroke is the most serious of the heat injuries. It occurs when a person is seriously overheated (104 degrees Fahrenheit or 40 degrees Celsius) and can lead to paralysis and death.

THE SIGNS AND SYMPTOMS OF HEATSTROKE ARE:
- **High body temperature**
- **Altered mental state**
- **Absence of sweat**
- **Nausea and vomiting**
- **Pale skin**
- **Panting**
- **Elevated heart rate or tachycardia**
- **Headache**

A heat stroke can be brought on by a high ambient temperature or by excessive physical exertion. It is exacerbated by dehydration. If it is caused by ambient temperature, the skin will be hot and dry. If it is brought on by physical exertion, the skin may feel tacky.

In all cases, heat stroke is a life-threatening injury and needs emergency medical care. When left untreated, it can damage the kidneys, heart, brain and muscles.

IF YOU HAVE THESE SIGNS OR SYMPTOMS, IMMEDIATELY:
- **Stop all work.**
- **Get to the coldest possible place.**
- **Remove all excess clothing.**
- **Get the body temperature down by any means necessary: ice, water, fan, air conditioner, etc.**
- **Place ice or cold, wet towels under the armpits, on the groin, on the head and on the back of the neck.**
- **Call EMS and get to a hospital.**

▶▶ HYPOTHERMIA

A common misconception about hypothermia is that it can only occur in seriously cold weather. When you consider that the average body temperature needs to remain at 98.6 degrees Fahrenheit, you can see how hypothermia can actually occur in temperatures that feel completely comfortable. Hypothermia is simply the condition where the body loses heat faster than it can replace it. Believe it or not, a person is technically hypothermic when their body temperature reaches 95 degrees Fahrenheit. Hypothermia is a medical emergency and requires immediate intervention and treatment.

SIGNS OF HYPOTHERMIA INCLUDE:
- Shivering
- Slurred speech
- Slow, shallow breathing
- Weak pulse
- Clumsiness/lack of coordination
- Drowsiness
- Low energy
- Confusion
- Loss of consciousness
- Bright red, cold skin (in babies)
- A feeling of warmth

IF YOU ENCOUNTER THIS:
- Get the person to a warmer place.
- Move them gently as jarring movements can trigger irregular heartbeats.
- Remove wet clothing.
- Wrap the person in warm, dry blankets.
- Call EMS.
- Watch them for confused or risky behavior and intervene as necessary.

A person suffering from hypothermia is usually confused and will not be able to make productive decisions. In fact, since they are already feeling warm, they may begin to remove clothing and/or try to immerse themselves in cold water.

Be prepared to stop them. If you are in a wilderness setting, keep them moving. The warm, drowsy feeling they are experiencing will cause them to want to lay down and sleep. DO NOT ALLOW THEM TO SLEEP. Build a fire and get them close to it. It is better that they go naked than stay in wet clothes. Your priorities are heat, dry clothing or blankets, and preventing impaired decisions.

›› FROSTBITE

Frostbite is a very serious condition that often results in losing body parts. It is a literal freezing of the skin and underlying tissue. It is most common in fingers, toes, nose, ears, cheeks and chin, but know that it can occur anywhere.

THE SIGNS OF FROSTBITE INCLUDE:

- Cold skin with a prickly sensation (initial feeling)
- Numbness
- Red, white, blue, gray or yellow skin
- Hard and waxy-looking skin
- Clumsiness due to muscle stiffness
- Blistering after rewarming

IF YOU ENCOUNTER FROSTBITE:

- Move to a warmer place.
- Add layers of thermal clothing.
- Never rub the skin as it can damage the tissue.
- Place the affected area in between your legs or under your arms.
- Bring the temperature up slowly with lukewarm water.
- Follow up with medical care to ensure damage control.

IMPROVISATION

HOW TO TURN EVERYDAY OBJECTS INTO INVALUABLE TOOLS.

THERE WILL COME a day when you need to scrounge around and turn whatever random items you have handy into a whole new device. Maybe you forgot to pack something in your bug-out bag, or maybe an unforeseen circumstance managed to catch you completely off guard and unprepared. Either way, from learning how to create a solar still out of a plastic bottle to fashioning a tourniquet out of duct tape to the many uses of paracord, these hacks will help you see just how effective mundane household items can be in a moment of crisis.

DIY SOLAR STILL

Have you ever seen a movie where the main character was marooned on a raft in the middle of the ocean? Outside of hoping it rains, how does someone like that survive without anything to drink? Look no further than this solar still you can make with just a few handy items from your bug-out bag.

YOU WILL NEED

- A water bottle
- A knife or multi-tool
- A soda or beer can

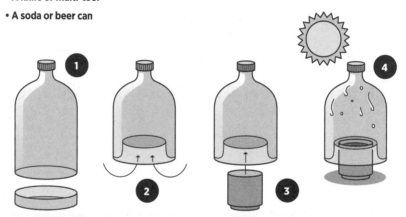

TO GET STARTED

1. Leave the cap on the water bottle and cut the bottom of the bottle off. Do not cut much, just the very bottom itself.

2. Once the bottom is cut away, carefully curl the plastic inward back up into itself by a few inches. Make sure you do not curl it outward.

3. Next, cut the top off the soda can, so that the can stands wide open, and fill it with seawater.

4. Take the plastic bottle and slide it down over the open soda can. Put your contraption in direct sunlight.

As the seawater in the can evaporates, the sun will cause the water in the air to condense and form droplets on the inside of the empty, plastic bottle. The drops will run down the insides of the bottle and catch in the tray you made by curling the bottle back into itself. Simply take the water bottle off of the soda can, unscrew the cap, and drink as you normally would.

Voilà! Fresh water.

MASTER TACTIC

Distilled water from solar stills does not need to be boiled, as the process has already removed heavy metals, salts and microbes.

HOW TO MAKE A WATER FILTRATION SYSTEM

Building your own portable water filtration system is easy with the right materials.

YOU WILL NEED

- A plastic water bottle
- A clean sock
- A knife or multi-tool
- Charcoal
- Sand
- Small and large gravel
- Small rocks (optional)

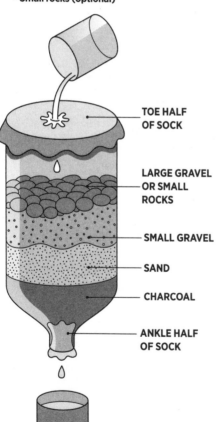

TOE HALF OF SOCK

LARGE GRAVEL OR SMALL ROCKS

SMALL GRAVEL

SAND

CHARCOAL

ANKLE HALF OF SOCK

TO GET STARTED

1. Cut the plastic bottom off the bottle and remove the cap. Turn the bottle upside down.

2. Cut the sock in half, then stuff the ankle half of the sock into the neck of the bottle.

3. Keeping the bottle upside down, add a layer of charcoal if possible.

4. On top of the charcoal, add a layer of sand.

5. On top of the sand, add a layer of small gravel.

6. On top of the layer of small gravel, add a layer of large gravel or small rocks.

7. Stretch the toe half of the sock over the wide opening of the water bottle.

8. Pour water through the sock and into your filtration system.

The upper sock will screen out visible dirt and each layer of filtration will screen out smaller and smaller particles. It will take a little while to drip through. Pour dirty water into the large opening and clean water will drip out of the small opening.

At this point you have cleaned the water of dirt and debris but you must still boil it to kill the bacteria before drinking it.

THE MANY USES OF STICKS

One of the most common of all found objects is the stick. Almost anywhere in the world, one can find a stick of some sort. Sticks make great improvised weapons and other tools. With a good stick you can:

- extend your reach in a fight, or swing it like a baseball bat.
- throw it at a target, if it is of sufficient weight.
- use it to stab or gouge.
- pin someone to the ground.
- reinforce a punch when gripped in your fist, giving it knock-out power.
- trip pursuers by suspending it near the ground.
- impale an unsuspecting foot by embedding it in the ground, pointy side facing upwards.
- light it on fire to ward off animal attacks.
- pick up and discard them anywhere without stealing or littering.
- make previously agreed upon signs for covert communications.
- build a fire.
- function as a writing instrument when burnt on one end.
- act as a bite holder for hanging a hammock.
- construct a timber shelter.
- make a slingshot or a hunting implement.
- make a spear.

Bottom line: Never take sticks for granted. You are limited only by your own ingenuity.

DUCT TAPE TOURNIQUET

There is a quick and simple way to create and apply a tourniquet to yourself or someone else in an emergency. You can make one from scratch and apply to a patient within 60 seconds with practice.

YOU WILL NEED

- **Duct tape**
- **Pen or pencil**

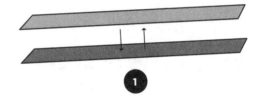

1

TO GET STARTED

1. Cut two one-yard lengths of duct tape and tape them to each other, front to front (sticky side to sticky side). You should wind up with one yard of double ply duct tape which is not sticky on either side.

2. Wrap the duct tape like you would a tourniquet, tying it as high and as tightly as possible around the limb, above the bleeding.

3. Make the first half of a square knot or an overhand knot. (Think of it as the first step in tying your shoe.)

4. Place the pen or pencil on the top of the half knot and and finish the square knot, trapping the pen/pencil inside it.

2-4

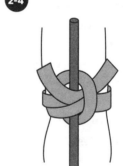

5. When you have the band of the tourniquet placed exactly where you want it, use the pen or pencil as a windlass and twist the knot to tighten the tourniquet down.

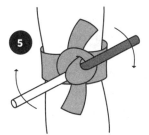

6. When it has reached the appropriate tightness (when all the bleeding stops and there is no pulse below the tourniquet), tuck an end of the pen or pencil under the strap to keep it locked and apply a piece of duct tape over top for security.

7. If you can, write the time and date on the forehead of the patient, so that medical personnel will know how long their limb has been out of circulation.

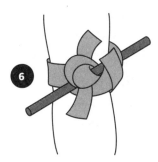

NOTE Never remove a tourniquet. Leave that for the hospital.

OPEN YOUR CLOSED GARAGE DOOR

Say the power goes out and you need to access your car, currently sitting in your detached garage. If there's no side door (or you lost your key to it), you can still get in. All you need is a metal coat hanger.

Note the small opening at the top of a closed garage door (usually in the middle). There is a thin rope that hangs down on the inside of this opening. It has a plastic T-handle hanging from the end.

1. Leaving the hook of the coat hanger intact, straighten the rest of the hanger.

2. Insert the hooked end of the hanger into the space at the top of your garage door. Fish around to find the T-handle hanging down.

3. Hook the T-handle with the hanger and pull it to manually release the mechanism.

4. Lift the unlocked garage door by hand.

Now, the opposite can also be employed as a home security measure. If so, you might want to consider cutting the T-handle off your release cable or tying the whole thing up so that no one can break into your garage by that method. You will have to decide whether it is more important to you to have the option of breaking into your own garage, or if you would rather employ a security measure to ensure no one else can. This may come in handy should you need to evacuate during a natural disaster or when taking a long trip away from home.

HOW TO MAKE PLASTIC

In all kinds of situations and environments, plastic comes in very handy. We use manufacturer-made plastic all day, every day as it is. Think of how useful it would be to be able to make your own plastic if you ever needed it. Now you can!

YOU WILL NEED

- 8 tablespoons of vinegar
- 18 ounces of milk
- 1 strainer
- 1 container

1. Heat the milk in the microwave or a saucepan but do not bring it to a boil.
2. Stir in the vinegar thoroughly.
3. Pour the mix through a strainer.
4. You will be left with a warm and pliable ball of plastic from which you can make whatever you need.

You can use homemade plastic to create funnels, valves, arrowheads, shivs, custom splints, containers, tools, drinking and eating vessels, utensils, traps, filters, waterproof casings, lids, projectiles for slingshots, pace counters and more.

Experiment with it in a non-survival situation so you know what you're capable of, and how durable it will be, when you're actually in need.

THE MIGHTY PONCHO

Waterproof ponchos are an essential piece of survival gear. They have as many uses as you can think of and they pack down small enough to go with you every time. They can be opened and wrapped around your gear to keep it dry, or they can be folded and stuffed into a pocket. One thing is certain: You will not want to get caught out there without one (or two). With a poncho, you can:

- create a raft to make gear and/or salvaged items waterproof and buoyant.
- create a water collector for a ground still.
- place it on the ground, enabling you to sit or sleep on a dry surface.
- form a dummy by stuffing it with leaves or straw to distract pursuers.
- use it as a signaling device or flag.
- use it as a marker.
- turn it into a sail for a boat.
- create a funnel to direct smoke signals.
- turn it into a tent.
- make it into a stretcher.
- wear it over or under your clothes for added warmth and waterproofing.
- create ground symbols for aerial search and rescue.
- make a chair.
- convert it into a bag for carrying gear/provisions which you can then hang above the ground, out of the reach of wildlife.
- stretch and suspend it flat between trees to create a makeshift table.
- make improvised clothing.
- hold water as a basin or a sink.
- stuff it with leaves or straw to create a mattress.
- create a parachute for small and light gear.
- protect yourself from the sun.
- make a hammock.
- create a rain collector.
- hang an improvised shower curtain.
- make a sling, splint or tourniquet.

You will not regret packing a poncho.

THE AMAZING PARACORD

In my humble opinion, paracord is the most versatile piece of equipment you will be carrying (yes, even more versatile than the poncho). I have several 1,000-foot spools of it around my home and office as well as hundreds of feet of it in my nine packs, five of which include one climbing/rappelling pack, one emergency medical pack, a day pack for hiking, a search and rescue pack, and a camping pack. I carry at least 100 feet in each pack and I keep about 100 feet in my car as well.

YOU CAN USE PARACORD TO MAKE:

- Anchor lines
- Backpacks
- Bands
- Baskets
- Belts
- Bow drills
- Bracelets
- Emergency dental floss (use one filament)
- Emergency rappel rope
- Escape tools
- Fishing line
- Fishing nets
- Game preparations
- Hammock straps
- Harnesses
- Jon lines
- Keychains
- Lashings
- Litters/stretchers
- Rafts
- Restraints
- Saws
- Seat belts
- Shoelaces
- Snares
- Static line
- Straps
- Suspenders
- Tethers
- Winch cables

As you can see, there are many, MANY uses for this particular item, which is worth its weight in gold to me. As a matter of fact, there is one particular place from which I always purchase my paracord: a company called TOUGH-GRID. Their product is outstanding and their customer service is unparalleled. I have bought their products exclusively for a number of years now and will be a loyal customer for life. As someone who does a fair amount of teaching, I send all my students to TOUGH-GRID for their paracord needs. Their product is made in the USA and the quality keeps me coming back over and over again.

ALTERNATE USES FOR EVERYDAY THINGS

▶▶ PERSONAL LUBRICANT

There are numerous alternate uses for items like personal lubricant and condoms that may surprise you. In a shelter-in-place or bug-out situation, having some personal lubricant around may help you in more ways than one. With personal lubricant you can:

- **prevent or treat chafing by applying it to underarms or the insides of thighs.**
- **moisturize dry skin.**
- **heal painfully dry or cracked lips quickly.**
- **use the tube to create a make-shift catheter or nasopharyngeal airway insertion in a medical situation.**
- **remove painfully stuck-on bandages.**
- **lubricate stuck fishing reels and similar mechanical contraptions.**
- **loosen a stuck screw or bolt.**
- **grease stuck zippers.**
- **provide symptomatic relief after being heated and massaged into strained muscles.**
- **lubricate stuck locks.**

A small amount of lubricant, carefully packed and double-sealed in a freezer bag, makes a great addition to bug-out bags. Again, be sure to pack it carefully so it does not leak out and soil the rest of your gear.

▶▶ CONDOMS

So...condoms. They're almost as versatile as paracord, with three additional advantages. They are watertight, elastic and fillable. Condoms can be used:

- **as a glove in a medical situation instead of handling someone else's blood directly.**

- over your socks to waterproof your feet.
- over socks or mittens to trap heat and fight frostbite.
- as a water reservoir. This will require reinforcing with a sock, backpack or other sturdier container.
- as a float (bobber) for a fishing line.
- to make a slingshot for self-defense or to kill small game.
- to make a bow drill.
- to waterproof your tinder.
- as a fire starter as they are flammable.
- as a water bottle or magnifying glass to start a fire by filling with water.
- as a support flotation device.
- as a signaling device.
- as a constricting band.
- to waterproof a wound dressing.
- to occlude a sucking chest wound.
- to waterproof a cell phone or handheld radio.
- to seal an open can of food.
- as a tie-down for your gear.
- to protect your food.
- to tie splints.

MASTER TACTIC

Be sure to buy NON-lubricated condoms. You will not want to drink water that has been contaminated by lubricant. Invest in a higher-quality brand that will not tear easily.

» EXPENDED SHELLS

Did you know that you can actually convert an empty rifle shell into a signaling device like a whistle? It takes a little patience but could save your life or someone else's.

TO GET STARTED

1. If the shell has a neck, file it off until the entire length of the shell has the same diameter.

2. Deburr the opening with a small rock to prevent getting metal splinters. Pick a rock and rub the shell back and forth on it until the job is done.

3. Cut or file an opening near the open end in the side of the shell, angled toward the closed end. If you do not have a file, an edged rock will work. Simply find an edge as close to 90 degrees as you can, then slide the shell back and forth until the opening appears. Deburr this new opening as well.

4. Find a piece of wood that fits snugly into the opening but allows air to pass over the top of it. Push the piece of wood into the hole, but not past the opening you made.

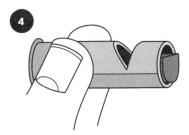

Now you have a whistle to signal for help.

❱❱ PAPERCLIPS, SAFETY PINS AND BOBBY PINS

These little gems are the unsung heroes of the bug-out bag. Tiny and light, you can afford to throw a dozen of these in each of your bags, coat pockets, purses, etc. If you ever need them, you will be glad you have them. Paperclips, safety pins and bobby pins can be used as:

- Fishing hooks
- Radio antennae
- Sewing needles
- Finger/toe splints
- Zipper pulls
- Compass needles

- Hooks for suspending things
- Gear fasteners
- Lock picks
- Shims
- Sutures
- Tools for gear repair

You will never notice their weight and they take up no real estate in your bag. Just throw them in and see what good they can do.

❱❱ KNEE HIGHS AND PANTY HOSE

Simply put, knee highs and panty hose have a plethora of survival uses, not the least of which is blister prevention. Knee highs and panty hose can be used to:

- create a water filtration system.
- prevent blisters or chafing by wearing them under socks.
- build a fish trap.
- conceal your face.
- replace or repair mosquito netting.
- provide a base layer for warmth.
- provide bug bite protection.
- act as a mask for filtering out particulate matter from your nose and mouth.
- make a sling.
- bandage over a dressing.
- act as a tourniquet.
- function as a rope.
- dry wet things by placing them in the hose and hanging them up off the ground.

• replace a belt.

• act as lashings.

These amazing pieces of gear are not just for the ladies anymore! Again, small and very light, they can easily be added to your pack.

›› TAMPONS

Look, everyone knows why they were designed. But put that aside for a moment and consider how helpful these can be in a pinch. With a tampon, you can:

• stop nosebleeds.	• filter water.
• pack a wound.	• bandage a wound.
• make tinder.	• clean your teeth.
• create ear plugs.	• cork a bottle.
• form cotton balls.	• create a windsock.

Do not let the thought of their original purpose keep you from carrying these pocket-sized and versatile medical and hygiene tools.

›› COTTON SWABS

These little buggers are the tiny counterpart to tampons. Whereas tampons can be used to pack wounds and stop bleeds, cotton swabs are used to clean and assist with medical and hygiene needs. You can use cotton swabs to:

• clean debris from eyes.

• pack gauze or a tampon into a wound.

• apply medication.

• brush teeth.

• replicate a candle wick when dipped in alcohol or petroleum jelly.

• splint fingers or toes.

• clean wounds.

• stir liquid.

• apply lubricant to stuck zippers.

• provide tinder for a fire.

The best way to pack these is to put a dozen or so loose cotton swabs in a zippered sandwich bag and seal them. Keep them as clean and dry as possible for when you have hygienic or medical need for them.

» DUCT TAPE

Duct tape is like the Force: It has a light side and a dark side and binds the universe together. Every fix-it guy, handyman and homeowner already knows the incredible potential of duct tape. Its applications are boundless. Duct tape can be used to:

- bandage wounds.
- splint broken bones.
- create a sling.
- repair gear.
- make tourniquets.
- restrain loose items.
- signal others.
- make plates.
- make cups.
- mark or label things.
- provide ground cover.
- repair clothing.
- build a shelter.
- make a blanket.
- waterproof equipment.
- fletch arrows.
- tie things.
- lash things down.
- stitch wounds.
- make shoes.

Just use your imagination. Pack a roll, and may the Force be with you.

» PENS

Pens are unique and quite diverse in their utility. Aside from writing, a pen can be used as a:

- stabbing weapon.
- projectile from a slingshot or bow.
- chopsticks, if you have two.
- stirrer for liquid.
- whistle (same as with a bullet cartridge).
- bite when suspending something from rope or paracord.

• shim (the metal clip).

• fishing hook (inner spring).

• awl.

WHEN EMPTIED, YOU CAN USE A PEN AS A:

• straw.

• trachea tube.

• blow dart sheath.

You will find that different styles of pens have unique capabilities. Throw a handful into your go-bag for maximum utility.

» PENCILS

Pencils are not very grand or glorious but they sure can come in handy beyond the occasional crossword puzzle. In a survival situation, use pencils to:

• provide tinder (i.e. the shavings) for a fire.

• lubricate a stuck lock by rubbing the eraser on the teeth of the key.

• stab an attacker with the sharpened end (the sharper the better).

• fashion a projectile for a bow or a slingshot.

• replace chopsticks.

• splint a broken finger, toe or wrist.

• function as an awl.

• stir things.

• start a fire by connecting both leads from your car battery.

• provide a bite for rope or paracord.

• provide a windlass for a tourniquet.

You will never look at these humble writing instruments the same way again.

» RUBBER BANDS

Almost everyone already has these on hand somewhere and, if you are anything like me, you have various sizes, too. You can use rubber bands to:

- cinch things down.
- keep things together.
- strap things to your pack.
- open stuck things.
- blouse your trouser legs or sleeves.
- make a slingshot.
- make a handle.
- make a strap.
- hold a roll of paracord together.
- get your hair up off of your neck.

» T-SHIRTS

Everyone, and I do mean that quite literally, has at least one t-shirt. They are the world's de facto uniform and have quite a few handy survival applications as well. You can use a t-shirt to:

- provide tinder for a fire.
- replicate medical equipment by cutting or tearing it into strips and using them for bandages, dressings, tourniquets, splints and slings.
- carry things by converting it into a bag.
- filter smoke and debris from the air by wearing it over your mouth and nose like a mask.
- protect your head or neck from the sun.
- create a pillow by stuffing it with leaves.
- make a char cloth.
- wipe down or dry wet things.
- make a chair by stretching it across branches or limbs.
- make a water filter.
- make a torch. Dip it in oil or alcohol, tie it to the end of a large stick, and light it up.
- mark your trail.

- make a flag and signal for help.
- clean people or gear.
- tie things together.
- handle hot cooking equipment.
- create a makeshift cord by cutting it into strips and braiding it.

WET T-SHIRTS IN PARTICULAR CAN BE USED TO:
- help treat overheating and heat-related injuries.
- assist in flotation. Tie the neck and sleeves closed with a simple knot. On the surface of the water, hold the untied end open and snap the spread T-shirt up into the air and back down again to trap a pocket of air inside. Tie the waist (open) end of the shirt closed, trapping the pillow of air and creating a flotation device.
- replicate a vice by twisting it around something.
- make an even more effective smoke-filtering mask than when dry.

Why not throw one or two in your bag?

›› NEWSPAPER

Who has newspapers anymore? Well, you might be surprised. Almost every town and county delivers a weekly newspaper, whether you want one or not. However, I am not advocating becoming a newspaper hoarder. But think of it this way: Just like many other types of material, newspapers will spontaneously combust under the right conditions. Considering the number you choose to keep, it is imperative that you are deliberate regarding where and how you store and maintain them. In a pinch, you can use newspaper to:

- line your clothes for personal insulation.
- line your walls for shelter insulation.
- provide tinder and kindling for a fire.
- replace toilet paper.
- provide a mattress or ground cover beneath a blanket or sleeping bag.
- fashion a makeshift pillow by stuffing a bag or pillowcase.
- insulate pipes to help them resist freezing.
- make your house or car more private, insulated or unappealing (to thieves) by wetting

the pages and sticking them to your windows.
- wick the moisture out of your shoes by stuffing the paper inside and letting them sit overnight.
- line your baby's cloth diapers, turning them into disposable ones.
- break glass or bludgeon an attacker by rolling it up tightly, bending the roll in half, and compressing it as solidly as you can.
- stop cold drafts by stuffing it under doors or in cracks and gaps.
- make papier mâché, which can be used to form casts, containers, hiding spots, blinds and decoys.
- absorb odors by soaking it in white vinegar.
- chock your wheels to keep your vehicle from rolling away.
- clean dirty windows.

As I said, be judicious when it comes to where and how you store them, but you may want to start keeping a few of the ones that wind up on your doorstep, instead of tossing them all in the recycling bin.

❱❱ COLA

We all know that syrupy soft drinks are not very healthy for us, but did you know how many ways it can come in handy during a crisis? No wonder it was formulated by a pharmacist. You can use cola to:

- remove blood stains.
- remove rust.
- remove E. Coli bacteria from your intestines and stop diarrhea.
- remove oil from things.
- soothe bites and stings when applied topically.
- tenderize meat.
- relieve nausea.
- relieve headaches.
- clean mold and mildew.
- soothe sore throats.
- neutralize skunk odor, if you soak in it.
- clean the carbon buildup off of a rifle or shotgun.

• defrost glass.

• tone down loud and unwanted hair dye if used as a shampoo (should you find you need to blend in with the local baseline).

Having some cola in your pantry would be a boon in a shelter-in-place situation (pg. 24).

MASTER TACTIC

The caffeine from two cans of cola can be used to prevent an asthma attack before you get to the hospital or access an inhaler. Be sure to keep a few cans in your gear, just in case.

» "TIN" CANS

Tin cans are so much fun! Soda cans work well, too. You can use a tin can to:

• make a fish hook with the tab.
• make a shim for bypassing locks.
• create a lantern by cutting one side of the can away and place a tea candle inside.
• create a great signaling device by using the concave bottom of the can as a reflector.
• store loose items.
• contain and drink liquids.
• cook small food items.
• function as a stove.
• slice things with the lid.
• make arrowheads—simply cut the shapes out of the metal.
• create a water filtration device by cutting a small hole in the bottom, then filling it with materials as detailed on pg. 240.
• create a fishing lure (the shinier, the better).
• geocache gear or cash.
• bury human waste.
• replicate a shower head by poking holes in the bottom and attaching it to a spigot.

- create an effective perimeter alarm by tying a bunch of empty cans together and hanging them along your property line.
- start a fire by using the concave bottom of the can to focus the sun on something flammable as shown on pg.196.
- work as a fishing line float (when whole and empty).
- provide the socket for stabilizing a bow drill (when crunched).
- keep your toilet paper dry when in the wild (coffee cans are best as they are resealable).

Use your imagination and don't be too quick to throw those cans away after you consume the contents.

» ALUMINUM FOIL

Chances are, you already have a roll or two of this stuff in your kitchen this very moment. Aluminum foil is handy enough in normal life. But what can it do for us in a crisis? Aluminum foil can be used to:

- create a reflective signaling device.
- mark a trail.
- boil water by shaping it into a pot.
- make a cup.
- fry food after shaping it into a pan.
- wrap meat and vegetables so that you can put them under a bed of hot coals to cook.
- make a fishing lure.
- sharpen scissors, which you can do by cutting through multiple layers of foil.
- remove rust by using the foil to scrub.
- collect and direct rain water to a container.
- erect a wind break around a small fire.
- erect a reflective wall on one side of your fire to direct the heat at you.
- fill a gap between a battery and its contacts.
- waterproof books or boxes of matches.
- help you get off the grid by wrapping four layers around your cell phone.
- make a funnel.
- waterproof the ground beneath your sleeping bag.
- make a lid for another container.

• insulate your shelter.

• make a crude mirror.

Foil is cheap and easy to come by, so why not have it on you just in case?

» ALCOHOL

This may sound like fun and games but, believe it or not, this item is a heavy hitter in the alternate uses category. You can use alcohol to:

• disinfect wounds, gear or surfaces.

• start a fire.

• deodorize.

• keep yourself warm.

• maintain a small fire.

• clean your teeth.

• relieve oral pain.

• relieve pain and itching from bug bites and poison ivy.

• melt snow and ice.

• suppress a cough.

• kill mold, mildew and fungus.

• sterilize instruments.

• dry the water from your inner ear.

• kill odors.

• degrease surfaces.

• repel bugs by applying it to your skin.

• cook eggs in about an hour by soaking a cracked egg in the liquid.

• clean your gun.

• barter for what you need most.

• clear your sinuses.

However you use it, make sure you do so responsibly.

❯❯ PLASTIC BAGS

This may be the most mundane item of them all. However, I have been caught without one enough times to know just how valuable they can be. Plastic bags can be used to:

- secure human waste or vomit.
- carry just about anything.
- make a pillow by stuffing it with leaves.
- make a rope by tying several together.
- mark a trail.
- make a signal device like a flag.
- make a solar still.
- collect rainwater.
- collect foraged food.
- waterproof your gear.
- make a sling.
- waterproof your feet.
- insulate your body.
- stop a draft.
- make a bandage.
- function as a floatation device by filling it with air then tying off the end.
- tie a splint.
- improvise a shower by filling it with water, poking holes in it and hanging it from a tree.
- pick up or hold messy, dangerous or soiled items.
- cover or plug a leak in your shelter.

Things do not have to be exciting in order to be useful or even life-saving—in fact, sometimes the best items are the most mundane. Their utility cannot be beat for the price and the convenience.

SURVIVAL IN THE DIGITAL AGE

KNOW THE RISKS OF A TECH-HEAVY WORLD.

TECHNOLOGY IS EVERYWHERE, and whether or not you are savvy to the pitfalls of digital devices can make or break your ability to go gray. You can assume you are being watched in public spaces at all times, sure. But do you know how to create static in a pinch? And how can you check whether or not you have been bugged? From understanding audio and video surveillance to destroying your laptop should you become compromised, these tips will help you keep a low profile whenever technology is involved.

PERSEC

We have already discussed the concept of OPSEC, or Operational Security (pg. 18). Now, we will discuss PERSEC, which as you may have guessed refers to Personal Security. Like OPSEC, PERSEC is about both information and physical security. PERSEC is about you, personally. Remember how to dress defensively (pg. 167)? Remember your Every Day Carry items (pg. 19)? These are all PERSEC issues.

Years ago, a friend and I were in the parking lot of a shopping mall, walking from my car toward the stores. A lady who was leaving the mall spotted me and hurried my way. Sizing up the situation, I pushed my companion behind me and got ready for anything this woman might have had in mind. As soon as the lady was close enough to speak to me without being overheard, however, she frantically asked for my help. She said she noticed a man watching her in the mall and went into what I have referred to as condition orange. She continued to shop and, as she moved from store to store, he kept appearing. Realizing she was being followed, the woman grew worried and left the mall but he followed her out. She was too scared to go to her car, for fear that he would follow her and she would lead him to her house. I had her point the man out to me, then escorted her to her car. Standing guard, I stayed there as she drove away, watching to be sure he did not follow her. He eventually turned around and went back into the mall.

This woman made a number of very sound PERSEC decisions that day. She kept herself in condition yellow as she shopped. Her situational awareness was good and she noticed she was being followed. She tested her follower by moving around and, after verifying that he kept showing up, she got off the X. When he continued to follow her, she got help and saved herself from an unpleasant encounter that day.

Part of PERSEC is also how dutifully you guard your information. Do you post about your life on social media? Do you talk with friends and acquaintances about your life, routine and plans? Are you judicious in the use of personally identifying information? Do not make it easy for the bad guys to target you. Live every day with good PERSEC habits and make yourself a hardened target. If you prove to be too much trouble, the bad guys will move on to an easier mark.

INFOSEC

These days, we have considerably more options for broadcasting information than they did during WWII. In addition to guarding against careless talk (pg. 80), we now have to consider the security implications of careless emails, text messages, social media posts and a host of other communication options. INFOSEC, or Information Security, is the backbone of all security. Ultimately, all operations and all security measures run on information. There can be no exceptions.

Your personal security, facility security and operational security begin and end with information security. If anyone is targeting you, physically or virtually, they will spend untold amounts of time gathering information about you. The goal here, of course, is to make that as difficult for them as possible.

A gold mine for data collection is social media. Social media platforms are places where people keep in touch and share stories, news, photographs, opinions and other pieces of information with their social circle. It was designed to work that way, but it can create a vulnerability for those who use it too freely.

HERE ARE MY TIPS FOR BEST INFOSEC PRACTICES

• **RESTRICT YOUR VIEWING AUDIENCE TO THOSE YOU KNOW OR HAVE A REASON TO TRUST.** Do not allow your site or your page to be unrestrictedly accessible.

• **USE GOOD JUDGEMENT WHEN YOU CHOOSE TO POST INFORMATION.** It may seem harmless to post about walking your dog after work every day, but that tells people two things: where you will be at the same time every day and when you will not be in your house. If anyone is targeting you, discovering this intel is like striking gold.

Everyone wants to post photos right away these days: vacation photos, wedding photos, restaurant photos, etc. When you do this real time, it shows people that you are not at home. You are at this vacation destination, or that wedding venue, or this restaurant. We have already discussed how you are helping the people targeting you specifically by advertising your location. However, if their intent is burglarizing your home, you are making that easy for them, too.

Likewise, if a criminal targets your child for abduction, all they need to do is find out where that child goes to school. From there, they can easily ascertain school hours. If you post about your child's school, schedule and activities, you are making their targeting that much easier.

Posting excitedly about your brand new car and adding photos feels so good. You have great news and you want to share it with your circle of friends. However, you are also tipping your hand about your financial situation and criminals are very interested to know how much they might be able to get from you. Remember that your real estate and vehicle taxes are public information. Any person can begin to construct an accurate picture of your net worth if you supplement the information they can obtain publicly by your social media posts.

• **IF YOU ARE PLANNING TO TRAVEL, BE DISCREET AND DISCERNING ABOUT WHO YOU TELL.** Travelers are of keen interest to certain criminal elements. Traveling puts you at a security disadvantage. Guard your information and itinerary closely.

• **PAY ATTENTION TO WHAT YOU THROW AWAY OR RECYCLE.** Do you shred personally identifying information? If you throw away a white paper pharmacy bag with the drug facts sheet stapled to it, it shows your name, address, birthdate, prescription and dosage, refills and expiration, pharmacy name, phone number and address. From that information, a criminal can develop a plan for how to gain placement and access to you.

Remember that the backbone of all operations is information, whether the operation is for good or for evil. All security measures depend on information. Guard your operations and your security by guarding your information. Take a moment to think through the potential implications of divulging information before you do it. Be judicious, not paranoid. Live in condition yellow, relaxed but aware. Be your own ally, not your own liability.

THE RISK OF PUBLIC WIFI

We all depend heavily on devices that connect to the internet. That is all well and good, but what about public wifi?

Password protected or not, public wifi is the least secure way of accessing the internet. Any hacker can skim all the data they like from the abundant phishing grounds. In fact, some hackers will set up a hotspot that has a very similar name to the local hotspot and inattentive people will jump on without so much as a second thought. All the hacker has to do is sit back and collect data.

If you are going to use the internet in public, I would recommend that you go through your cell service and not through public wifi. I realize that eats up data and costs something. If that is not feasible for you, use a VPN (Virtual Private Network). This also has a small, monthly fee but it sends all incoming and outgoing communication through an encryption, making you a much harder target.

If you must use public wifi, make sure that you do not access any financial accounts or personal information. Identity theft is still an issue, not to mention bank account and credit card fraud.

Look at it this way: Public wifi is about as private as your neighborhood swimming pool. While you might elect to use the pool in proper attire, you cannot consider it the same as your bathtub. One has guaranteed privacy. The other does not.

SAME OLD PASSWORD

Setting up a great password that you will always remember, and then never changing it, is a dead giveaway.

No matter how good your password may be, it needs to be changed on a periodic and unpredictable basis. Never choose words or numbers that are easily associated with you like birthdates, street addresses, phone numbers, social security numbers or anything that is part of your public record. Choose things only you would know. Be sure to use a combination of upper and lowercase letters, numbers and symbols if your password allows. Do not simply keep the same word, perhaps, and add a "1," "2," etc. every time you update that password. That makes for an easy guess, should anyone be trying to access your information without your knowledge. If you need to make a memory jogger, do so, but leave it in a secure place like a safe or safety deposit box. Ideally, of course, you will want to commit that information to memory.

After entering your password, some of your personal accounts may also give you the option of using a two-step verification system, in which a text will be sent to your provided phone number so that you can confirm your identity by entering a given code, or answering security questions. This is your call, but any added layer of security is a win in my book. Having a verification system in place can still help keep your information safe should your password be stolen or compromised.

A password is a critical layer of privacy, but it is only as strong as you make it.

HOW TO DESTROY A LAPTOP

Most of us will never need to destroy a laptop computer with little to no notice. However, the following scenarios are potential instances in which you might consider otherwise:

- **A break-in**
- **Burglary**
- **Identity theft**
- **Bullying**
- **imminent kidnapping**
- **A dictatorial regime**
- **Corporate espionage**
- **Compromised sensitive or medical information**

In the case of kidnapping, if your laptop has also been taken, this is likely because your captors want to acquire sensitive information that could endanger others, critical systems, etc. and you will want to destroy it when the opportunity presents itself.

If you ever do find yourself in any of these unenviable situations, there is one instant solution.

1. Take the battery out and put the computer in the microwave for a few seconds on high.

2. Stand back.

The metal may spark but the result will be unrecoverable data. Be advised that this may disable the microwave as well, but I have a feeling if things get to this point, your primary concern will not be the microwave.

NOTE If you do not take the battery out of the computer, it may explode. Use extreme caution. This technique should be a last resort in a dire circumstance.

AUDIO SURVEILLANCE

There are several ways in which targeting for audio surveillance occurs. If the person conducting the surveillance is good at their job, the target will never know it is happening and never see a thing. Here are just some of the techniques bad guys might use in the intelligence collection phase of their targeting cycle:

- **Laser microphones**
- **RF flooding**
- **Parabolic microphones**
- **Recording devices**
- **Phone taps**
- **Bugs**
- **Human placement**

The first three things are carried out from a distance. The second three are planted, but minuscule and concealed. The last one is neither from a distance, minuscule, nor concealed. However, a trained observer will not appear to be such. They will be the next customer in the grocery store or a jogger running past or a person enjoying a walk on a sunny day, or anything else you can imagine. The point is, any of these things could be in operation in any place, regardless of whether or not you are the specific target. Since you have no way of knowing, it is a best practice to conduct yourself as though every word you say is being overheard. We all know that integrity means doing the right thing even when no one is watching. Well, if you conduct yourself with integrity at all times, you need not worry. For a person with nothing to hide, it does not matter if they are overheard.

VIDEO SURVEILLANCE

Just like with audio surveillance, there are many ways to conduct video/visual surveillance. Where microphones and ears need to hear, cameras and eyes need to see. Hiding places that work for planted audio surveillance will not work for video surveillance, unless they have line of sight. Here are just some of the techniques bad guys might use in the intelligence collection phase of their targeting cycle:

- Infrared imaging
- X-Ray imaging
- Gamma ray imaging
- Security cameras
- Cell phone cameras
- Night vision imaging
- Human observation
- Automobile cameras
- Satellite imaging
- Facial recognition computers
- Concealed microelectronic cameras

Again, if you conduct yourself with integrity, you need not have fear. In today's age of technology dependence, we are never guaranteed to be completely un-surveilled. They say the average urban or suburban resident is on camera 10 times a day, unbeknownst to them. Always conduct yourself as if you are being recorded.

DISGUISE FOR A VIDEO CAMERA

We are all being recorded every day as we go about our lives in modern society. Every store, bank and place of business has cameras recording all day. Many homes have them as well. People are using their phones to record in public. Cars have backup cameras. Even Google has cars, planes and satellites making recordings to keep an updated map of the Earth. Not all of us are keen on being on camera everywhere we turn, but there are a few things you can do about it.

The word "disguise" brings a funny false nose and glasses to mind. However, you can employ much more subtle ways to shield your identity from constant surveillance.

- **Wear a hat and keep the brim down low over your eyes.**
- **Wear glasses or sunglasses.**
- **Wear a headscarf.**
- **Smile.**
- **Keep your head down or turned away from high-placed cameras.**

DISALLOW VIDEO RECORDING WITH LIGHT

Perhaps, for one reason or another, you will one day need to disrupt a video recording of your person. To do this, you will first have to know where the camera you are avoiding is located.

A camera can see no more detail when "looking" directly into a light than you can. If you feel you are being intrusively surveilled, you can hold a flashlight next to your face, pointed forward, to shine the light directly into the camera. The auto exposure feature constricts or closes the aperture in bright light and hampers the ability of the camera to get a good image, much the same way your pupils constrict when you look into light.

CREATING STATIC

You must be careful with this method as you will be harming someone else's property, and I do not say that lightly. This technique, which you can do with gloves or barehanded, should be reserved for criminal threats to your life, limb, eyesight, freedom or property. Perhaps someone is following you or setting up surveillance to learn your pattern of life as they gather intelligence in an effort to threaten, kidnap, extort or kill.

1. Locate the wire to the camera. You will find that it is sheathed in either rubber or metal.

2. Inside that sheath is a copper conductor. Take a razor blade and slice the wire just deeply enough to cut into the copper.

The result will be a static filled video feed as long as the razor stays in contact with the copper, meaning **you must leave the blade there for the duration of the time that you need the feed disrupted**. The feed should return to normal once the razor is removed.

Either way, you will want to leave as soon as possible once the work is done.

SIGNAL SURVEILLANCE

Signal surveillance is employed in two different ways. One is to monitor something that you are already carrying, like your cell phone and credit cards. The other is to plant something like a tracking device and follow the signal. Here are just some of the techniques bad guys might use in the intelligence collection phase of their targeting cycle:

- Cell phones
- GPS units
- RF signatures
- RFID tags
- GPS tags
- TTL technology (tag, track and locate)
- IMEI addresses
- IP addresses
- Computer viruses
- Radios

In short, everything you say, do and write has the potential of being witnessed and even recorded by networks who do not have your best interest at heart. Always be mindful. Live in condition yellow.

VISUALLY DISCOVERING VEHICLE-BASED TRACKING DEVICES

Vehicle tracking devices have gotten smaller, cheaper and more readily available over time. Unfortunately, they are also more difficult than ever to detect. If you believe that you are being followed and tracked, the first thing you should do is visually inspect your vehicle for bugs. I would recommend doing this in your home garage with the door closed in order to avoid alerting your surveillance team of their detection. Do not let them know that you know if you can help it.

The most likely placements of tracking devices on your vehicle, which might look like a button, strip or any other kind of tiny electronic device, will be:

- on top of the roof.
- under the rear dashboard fabric.
- under the center brake light.
- inside the plastic of one of the bumpers.
- under any of the seats.
- inside the glove compartment.
- under the bug shield or grill.
- between the windshield and the hood.
- under the dashboard.
- in a speaker.

You might be surprised to learn that bugs can be placed anywhere except the engine, so be thorough in your search.

If you do find a bug in your vehicle, you have a few options. You can:

- report it to law enforcement.
- disable it.
- remove it.

• leave it in place and know you are being monitored.

Assess your situation and go with your gut.

USING TECHNOLOGY TO DETECT VEHICLE-BASED TRACKING DEVICES

Aside from doing a visual inspection of your vehicle, you can confirm the presence of a tracking or listening device by using your vehicle's radio.

1. Get into the vehicle and close the door. Turn all cell phones off.
2. Set the radio to an AM station that is staticky and out of range.
3. Listen through the static. If you hear a rhythmic clicking or ticking behind the static, there is a cellular device somewhere in or on your vehicle. The most likely culprits are tracking devices and listening devices. In extreme or crisis situations, this could also be a remotely-controlled explosive device, in which case you must EXERCISE EXTREME CAUTION.

Once you have detected its presence, you must decide how to proceed. You can visually search for the device, alert the authorities, alert the surveillance team of their discovery, remove or disable the device, or leave it alone and operate with the knowledge that it is there.

TRAVEL WITH CARE

KNOW WHAT TO LOOK OUT FOR WHEN YOU LEAVE HOME.

PREPPING FOR TRAVEL does not end with a packed bag. Did you book a hotel room between the third and fifth floors? Do you know where the nearest embassy is? Did you bring a towel? If your answer to all of these questions is "No," you might want to rethink your plans. From understanding how to keep an eye on your hotel room while you are not there to staying one step ahead of counterfeit scams to knowing how to create a three-point harness in case you ever need to rappel out of a window James Bond-style, these skills will serve you well whenever you leave your home turf.

WHAT TO PACK

Learn what items get top priority in your bag when traveling.

▶▶ PACK LIGHT

This is quite possibly the granddaddy of preparedness rules when it comes to travel, but it carries plenty of weight in everyday applications as well. You need not bring the kitchen sink. **Pack no more than you can carry for a mile by yourself.** Keeping this in mind will help you decide what goes and what stays long before circumstance makes that choice for you. Being able to haul all your own items by yourself may come in handy if you suddenly and unexpectedly need to evacuate in a hurry.

That said, what follows is a list of items for which you will certainly be glad you left room.

A TOWEL

You would be amazed how many times I have been grateful to have my own trusty towel when traveling. There have been plenty of unfortunate instances in which no towel was provided at all. (Let me just say it takes a long time to air dry after a shower.) There have also been times when there were too few towels and sometimes housekeeping is not as reliable as you would hope. Why bring a towel?

A TOWEL CAN:
- double as a blanket.
- create a makeshift seat or cushion.
- pack wounds.
- work as a dressing, bandage, splint or sling.
- mop up spills.
- be hung as a room divider for privacy.

Camping towels are small and amazingly light. All in all, it takes little effort, space or weight to pack a towel when you travel and, if you need it, you will be glad you have one.

A JACKET

For all of you like me who are confirmed minimalists (and there is nothing wrong with that), you may be tempted not to pack a jacket for certain trips and I certainly do not blame you for wanting to travel light. However, I can attest to the fact that I have always regretted the times where I have failed to bring a jacket. Every time I leave home without one, I wish I had not. For this reason, it is now a mandatory item on my minimum equipment list.

A JACKET CAN:
- keep you warm.
- keep you dry.
- rapidly change your look.
- camouflage you to the baseline.
- help you carry extra cargo in your pockets.
- be converted into a makeshift bag.
- keep you clean.
- conceal an item you are carrying.
- be used as a rope to extend your reach.
- be used a weapon.
- be slipped to someone else to don as a decoy.

You, dear reader, have a golden opportunity to learn from my mistakes. Allow me to put it bluntly: Never travel without a jacket!

SUNSCREEN

Whether summer, winter, spring or fall, sunscreen is a must-have. It does not matter where you are traveling or when; so long as there is sun, there will be sunlight. Inevitably, you will be outdoors for some portion of your trip. Melanoma is no joke. It is your job and your job alone to protect the largest organ of your body: your skin. At the end of the day, your most vital asset is your health.

EARPLUGS

No matter how skilled you might be when it comes to researching and planning a trip, no matter how many reviews you might pore over, you simply cannot know in advance how noisy or quiet your sleeping arrangements will be. Whether due to construction, traffic, noisy neighbors or rioting in the streets, whatever the case may be, you will need to get the best shut-eye you can. That means packing earplugs.

Earplugs are cheap, tiny and light. Keep a pair in your pocket. If you do not need them after all, you have not lost anything by bringing them. But believe me when I say nothing ruins an otherwise good trip like sleeplessness and fatigue. You will be thrilled to have them. And remember, earplugs are not just for nighttime: If you find yourself in a particularly loud locale, you can use them to drown out the noise a bit. So long as you stay aware of your surroundings and live in condition yellow, earplugs will serve you well.

A SLEEP MASK

Just like earplugs, this item is small, light, relatively cheap and a life-saver in terms of getting good rest. For me, however, this is a much more important item than earplugs because light bothers me far more than sound. I can sleep better in noise than I can in bright light. Sleep masks cause you to think you are in total darkness. This tricks your brain into releasing more serotonin, which helps regulate your sleep. As I said before, nothing interferes with travel as much as fatigue. Do what you can to stay ahead of the curve and your body and mood will thank you.

GOOD SHOES

Either pack them, wear them or both. You will be doing some walking no matter where you go. Most airports are expansive and require each traveler to do a fair amount of hustling to terminals, security and the like before ever leaving home. Make sure to take care of your feet, knees, hips and back with good quality and supportive shoes. Pack a pair you can run in should the need arise. (You can have your flip flops, but bring athletic shoes, hiking boots, loafers or some other high quality shoe, too. I would suggest leaving the flip flops in your bag until you arrive at your destination.) Good shoes are not only a good travel item, they are a necessary personal security item.

FLASHLIGHT

You simply never know when you might need to make your own light, and the pitch black darkness can definitely pose a threat to your safety. Emergencies arise. You may be roused from your sleep in the middle of the night and have no clue how to navigate out of wherever you are staying because you have not yet committed it to memory. Perhaps your cellphone is dead or you are trying to conserve what little battery remains to make a call for help. Or maybe you do not want to alert anyone to your presence as you fumble your way through the dark (pg. 225). Some places on earth may not have electricity to offer you, in which case you had better be prepared to make do. A flashlight also doubles as a good improvised weapon. Stay ahead of the need and bring a small, inexpensive one with you. It will be a lifesaver if you need one.

A BOOK

You may encounter a no-electricity situation and you will still require mental stimulation. Having a book amongst your belongings allows you to entertain yourself anywhere. Broaden your horizons, brush up on your vocabulary, lose yourself in pages of well-written prose or make it look like you are occupied when you would rather not be bothered. Keeping a low profile has never been easier.

A MAP

Do not be afraid to use it! Up until only a decade ago, maps were quite common. Without having to rely on these paper-based tools, we have been lulled into laziness by the siren song of technology, forgetting how to think for ourselves. On a personal note, I know I get mentally lazy when I do not have to use my gray matter too much. Packing and using a map is an excellent practical exercise and will help you stay sharp. It is a necessary skill for survival and may become necessary if you have no GPS for any reason. There is no harm in preparing your mental map of an area before you arrive.

A COMPASS

If you acquire a local map, having a compass will make life so much easier. Even in an urban environment, a compass is a sure way to navigate once you know which direction you are facing. Maps and compasses go together. If you have one, you should have the other. Like many incredibly useful items on this list, compasses are small, lightweight and relatively inexpensive. In fact, you can buy a "button" compass which has a face about the size of a nickel. While this is meant to be mounted on your watch strap (unless your watch strap is metal), it can easily be mounted on your shoelaces or carried in your pocket (away from metal). It is unobtrusively tiny and will be a life-saver should you need it.

SPARE DOCUMENTS

If you are traveling overseas, one of the best tips I can offer you is to carry multiple copies of your passport. My personal practice is to keep my actual passport on my person, but I will also put two photocopies in my bag(s), have a digital copy on my phone and another digital copy in email, which is accessible from anywhere. If you should lose your documents for any reason, you will need to visit a U.S. consulate or embassy. (You may want to contact them before your visit, and I highly recommend you read up on all travel advisories regarding your destination before and during your trip.) It will be far easier for them to help you by issuing you a temporary passport if you have brought copies of the original.

A BACKPACK OR MESSENGER BAG

By which I mean bring an empty bag. This may seem like an odd piece of advice, but very few people walk around on a trip with their hands empty. We are all usually carrying something. It will increase your enjoyment of the trip and your quality of life if you bring a backpack. This gives you a way to carry your jacket, flashlight, sunscreen, hat, umbrella and anything you purchase in a hands-free and comfortable way. It will help you go the distance when you are out of your hotel all day long. Like a jacket, a backpack can act as a weapon, a concealment or an accessory to rapidly change your look. If a backpack is too uncommon in your destination area, consider using a messenger bag instead.

EMERGENCY CASH

I know the goal is to travel light, to make yourself as gray as possible, to not put anything on your person that makes you a liability should it come to that.

While I will grant you that it is operationally safer not to carry much cash, there are some cases where cash is king. Emergencies happen. I recommend carrying a couple hundred dollars that you earmark exclusively for emergency use only. Put it somewhere inconspicuous, by which I mean do not carry it in your wallet. Find another place where even a seasoned mugger would be likely to overlook it: in your shoe, a zippered or buttoned pocket, a shirt pocket, an evasion belt, a tactical or conceal carry shirt or even your bra. Do not factor it into your resources when you are calculating expenses. Just place it and forget it. Regard it as a tool for getting yourself out of trouble.

PARACORD

Practically speaking, paracord has a thousand uses. It can:

- **serve as your ad hoc clothesline for drying things out.**
- **secure your room as a tension lock.**
- **lower things, and, in extreme emergencies, people to the ground.**
- **bind things together.**
- **make a seat belt.**
- **make a lanyard.**
- **replace shoelaces, purse straps and luggage handles.**

Even in an urban setting, paracord can be a trip saver by fixing or replacing many items you may not be able to buy at your destination.

TWO CARABINERS

This goes along with the paracord. If you have to exit a building in a hurry from anywhere other than the ground floor, you will need a carabiner to do so. Carabiners can also replace handles and straps in a hurry. They can be used to clip things off and free your hands. Two can be used to create a makeshift seatbelt. If you do intend to carry a carabiner that will work for rappelling, make sure that it was made for that purpose. Not every carabiner that is capable of holding your weight can withstand the G forces of a fall. If you have questions about this, ask your local outdoor store for tips. They will point you in the right direction.

DUCT TAPE

I can't say it enough: Duct tape is like the Force. It has a light side and a dark side and it binds the universe together. Where would we be without duct tape? You do not need to pack a whole, big, heavy roll—just take a few feet. Simply wrap the duct tape around a pencil over and over, creating a tiny (6-foot) roll of your own with the pencil in the center. If you are worried about stickiness, throw the duct tape in a plastic sandwich bag. Duct tape can be used as a makeshift tourniquet or bandage. It can patch holes, waterproof things, hold things up or keep them down. The possibilities are just about endless. Wrap 6 feet of duct tape around a pencil, throw it in your luggage and you will be good to go.

SMOKE HOOD AND TOURNIQUET

Always pack a smoke hood (pg. 97) and a tourniquet. These two items will see you through the two deadliest hotel emergencies: fire and bleeding. If you are prepared to handle these two, life-threatening emergencies, you will be able to handle anything less than that with ease.

BEACONS

Nowadays, you can opt to carry a personal locator beacon with you wherever you travel. This is a device that can track your location and send out a distress call should your situation require it. Depending on the brand and capabilities, these devices can also be programmed to send out routine messages that you are safe when you are out of cell coverage. With some, you can choose to alert a specific person or organization of your whereabouts. With others, only the Air Force Rescue Coordination Center gets the alert. Either way, someone will know where you are.

No matter which one you choose, all conscientious travelers should carry a beacon. They are several generations old now. Their size and price have decreased and their capabilities have increased. These unobtrusive, light items provide a huge peace of mind factor for both the traveler and their loved ones. I have carried one for more than a decade now. It has accompanied me all over the world and into all kinds of situations. I recommend you do the same. As always, it is far better to have it and never need it than to need it and not have it.

SELECTING A HOTEL

When you need a place to rest your head abroad, it pays to do your research.

» ACCESSIBILITY

As a conscientious traveler, I am certain you always do your research prior to selecting the places where you will stay. One of the criteria of a thorough vetting process should be how many routes there are to and from the hotel of your choosing.

You do not want to choose a hotel which has access in only one direction. One way in and one way out leaves you trapped in the event a crisis occurs. Whether that crisis is a natural disaster, a health epidemic or a terrorist attack, always leave yourself multiple routes of escape. Before you book, do a bit of digging and find out if any construction or other projects have closed roads or restricted routes to and from your hotel. Even well situated hotels with multiple entrances and exits can find themselves cut off during construction projects. Make sure you have multiple route options for leaving before you commit to staying anywhere.

» SECURITY FEATURES

See what you can find out about the building's security features. Physical layout is of premium importance as you consider how easy it is to enter the building, access the rooms and escape in the event of a fire, flood, earthquake or attack.

Good security features include gates with guards, card or ID-only access, cameras, security guards, a fire-escape plan, a hotel detective, safes and known proximity to criminal activity areas.

» PROXIMITY

How close is this place to emergency services? How quickly could the fire department, police or EMTs show up in a crisis? Ideally, you want to select a hotel within easy access from a hospital, police station and fire department. At the very least, make sure you know exactly where each of those are located relative to your hotel so if you need to get there on your own you can do so. If you have that map handy, you may want to go ahead and highlight the routes yourself. Do it before you need it.

❱❱ SHELTER

The hotel of your choosing should have a below-ground level you can use as shelter in the event of bombs or hurricanes. If it does not, look at the surrounding buildings. Do any of the other buildings within sprinting distance have an underground level that you can access in an emergency? If the answer to all of these is no, are there concrete or cement above-ground structures that will provide cover in a storm? In a coastal setting, this is going to be the likely option. If the answer to all of these questions is no, re-evaluate your plan.

❱❱ NEIGHBORS

Is the hotel you are considering in close proximity to a high value target like an embassy, consulate, government building or military area? In these cases, sometimes proximity can be a liability because your risk level is higher. These locations are regarded as fair game in terrorist attacks, military actions, police actions, political actions, demonstrations, protests and coups. While security is heavier in these locations and forces are quicker to respond, for the bad guys, the value of those targets can be downright irresistible in terms of sending a message. Get off the X. Know your neighbors and factor that into your choice. Location, location, location.

❱❱ QUALITY

Quality can be a surprising indicator of higher security. When a hotel invests money in creature comforts and modernization, they usually protect that investment by adding state of the art security features. They also tend to show more concern for the well being of their guests than, say, older run-down hotels do. Likewise, charging higher prices tends to discourage the presence of petty criminals and the types of activity associated with them, i.e. prostitution, drugs, trafficking and gang activity. Choosing a modern and high quality hotel is always going to be a better security decision than choosing a hole in the wall. I believe you more often than not get what you pay for. This could make all the difference if things were to go sideways.

›› SELF-SUFFICIENCY

Good quality hotels care about their guests. They also care about their reputation and they want their guests to return. They care about their income and they want their guests to recommend them to others. To that end, they take measures to ensure as little interruption of services as possible. In the event of a natural disaster, coup or attack, they want to continue to provide food, water and electricity to their guests with as few interruptions as possible.

When selecting a hotel, see what you can find out about their emergency continuity of service plan. By that I mean they should have multiple backup generators for electricity, fuel reserves, potable water in storage tanks, water filtration systems, trash removal and/or an incinerator and a well-stocked pantry. You want to choose a hotel that can likely handle it if their guests need to shelter in place for up to three days. I realize you do not want to ask these questions to staff directly, but see what you can learn on your own. If you are staying in a coastal area, you may want to ask how they managed during the last severe hurricane season. This is a common item of discussion in those areas and asking this will not peg you as a potential threat.

›› BRAND NAME

A brand name hotel you recognize can save you a lot of questions, anxiety and problems down the line. As a matter of fact, Western hotel chains have standards and regulate themselves accordingly. When you book a hotel overseas and you recognize the brand, you are setting yourself up for a much better overall experience. It is the same concept as using a brand name taxi service, for example, whose company does regular business with the hotels and airports. You will know a bit about what to expect by the company's own regulations, safeguards and policies. More importantly, you will also have a clear picture of your rights and your recourse in the event of a crisis.

›› CHOOSING A HOTEL ROOM

In my entire life, I have only ever met one person who did not like to travel: my grandfather. I never could figure it out. I personally love the idea of going anywhere for any reason to do anything for any length of time. Frankly, I fantasized for the first 23 years of my life about what it would be like to travel abroad before my chance actually came. I am happy to say I have now visited 49 states and 22 countries, and the list keeps growing. I never tire of traveling to new places and meeting new people. However, travel requires prior planning and plenty of situational awareness in order to return safely.

Your careful planning does not end with choosing the best hotel to meet your needs, not by a long shot. As it turns out, you still need to suss out which room will benefit you most in any given scenario. It is an unfortunate truth that the world is getting more chaotic with every passing day. Violence, organized crime, war, terrorism, disease, scamming, kidnapping for ransom, express kidnapping, robbery, human trafficking and narcotics can make traveling far trickier and more nuanced than it used to be. There are so many more things to take into account these days. Do your research, educate yourself and decide in advance which safety precautions are non-negotiable to you.

In many developing countries, there is a black market for data on tourists. This information is collected for a number of nefarious reasons, the most common ones being kidnapping for ransom and extortion. To this end, many hotels are able to supplement their income by covertly collecting and selling intelligence on their foreign guests. Often, the rooms are under electronic surveillance, both from within and without. As a rule, it is best to assume that this is going to be the case anywhere you go. You must approach it with the mindset that the hotel staff, front desk, management and even police will not help you. You will need to do your own planning and rely only on yourself and your traveling companions while in-country.

With terrorist attacks on the rise, hotels are a common target. There are three possibilities for entry: the ground floor, the roof and a floor that can be accessed either by climbing or rappelling from the outside. By far, the most common point of entry is the ground floor. This is precisely why you DO NOT want to accept a room on the ground floor. Because the second floor can be accessed from the outside with a low-risk climb, I would not recommend a room on the second floor either. In the event of a fire, hook and ladder trucks can only reach the sixth floor at the absolute most. Most commonly, they can only reach the fifth floor. I have been in a hotel fire and you definitely do not want to be out of the reach of rescue should you need it. Therefore, your ideal hotel room should be located somewhere between the third and the fifth floors.

MASTER TACTIC

Do not think just because you are in your hotel room you are safe. Assume you are being monitored and conduct yourself accordingly. Familiarize yourself with your surroundings as quickly as possible.

Kidnapping for ransom has become the favorite income stream of cartels, terrorists, gangs, drug lords and other organized crime rings. Easy and lucrative targets usually present themselves in the form of foreign visitors, whether on business travel or holiday, and naturally such targets can be found in abundance in and around hotels. When selecting a room, you must balance ease of access for the bad guys against ease of escape for you. We have already decided to stay on floor three, four or five. Now we need to select the exact room. Do not accept a room at the very end of the hallway, nearest the stairwell or fire escape. These routes are so easy to access that kidnappers target these rooms first in order to minimize their own risk of exposure. Likewise, a room that is too close to the elevator presents the same problem. Ideally, you will want a room halfway between the elevator and the stairs. This provides you with maximum security while giving you two potential avenues of escape.

It is a very good practice to familiarize yourself with all exits and possible escape routes as soon as you check in. Take a stroll around the place and get to know the grounds. Know how to get out and away from the scene prior to going to bed that first night and do not forget your "what if" scenario drills. Take a few minutes to run through possible scenarios in your mind and what you would do in each case. That way, if something wakes you up in the middle of the night, you will be able to act right away based on the plan you already have.

You will also want to choose a room with a king-sized bed, as the bedsheet can be used to create a harness, should you need to make a daring escape (pg. 288).

HOTEL SECURITY

Make the best of your stay with these tips.

» ROOM KEYS

Once, I found a set of hotel room key cards. Not an unusual sight while traveling, however, this set was still in its original paper sheath with the room number written on it. I picked it up, keenly aware that I not only had the means to enter someone's room, I also knew exactly which room it was. Had I been a bad guy, this would have been my lucky day. **NEVER LEAVE ANY INDICATION OF YOUR ROOM NUMBER WITH YOUR HOTEL KEY(S).**

When the front desk hands you your keys in that little folder or envelope, remove your keys right away. Leave the envelope in your room. Even if the key never leaves your wallet, remove the location of the room from the equation. Thieves will have a field day if they find both together.

» DO NOT DISTURB

Whenever I travel, I always opt to keep housekeeping out of my room when I am not there. Unfortunately, this is not always a viable option. There are localities where the law mandates that an official hotel employee must visually inspect the inside of each room every day, two days or once a week. These laws are meant to prevent some illegal activities like setting up temporary methamphetamine or bomb-making labs, or in the case of the 2017 Las Vegas shooting at the Mandalay Bay Hotel, to prevent people from stockpiling firearms in their rooms. There are other locations that will promise to stay out of your room and respect the Do Not Disturb sign but will instead attempt to access your room covertly. The good news is there are some actions you can take to find out whether or not your room was accessed while you were out.

- **Close the Do Not Disturb sign partially in the door. If it is not closed in the door when you return to your room, the door was most likely opened since you left.**

- **Leave lint, fuzz or hair at the top of each door to and in the room, as well as on the top** edges of all the drawers. If they are gone or on the floor when you return, the doors and drawers were likely opened.

- Using a compass or a compass application on your phone, determine the cardinal directions of North, South, East and West. Take your suitcase and carefully align it in a North/South or East/West orientation. Upon your return, before you touch your suitcase, take your compass out and compare its position to the way you left it.

- Leave your laptop computer perfectly square to and exactly one thumb's width away from the edge of the table or desk. Measure it when you get back.

- Obstruct your USB port with paperwork, a coaster, glass, mug or anything else you can use. Position everything and then take a photo of it prior to leaving your room. Compare the photo to the actual laptop once you return to your room.

- Take a photo of your room before you depart and then again when you return, being careful to take the photo from the exact same spot both times. Compare the two and look for any discrepancies.

While it is certainly frustrating to know you cannot completely prevent people from entering your room, these tips can help you stay one step ahead of the bad guys.

» THE HOTEL SAFE

There are two kinds of hotel safes: the one in your room and the one in the manager's office. As with most things, there are pros and cons to using these safes. You must weigh your options and decide what to do.

PROS

- Items you do not take with you cannot be pickpocketed from you.
- Items you do not carry around cannot be seen or create temptation.
- Items not found on your person cannot be taken in a mugging or robbery.
- Items you do not have on you are not susceptible to being inadvertently dropped or lost.

CONS

- Someone on the hotel staff has access to the safe(s) and items can still be stolen.
- Documents can be removed, copied and replaced without your knowledge.
- You may wind up needing more cash or your passport while you are out.

There is no wrong answer, as long as you make an informed decision.

» EXITS

Know where ALL possible exits are and think outside the box. Obviously, doors are, in many scenarios, the most ideal exits. Windows are also viable exits in an emergency. Stairwells lead up and down. In the event of a fire, you will usually go down. However, other emergencies might require different decisions. Fire escapes still exist in some places, while tunnels or passageways are another possibility. In an extreme situation, ventilation ducts can get you out. Laundry chutes, garbage chutes and broken elevator shafts can be exploited in emergencies, but options like these should be a last resort.

Before you go to sleep on the first night, inspect all the stairwells between your room and exiting the building. Check for obstructions on the stairs as well as chained or padlocked exit doors. You may be surprised to learn many countries do not have mandatory and unobstructed fire escapes. Make sure you know what your options are and run some what-if scenarios to get comfortable with your likely reactions.

» HOW TO MAKE A THREE-POINT HARNESS

Aside from being a particularly comfy and spacious option in terms of bedding, the king-sized bed serves a practical purpose as well: the flat sheet can be used to create a rappelling harness for an adult in under three minutes.

If you don't have a rope for your carabiner, you can create a makeshift one using sheets, towels, clothes or paracord. Make sure you use the correct length for your "rope" to let yourself down all the way safely to the ground.

NOTE This is an extremely dangerous maneuver and should only be used in a life and death emergency. If possible, I recommend taking rappelling lessons to get familiar and comfortable with rappelling concepts prior to attempting this kind of self-rescue in the real world.

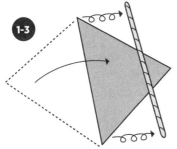

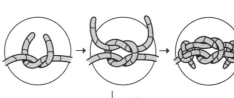

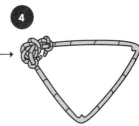

HOW TO DO IT

1. Take the king-sized flat sheet and lay it out flat on the bed or the floor.

2. Fold it in half, diagonally so that you have made a triangle.

3. Roll it up, starting at the wide end (just like Pillsbury crescent rolls in a can).

4. Tie a secure knot (I recommend a square knot backed up by an overhand knot on each side). The knot MUST be secure. Your life depends on it.

5. Put the securely-tied harness on the floor and position it into the shape of a triangle.

6. Stand over it, straddling it with one of the points of the triangle between your feet.

7. Pick the harness up—one point of the triangle between your legs, one point of the triangle on your left and one point of the triangle on your right.

8. Use a rappelling grade carabiner to gather all three sections and clip them together.

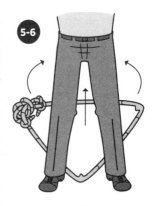

» ALARMED DOOR STOPS

These simple rubber wedges are very cheap and can be ordered online. While standing inside your hotel room, simply close the door and insert the device under the door. If the door is opened into the wedge while you are asleep, the alarm in the wedge will sound off loudly, waking you up and giving you a chance to react and call for help.

» LOCKS

Always use all of the door locks plus the alarmed door stop when you are inside your room.

If the door opens outward from the room, use a tension lock. You can do this by tying a length of paracord around the doorknob and anchoring it to something solid and immovable in the room. This creates a backup for locks that fail, are picked or unlocked by someone unfriendly.

If the door opens inward to the room, you can barricade it with a chair, room furniture, multiple door stops or even a door bar. These are not recommended for routine nights in your hotel room but to counter the actual threat of intrusion.

» ANTI-VISUAL SURVEILLANCE

This one is simple to do but easy to forget: Cover the television when it is not in use. Modern televisions have two-way cameras. They can be used to watch you when you are unaware. Simply drop a towel over the television to obscure the camera when you are not watching it.

To prevent anyone in the hallway from looking through the peephole of the room door, push a wad of tissue paper into the peephole to obscure their view.

Put a rolled up towel in front of the closed door on the floor, to prevent someone from feeding in a surreptitious borescope (otherwise known as a snake camera) while you sleep.

» ANTI-AUDIO SURVEILLANCE

To prevent others from listening in on your stay, you have a few options:

- **Conduct sensitive phone calls in the bathroom with the shower running.**

- **Unplug the room telephone.**
- **Turn the television on to create white noise.**
- **Do not accept a room with a door connecting to the next room unless you know the occupant. This can be not only a platform for audio surveillance but also video surveillance, and even intrusive entry.**

Bear in mind that Westerners are often put into rooms which are prewired for surveillance. Some organizations pay hefty amounts of money for solid intelligence on Westerners' habits and patterns. The hotel may or may not be a willing participant in this data collection. Best to assume they are and take preventive measures.

›› ROUTES

As with all ongoing security measures at home and abroad, vary the routes and times as you come and go from the hotel. Be as unpredictable as possible. Before you venture out alone, however, let the front desk or concierge know of your intended destination and timeline. If anything were to happen to you, doing this would at least give the police a crucial starting point.

Familiarize yourself with the quickest way out of the building and away from the scene. If anything should happen, merely clearing the building will not be enough. You will need to know in advance which direction to take once you exit and how far you need to go in order to reach safety. Are there people or organizations in the area who would be sympathetic to you in an emergency? Know where they are and how to get there in a hurry.

›› UNPACK ONLY WHAT YOU NEED

I told you in Fires Grow Fast (pg. 95) I have been in both a house fire and a hotel fire. For the latter, the hotel fire alarm roused me from my sleep early in the morning. Despite being woken from my slumber, I had one major advantage: I had not unpacked anything beyond what was absolutely necessary. Thanks to this prior planning, I was able to grab my phone charger, toiletry bag and luggage, and quickly evacuated to safety. I did not waste precious seconds rushing around trying to find all of my gear.

The best advice I can give you is to not empty your luggage and leave your personal items strewn about the hotel room. For all intents and purposes, think like you are living out of your suitcase. This will allow you to evacuate with all your belongings in under a minute.

» FLASHLIGHT

Remember how I told you to pack a flashlight? Once you unpack, keep that flashlight within arm's reach all night. Whether you face a room intrusion, an attack, a natural disaster, a medical emergency or a simple power outage, a flashlight is an invaluable travel tool. It can be used to provide light for you and others, temporarily blind an assailant, signal for help or be used as an improvised weapon. It does not have to be big, but it should have multiple settings like strobe and steady, high and low intensity, clear and red light options. It should be LED for maximum reliability and longevity. Remember to pack extra batteries unless it is hand cranked or solar charged.

» HOW TO CREATE A BULLETPROOF VEST

To create a makeshift (albeit small) bulletproof vest, tape together the Bible and the Book of Mormon. Most hotel rooms have these two books in them. A phone book also works nicely but may not be as readily available.

If you need to use this, after binding the books together, place them over your heart. Affix them inside your clothing with duct tape, then stay low and out of sight. Keep covered or concealed as long as possible and do not take any chances. Your bullet proof vest is only a backup to your decision to stay hidden.

This is something you should craft when you know an attack or kidnapping is imminent, in which case you should also consider destroying your laptop and any other sensitive information while there is time (pg. 266).

AIRPLANE SECURITY

Be aware of the threats and other dangers you face when flying to maximize your personal security.

❱❱ CHOOSING A SEAT

Aim to book an aisle seat as close to an exit as possible. In the event of an emergency of any kind, you want to ensure your own easy egress from the aircraft. Always be prepared to help the people around you if you can, but set yourself up for success by strategically positioning yourself to take full advantage of the quickest and easiest way out.

❱❱ PAY ATTENTION

Situational awareness is key in every situation. Most people want to zone out and do their own thing during the preflight briefing. This is a bad idea. The information being presented is critical to your own survival if anything should happen during the flight. Read the information card and pay attention to the safety briefing. I realize we seasoned travelers have heard it many, many times, but this is actually a good thing. I believe you should consider yourself pre-programmed to take decisive, meaningful action. Having heard it so many times and then having a refresher right before each flight means, if something happens, you are already equipped with the proper knowledge to know exactly how to respond in a crisis. What you have been taught will take over and you will find yourself carrying out the instructions without thinking about them. It's only your life (pg. 98.) How much is it worth?

❱❱ LETTING YOUR GUARD DOWN

Try not to get in vacation mode as soon as you set foot on the aircraft. More specifically, do not drink alcohol, take sleeping pills or fall asleep until you are 30 minutes into your flight. Allow me to illustrate why this could very well be counterproductive.

I once took sleeping pills an hour before a very long flight was scheduled to depart. I had already acclimated to the destination time zone, and by my calculations, it was time to go to bed. In a perfect world, this might make sense. But to my growing frustration, my flight was delayed, delayed and delayed and then ultimately cancelled. Believe me when I say it was sheer misery trying to keep myself awake while I waited in the terminal. Eventually, I had to stay overnight before getting rebooked on another flight the next day. To sum up my physical and mental state: I was in limbo between two polar opposite time zones, medicated for sleep in the middle of the day at my current location and totally unable to keep up my usual level of situational awareness and personal vigilance. Not good. But like a number of unpleasant experiences, it taught me several important lessons. Amongst them: Wait to drink alcohol, take sleeping pills or otherwise get some shuteye until at least half an hour after takeoff. Why? Because by then, you can be reasonably certain that you are going to continue on your way.

Granted, I realize that it is not at all practical to suggest you should never fall asleep on an airplane. If you travel very long distances, it is going to happen, period. However, you should take comfort in knowing the in-flight portion of your travel is actually the safest part of your trip. Conduct your scans of your surroundings and pay attention to people and details. Maintain condition yellow. Sleeping pills and alcohol lower your ability to think clearly and make accurate observations as well as slowing your reaction times. There is a time and a place for relaxing and unwinding, believe me. Traveling to the airport, going through security, sitting in the terminal and sitting in the plane on the ground are none of those places. Be your own advocate and make the right call to stay alert. Once the aircraft is safely en route and you are satisfied with your own observations, then and only then do I recommend taking these relaxing measures or falling asleep.

❯❯ WHAT TO KEEP ON YOUR PERSON

Keep your shoes on and essential items in your pockets. It is always prudent to think in terms of "What if something happens right now?" to minimize your reaction time and cut down on the number of decisions you will need to make in a crisis. I recommend keeping your shoes on your feet and certain items on your person for the entire duration of the flight. You will want your wallet, keys, passport, phone and charger as well as any important medication in your pockets. If there is a serious incident or accident, you will have no time to try to retrieve these things from your carry-on bag. You will not have much space to maneuver and will definitely want to have your hands free. To streamline your potential need to respond to anything, just ask yourself what you would need to have with you if you had to flee, then keep those things on you the whole time.

» THE PEN

This is one multi-tool that you are allowed to carry aboard any airplane anywhere in the world. Keep a pen on you. If you always have one of these in your pocket, you will at least have one line of defense if you should need it at any point along the way. I am never without mine and I use it to write every day. Mostly, it gives me the comfort of knowing I have some sort of weapon for stabbing, controlling, joint locking and reinforcing my punch, innocuously presented as a nonthreatening pen, always within easy reach, just in case.

» BE OBSERVANT

Notice the passengers around you. It does not take long. You are in a very confined space. What you are looking for in particular is how comfortable or agitated they seem. Are they interacting with anyone? If so, how? Notice their facial expressions, body language, eyes and hands. You will know very quickly if someone is on edge. If you do spot something amiss, you will then need to figure out the probable cause. Use your best judgment. Some people are afraid to fly and this manifests as irritability, nervousness, agitation, etc. Some people do not feel well for any number of reasons whether it is due to having imbibed one too many preflight drinks at the cantina or a destination-related reason like having to attend the funeral of a loved one. Others are grumpy travelers, plain and simple. Just get into the habit of observing the people sharing your flight and take note of any anomalies. Be prepared to respond if need be.

Make note of any potential obstructions between you and the exit. You will need to do this repeatedly throughout the flight as you are in a very dynamic situation. If there are any obstructions at any point during the flight, and there will be, ask yourself exactly what you would do if you needed to get around the obstacle right now. Play the what-if game and keep your brain engaged in problem-solving.

» BE READY

While I have already discussed being awake for at least 30 minutes after takeoff, I also recommend that you be awake for the landing. Rarely do things go wrong during the straight and level en route portion of the flight. It is the takeoff and landing that pose the riskiest times for the aircraft and its passengers. It is a best practice to be awake with your shoes on for the approach and landing phase of every flight. If any emergencies occur and there is anything abnormal about the landing at all, you will want to be aware of the problem and prepared to react or evacuate immediately. Simply being ready in advance of the potential need puts you one step ahead of everyone else.

TAXI SECURITY

Chances are, you will need to take a taxi. Know the risks to better guard yourself against potential threats.

» VETTING

When you travel, it is paramount that you know whom you can trust. When taking a taxi, always vet the taxi company through the airport or the hotel. Do not accept a ride from anyone who offers one to you, even if it appears to be a legitimate taxi. Treat taxis just as you would treat a suspect email: If something looks or seems off, do not open it. Conduct an independent search by looking them up yourself or by verifying the brand with airport or hotel staff.

Taxis are common platforms for cons and ruses of many kinds, up to and including kidnappings and murders. Stick to the companies that the hotels and airports recommend, and you will maximize your own personal security.

» VERIFY AT-WILL EXITS

Make sure that the taxi has door handles on the inside so that you can exit at will. If you start paying attention to this one detail, you will be amazed at how many do not. Never put yourself in any situation where you have no control over your own ability to egress. Aside from the kidnapping implications, if the vehicle gets into an accident, catches on fire or gets submerged in water, your ability to control your own exit will mean the difference between life and death.

» TRUST BUT VERIFY

Always verify the taxi driver's information card and study their face. Make sure that the face you see on the driver matches the face on the information placard. Anyone who is attempting to assume someone else's identity is definitely up to something and it is best not to get anywhere close. Take a photo of the identification placard in case you need to refer back to that driver at some later date. It could be for something good like trusting a driver you already had and requesting them again by name. It could be for something logistical like forgetting something in the taxi and needing to get a hold of the driver to arrange for the item's return. It could be for something bad like having a questionable experience with a driver and reporting them to the hotel or the taxi company. In any event, verify that the information is correct and accurate and take a photo to capture it for later use.

❯❯ LOCK UP

While traveling in a taxi, keep the doors locked and the windows up. (This applies to driving a rental car as well.) It is a common ploy for bad guys to throw something into cars via open windows while the vehicle is in motion. This could be anything from simple propaganda material to an IED. Stopped cars are at risk even when the windows are up. Consider how someone outside the vehicle could open the car door and toss something inside. Beat them to the punch by keeping the door locked.

Similarly, things are stolen out of cars through open windows all the time, even while the vehicle is in motion in slower traffic. Keeping the windows and doors closed and locked will encourage bad guys to look for another target.

AT YOUR DESTINATION

Advice for blending in with the locals, keeping a tab on things and staying safe wherever you go.

❯❯ AVOIDING COUNTERFEIT SCAMS

Unfortunately, there are a fair number of counterfeiting scams perpetrated on tourists at international vacation destinations. They are ingeniously conceived and flawlessly executed. The goal is to swap the counterfeit money in the pocket of the thief with the real money in the pocket of the tourist. Here are a few.

THE "FOUND" WALLET

Pickpockets with all denominations of counterfeit currency will lift the wallet of a tourist, quickly swap out all the real bills for fake ones, and then run after the tourist, yelling that they dropped their wallet. A grateful tourist will thank the scam artist for being so "honest" and returning the dropped wallet, then go on their way with a wallet full of illegal currency, never suspecting a thing.

THE TAXI SCAM

At the end of a taxi ride, the driver will state the fare that is due and the passenger will pull a bill out of their wallet to pay. The driver will accept the bill, deftly conceal it, and covertly produce a counterfeit of the same denomination. He will then hand it back to the passenger, stating that he cannot accept the bill because it is counterfeit. Now, the passenger has to come up with another real bill and is out twice the amount of the taxi fare.

FAKE CHANGE

Tourists will often carry larger denominations of currency. When they pay for a small item with a large bill, they are hoping to gain the usability of smaller bills in change. Often, the change they will receive for their genuine currency will be a fist full of small, counterfeit bills.

CURRENCY EXCHANGE

Scam artists will sometimes hang out on the street in the vicinity of genuine currency exchangers. They will approach tourists and offer to exchange their currency for local currency at a much better rate than the official currency exchange. The tourist, who wants to save money and cut expenses, will take advantage of this deal and will walk away with a stack of counterfeit bills.

So, what do we do? Well, of course we should not stop carrying cash. Here are some suggestions to make yourself harder to scam:

- **Carry small bills so you can pay with exact change. Do not rely on obtaining local change. Refuse to give more than you were originally asked for and do not be afraid to make a scene or call for help if pressed.**

- Use a dummy wallet. Put one credit card, one ID card and a little bit of cash in a cheap wallet and carry it where most people carry their wallets. Let that be your sacrificial pickpocket wallet.

- Leave most of your cash in a secure location and only take a limited amount out with you. Use the hotel safe or hide it in your room (in your luggage; in the pockets of your laundry; between the mattress and the box spring; in the pages of a book; under the couch or any other heavy furniture; in a vent; in the toilet tank; etc.).

- Use a money belt under layers of tucked-in clothes. If you want to have larger amounts of cash on your person, keep most of it there and only keep a small amount in your dummy wallet. **NEVER REFILL YOUR DUMMY WALLET FROM YOUR MONEY BELT IN PUBLIC.**

- Exchange currency before leaving your home country. If you need more local currency at the destination, go to a bank, ATM or an official currency exchange business.

- Do not pay for services upfront.

- Look at the serial number on your own bill before paying for anything.

- Use official taxi companies with actual taxi stands.

- Familiarize yourself with the look and feel of local currency.

- Be slow to believe the bill you just used to pay is a fake and even slower to replace it with another.

When something does not feel right, it usually is not right. Listen to your instincts. If you need to involve the police, do so. Pay attention and use your situational awareness to stay one step ahead of pickpockets and counterfeit scam artists.

» WORLDVIEW

A woman woke up one morning and discovered she only had three hairs left on her head. She carefully shampooed and dried them and then said to herself, "Today, I think I will part my hair on the left." She did that and had a great day. The next day when she woke up, she had only two hairs left. She carefully shampooed and dried them and said, "Today, I shall part my hair in the middle." She did that and had a great day. The next day, when she woke up, she had only one hair left. She carefully shampooed and dried it and said, "Today, I will wear a ponytail." She did that and she had a great day. The next day she woke up and she had no hair left at all. She was completely bald. She smiled and sighed contentedly as she said, "I am so grateful that I do not have to do my hair today!" and she had a great day. (Author unknown)

Our worldview determines everything about us, our decision making capabilities, as well as our ability to improvise, adapt and overcome. I know people who seem to be out of sync with the rest of the world. Everything they do is just a little bit off: They cannot connect with people or keep friends, succeed in a career or make a positive difference to the world around them. I believe that it comes down to their worldview. They live incredibly frustrated lives.

There is a place I love to go hiking. I know that the trails run north and south, along a river. When the terrain is going up, I know I am headed west, away from the river, and that when the terrain is going down, I know I am headed east, toward the river. This means once I get to the river, if I turn left, I am heading north and if I turn right, I am heading south. When I keep all of this in mind, it is impossible for me to get lost. My worldview matches with reality. I understand the geography. Even without a compass and a map, I know how the terrain is laid out and I understand where I am relative to everything else. This worldview allows me to navigate the trails with ease, take as long as I like, and head straight back to my car when I am done, with no fear of getting lost.

In order to live effective lives, we need to make sure that our worldview squares with reality. If we lived in 1940, in an idyllic, suburban community with no crime, we could afford to leave our doors unlocked and our kids unsupervised. The reality of a safe time in a safe location would have allowed us to live with our guard down and we would have been largely OK. But this is not that time, and we are far removed from the relative security of those days. The world has changed in leaps and bounds; it is chaotic and the news bears witness to some pretty unpleasant realities of life. We have been at war for the better part of two decades. What makes this world navigable today is having an accurate worldview.

IF I WANT OR NEED TO TRAVEL, I HAVE THREE OPTIONS. I CAN:
1. Refuse to go out of fear of how things are.
2. Go fearlessly with no prior planning, counting on things abroad to be just like things at home.
3. Be realistic about the state of the world, take the dangers and complexities into account, research and plan, and take my trip.

Having an accurate understanding of my destination and a worldview that matches reality will go far, not only in keeping me safe, but in contributing to my enjoyment.

Make no mistake: I do not recommend pessimism. That robs us of joy and and causes us to forego opportunities out of fear. It also goes against a lot of what I have already described in this book as pertaining to the mindset of a conqueror. But on a similar note, I do not recommend unrealistic optimism. That blinds us to real security concerns and leaves us wide open as soft targets. Take the realist route. It is OK, even accurate, to admit that there are security concerns when we travel. Knowing they exist and ascertaining what they are allows us to navigate our course with the greatest situational awareness and maximize our security and safety. It helps us to plan well, execute our plan and enjoy the experience.

Trust is a wonderful thing, and I definitely recommend having a healthy dose of respect and appreciation for all cultures but I would be remiss if I did not also suggest maintaining a reasonable amount of skepticism. Our world is complicated. In certain places it is dangerous, and it is also wildly beautiful, captivating, surprising and absolutely worth seeing. Beyond travel: Life is worth living. Take the journey. Keeping all of these things in mind and acknowledging real threats where they exist is the worldview that will allow you to go, see, do, touch, taste, smell, experience, live...

And return safely.

▶▶ MODESTY IS THE BEST POLICY

We have talked about living in the gray, meaning choosing not to stand out from the crowd and get noticed as a potential target. Dressing with modesty is one such way to discourage unwanted attention. This applies to men and women alike.

Catching someone's attention through your clothing choices may seem like a positive, but it can also have negative consequences. It will not just be the respectful and settled people whose attention we gain, it will be criminal elements, licentious hearts and those with selfish intent. In a kidnapping situation, the criminals will have two things on their minds: the potential ransom money they stand to gain and the fun the hostage will provide while they wait for the payout. The sad truth is, most people who are kidnapped are also sexually assaulted while in captivity. It is a natural progression.

It does not matter who you are, how you view yourself, your sexual orientation or your gender identification—when you choose to wear revealing or form-fitting clothes, you are likely to turn some heads. And turning heads is, by default, the opposite of going gray. In this case, it could have disastrous ramifications. I am not suggesting that you try to look ugly, but you can use your intellect to determine how much, or little, to reveal.

Look nice, by all means, but pay attention to the baseline. In the same way you might avoid wearing designer clothes in an area that's particularly impoverished, you should use common sense when making decisions about what constitutes proper attire for your situation. You should always dress in a way that does not attract extra attention. It is all part of your advanced preparation.

▶▶ CULTURAL AWARENESS

When operating in a foreign area, blending in and avoiding giving offense may necessitate removing or going without certain things from your wardrobe, accessories or carry items:

- **Bible, Quran, Torah or other sacred texts**
- **Class ring**
- **Colored clothing**
- **Facial hair**

- Hair dye
- Hat or other head covering
- Photos
- Religious jewelry
- Toupee or wig
- Visible brand names
- Visible icons or other religious symbols
- Wedding band on the "wrong" hand

THERE ARE ALSO PLACES WHERE YOU MAY HAVE TO ADD SOMETHING(S):
- Facial covering
- Facial hair
- Facial markings
- Foot covering
- Head covering
- Long pants
- Long sleeves
- Wedding band

Whether adding or removing, keep the cultural and religious norms in mind for the area in which you will be operating, and do your best to respect them by adopting locally accepted practices.

›› NO

There is a rule in hostage negotiation: "Never take responsibility for saying no." There will be times when you have to decline something, turn someone down or refuse someone a request, but the strongest "no" you can deliver is the one that is out of your hands. If someone asks me to host a loud party in my hotel room, I could say something like, "I'm sorry. The hotel says no loud parties." What can they say? It is very difficult to talk me out of my "no" when I am not the decision-making authority.

That is the very reason why, if you are married and agree to attend a timeshare sales presentation, the salesman will insist on speaking with both parties in the couple at the same time. They have no interest in wining and dining one person in an attempt to make a sale, only to have them say at the end of an expensive dinner that they need to go home and discuss it with their spouse.

When you travel, you may want to have ready-made answers to requests or invitations you wish to decline. Things do sometimes come up that leave us feeling cornered if we are not ready. You may meet people on an airplane, bus, train or at your hotel. They may get too chummy with you too fast and ask you to dinner. This is a red flag. You should have an answer in your back pocket that you can pull out and use when you are surprised. It could be something like, "I am fasting tonight," or "I have a phone meeting with my boss tonight," or "My husband/wife wants to have time with me alone." (This comes in handy on your home turf as well, but I digress.)

Now, in order to be a person of integrity, whichever answer you give should be the truth. If you tell them you are fasting tonight, you should actually follow through. Never use a patently false excuse. We call that backstopping. Make sure your story is accurate. If you refer back to God for fasting or your boss for a phone call or the hotel policy against loud parties, you have eliminated the temptation to talk you out of your answer. There is no need to have that discussion when you are not the actual decision maker.

▶▶ SPEED OF MOVEMENT

Have you ever stopped to consider the speed at which you move at any given time and what it might say about you?

Speed can tell us a lot about a person's intentions and general comfort level. When you see a person running, you can suppose that the cause is one of three primary reasons. People usually run for fitness. So, if their pace is rhythmic and they seem unconcerned, if their clothes are workout appropriate and they have headphones in, you can draw the conclusion that they are simply working out. People also run to chase someone or to flee. In these two cases, their pace will be erratic and their clothes are likely street clothes and not exercise clothes. In this case, although focused, they will likely be either scared or angry.

- If a person is walking fast, "with a purpose," we can surmise they are in a hurry. We may not know why, but they are hurrying toward or away from something. They usually come across as mildly uncomfortable in that they seem to be running late for something. Even if they are not late, they are unusually focused and intent upon reaching their goal.

- If a person is meandering, strolling lazily along and stopping to window shop, you can surmise they are unconcerned and quite comfortable in their surroundings.

- If a person is stopped, merely standing or sitting, it is more difficult to tell. They could be enjoying a cup of coffee and catching up on news and emails. Or, they could be surveilling the area. They could be waiting for someone or just trying to pass the time between meetings. They could be uncomfortable or completely comfortable.

If we know the baseline of an area, we can quickly spot the anomalies of speed all around us. We can see who stands out and why. Likewise, if we need to move from point A to point B undetected, we can adopt any of these to reach our intended destination.

For example:

- If I need to move rapidly from point A to B, but I cannot risk standing out, I can put on exercise clothes and headphones and running shoes and no one will think twice about a jogger moving fast.

- If I need to stay in one spot indefinitely, I can have a meal or a coffee or read the news and not stand out.

- If I wish to move a short distance without attracting notice and I wish to stay in street clothes, I can stroll and window shop my way there.

The important thing is to understand the local baseline, be able to identify anomalies around you and choose methods of movement that keep you in the gray.

▶▶ DEAD GIVEAWAYS

Years ago, upon arriving in Poland for a visit, I was going down an escalator
to exit the terminal and saw a sign warning visitors to guard their wallets and
valuables closely, citing that pickpocketing was a problem. As I looked down
the escalator ahead of me, everyone else was reading that sign, too. As soon as
they did, most people did exactly the same thing: the men patted their pockets
to check for their wallets and the ladies dug into their purses. Then I looked
all the way down to the floor where we were headed and saw a few local men
and children carefully observing everyone's arrival. They were all smiles as
they greeted people exiting the escalator and offering them rides or trying to
sell them candy and gum. Putting two and two together, I quickly saw the con.

The men and children watched every traveler who read the sign, knowing
that most if not all of them would immediately reach for their wallets. All the
bad guys had to do was choose a target and get close enough to offer a ride or
try to make a sale, and then deftly pick the pocket with the wallet in it. Most
people would not know their wallet was missing until the end of their taxi
ride, far away from that escalator.

That taught me a valuable lesson about discretion. I, too, wanted to know
that my wallet was safe, but instinct told me not to give its location away
publicly. I restrained myself from reaching for it, opting instead to affect
a casually unconcerned aura. Before I left the terminal, I went into the
restroom, into a stall, where I checked the status of my wallet and passport
in private. I chose a secure location for both, putting a little bit of cash in my
pocket, and headed out to grab a taxi. If anyone had picked my pocket, they
would have gotten my decoy cash and not my stash.

Think about the security implications of your own actions. Are any of your
actions dead giveaways?

▶▶ TALK LESS, LISTEN MORE

What do we learn when we talk? Very little. It is unusual for me to say
something that I did not already know. What do we learn when we listen?
Much. Sometimes more than you can imagine.

Whether you are traveling abroad or thinking about personal security,
get into the habit of listening. You will be amazed what you can pick up on

through simple observation and good listening skills. If you are conversing with someone overseas, they can tell you about exciting places to visit and things to do, bad neighborhoods of which you should steer clear, special events, cultural norms and nuances, where to get a good bargain, local trouble from gangs or cartels, high risk areas, weather patterns and dangers, how to dress for protection from the elements, who makes the best coffee in town, and many more things that will add to the security and enjoyability of your trip.

Hear them out. Always give serious weight to the words and opinions of the locals.

▶▶ POCKET LITTER

Most of us may not have heard this term. Pocket litter is exactly what it sounds like: the things most often found in the pockets of the average person. What you have in your pockets can say a lot about you.

RECEIPTS

Aside from telling a thief where you were and when, receipts can also tell him/her about your habits, preferences, routines and even your level of wealth.

CREDIT CARDS

Although they can help you make large purchases quickly before you report your card lost or stolen, credit cards can be used to access records about purchase history, by a savvy thief.

BANK RECEIPTS AND/OR DEBIT CARDS

A savvy thief can gain access to bank records and proceed to look up your real estate and tax records.

KEYS

Keys tell a lot about a person: what kind of car they drive, at least one layer of their home security apparatus, whether they have a P.O. box, where they shop and have memberships, whether their home mailbox locks, etc.

BUSINESS CARDS

People usually carry their own business cards and those of their professional contacts. This is incredibly valuable information. It tells a thief what company you work for and your position there, as well as the kinds of professional associations you have and your general level of income. People also carry business cards of the people whose services they need or use: hairdresser, plumber, daycare, etc.

None of these things on their own present a problem or other security risk. However, if you are going to spend time in any region of the world where kidnapping for ransom occurs, the things in your pockets paint a very comprehensive picture about you to the kidnappers. It tells them enough to demand everything you can pay and know, with some accuracy, what you can afford. When you travel abroad, consider keeping your pockets litter free, and keep your information to yourself.

‣ WHY ELICITATION WORKS

The world in which we now live is not like the one in which we grew up. It is much more difficult to navigate than it has ever been before and it is harder to know with absolute certainty that we are safe from information theft. One of the key ways in which foreign governments obtain useful and proprietary information is by using elicitation. This is a gentle probe for information which is so nonthreatening that an untrained person will never even know it has happened to them. Allow me to arm you with the knowledge base to understand, spot and avoid elicitation attempts.

The reason people succumb to elicitation is that it is designed to prey on certain facets of human nature. Some of these include:

- **Our tendency to believe that people are, by and large, honest and well-intentioned.**
- **Our belief that to be suspicious of other humans is to be a bad person.**
- **Our unflagging hopefulness to be able to convert people's opinions to match our own.**
- **Our desire to feel important.**
- **Our desire to not be rude.**
- **Our desire to appear intelligent.**
- **Our desire to be helpful to others.**
- **Our desire to be appreciated.**

- Our desire to contribute something useful and/or valuable.
- Our desire to appear knowledgeable.
- Our natural instinct to be honest.
- Our enjoyment at hearing our own voice.
- Ego gratification.
- Our eagerness to gossip.
- Our desire for praise.
- Our willingness to expound on a topic of interest to us.
- Our willingness to correct false impressions or misinformation.
- Our tendency to underestimate the value of what we know.

We are human beings with feelings and interests. This is the platform upon which all elicitation attempts are made. Keep these in mind when you interact with people in foreign countries.

» METHODS OF ELICITATION

The methods of elicitation are surprisingly natural. Some of those methods include:

- The three step: starting a conversation about something harmless, transitioning to the subject of interest, then transitioning back into harmless territory.

- The ruse of feigning a questionnaire or survey to gain placement and access.

- Expressing mutual interest in the subject of interest.

- Using active listening skills to encourage talking.

- Stroking the ego with flattery.

- Pretending to be a student of the subject of interest and affecting a deferential manner with the person, in hopes that they will proceed to teach.

- Telling the person a story in the hope that they will reciprocate and even top it.

- Pretending to divulge sensitive or confidential information in the hope that the person will reciprocate.

- Criticizing a "common enemy" and using that to develop rapport and encourage the person to divulge data.

- Criticizing a friendly organization in hopes that the person will defend them with useful information.

- Discussing an indirect but related topic in the hope that the person will reveal something usable.

- Creating a quid pro quo situation in which the person feels that they owe the elicitor something.

- Repeating key words the person has used to encourage them to expound.

- Creating a ruse of being a recruiter for a company that is interested in hiring the person.

- Pretending to have knowledge on the subject of interest already.

- Stating a low price and a high price and encouraging the person to be more specific.

- Making a deliberately false statement in the hope that the person will correct it.

- Asking about an organization to which the person does not belong.

- Quoting facts, statistics and references for open source data on the subject of interest.

- Making a statement that requires clarification and enticing the person to ask questions.

- Pretending to be completely ignorant of the subject of interest and encouraging the person to educate.

- Feigning disbelief in the subject of interest and encouraging the person to defend it with data.

- Opening the conversation broadly and gradually narrowing down the focus to the subject of interest.

- Asking a leading question with an accurate or inaccurate presupposition, in hopes that the person will confirm or deny it.

- Using the allure of an attractive man or woman and express interest on a personal level and use flirtation to encourage talking.

- Making a statement that is derogatory or dismissive of the person and encouraging them to defend themselves with information that will restore your high opinion of them.

Elicitation is a psychological game where the payoffs can be significant. But what do you do once you read the writing on the wall and realize an elicitation attempt is taking place?

▸▸ HOW TO HANDLE ELICITATION ATTEMPTS

There are four basic categories of potential responses to an elicitation attempt: ignore, evade, engage or outmaneuver.

IGNORE

You can ignore the encounter entirely, but this is very difficult to do. It flies in the face of our desire not to be rude.

EVADE

You can evade by giving a vague answer, stating that you do not know the information, referring the elicitor to open source material, asking why they want to know, or even claiming not to have time to talk. This is the middle ground choice. It is easier to do than ignoring and not nearly as dangerous as engaging.

ENGAGE

This is the most dangerous choice because this pings the radar of the elicitor and any possible superiors. However, you can directly state that you cannot discuss the subject with them. If you choose this response, raise your level of situational awareness for a time to ascertain if you are under surveillance. Someone may try to follow you.

OUTMANEUVER

This response requires training. At this stage of the encounter, you are willingly entering the arena and agreeing to play the game. The risk you run is inadvertently giving away the information you are trying to protect.

If you encounter a serious elicitation attempt or threat, report it to the authorities right away. If you already have a clearance job, report it to your security officer. Do not brush it off lightly.

EXTREME SURVIVAL SITUATIONS

LIFE-SAVING TIPS DESIGNED FOR WORST-CASE SCENARIOS.

THESE ARE ARGUABLY the most nightmarish situations you could ever encounter when it comes to fighting for your life. Familiarizing yourself with their risks and developing a survivor (or, more accurately, conqueror) mentality now means considerably increasing your chances of survival should you find yourself in mortal danger later. Whether it be kidnapping, volcanoes, avalanches, sinking cars or acts of terrorism, know your options when it comes to avoiding and outlasting the worst.

HOW TO HANDLE A SINKING CAR

Being trapped in a vehicle while it sinks in water is any human being's idea of a nightmare. It is a horrifying scenario, but take heart: It is survivable. The key is you must immediately acknowledge what is happening and respond as it unfolds. In a slow and gentle sinking, you have less to worry about, but not more time. However, most vehicular water tragedies begin with a real impact.

IF YOU SEE THE IMPACT COMING:
- Sit up straight.
- Wear your seatbelt.
- Look straight ahead.
- Rest your head back against the headrest.
- Give yourself ample space from the steering wheel. Do not lock your elbows as you hold the steering wheel. As hard as this might be to imagine, relax your body. The reason drunk drivers and babies sustain a lower rate of injuries in accidents is that they do not tense up and brace for impact.
- As soon as your vehicle hits the water, unbuckle your seatbelt, unlock the doors and immediately lower the window. The water will very quickly damage the electrical system and the windows will cease to work, not to mention the fact that the pressure of the water on the doors seals them shut. Even if the car takes a minute to sink, you lose your ability to control windows and locks immediately. For this reason, it is prudent to stow a seat belt cutter and a glass breaker in your vehicle within reach of the driver's seat. You should have multiple methods of releasing yourself.
- Do not wait one nanosecond.
- Do not open the door.
- Swim out of the window you opened. The space you gave yourself by distancing yourself from the steering wheel will give you the ability to maneuver your way out. Break free and get to the surface. If there are multiple people in the car, everyone needs to do the same thing: ditch their own seatbelt, open their window and swim out. If there are young children in the car, open their windows for them and start freeing them immediately.

If you have gulped down the air trapped in the car with you, make sure to exhale on your swim to the surface to avoid a lung overexpansion injury. Get clear of the wreckage and the water and seek help. All of this requires having a cool head. Remember that panic kills but calm is contagious. You can do this.

COOPERATIVE EVACUEE

Hurricanes abound. One of the best things we can do is to behave as cooperative evacuees. If local law enforcement issues a mandatory evacuation order, we need to comply. Depending on how much advance notice you have or the intensity of the storm, you may be able to do all of these things or a select few. The priority is making it to safety, so you will need to choose wisely.

When it comes to evacuations, you will want to heed warnings, pack and head away from the affected area as soon as humanly possible to avoid getting stuck in departing traffic.

- Maintain an orderly departure and stay calm. Do not cause chaos or create panic.
- Take all the supplies with you that you will need for your own survival and comfort.
- Take your most precious possessions with you. If you are being told to evacuate, there is a fair chance your home and belongings might be destroyed as the storm progresses. Chances are you will not have enough room to take everything with you, so grab your top priority items and secure the rest at home.
- Move your valuable or irreplaceable items as high up in your home as you can if flooding is expected.
- Turn off the water, gas and electricity before you go.
- Take your pets with you.
- Take all your medications and medical devices with you.
- Bring anything that can be blown away by hurricane force winds inside your home, like patio furniture, small potted plants, grills, etc.
- Board your windows.
- Tie down your roof.
- As you travel away from the area, stay clear of high water, flooded roads and downed power lines.
- Pay attention to detours, emergency routes and changes of travel direction.
- Head inland.
- Let people know you are safely out of harm's way.

MASTER TACTIC

HERE ARE SOME TIPS FOR ENSURING YOUR HOME IS HURRICANE-READY YEAR-ROUND:

• Ensure your sump pump is working.

• Clear your gutters of debris.

• Cut down the dead limbs on your trees.

• Cut your bushes back.

SURVIVING VOLCANOES

To many of us, this will seem pretty far-fetched as far as threats are concerned, but there are places in the world where volcanic eruptions are a very real concern. Here are some things you can do ahead of time, during the event and afterwards to maximize your safety.

BEFORE

• Do some research. Is your home or intended destination located inside the "ring of fire" of the Pacific Rim, in Mexico or in the Rift Valley of East Africa? Have there been any known volcanic eruptions recently? If so, have there been any alerts issued?

• Procure certain items and keep them handy: face mask or smoke hood, goggles that seal, long-sleeved shirt, long pants, medical supplies, flashlights, radio, water and food.

• Have a plan for evacuation and communications.

• Prepare a bug-out bag (pg. 22).

DURING

• Wear your goggles, face mask, long pants and long-sleeved shirt.

• Evacuate to a safe indoor location.

• Take your pets with you or bring them inside.

• Have an alternate plan of evacuation that does not include motor vehicles or airplanes, since ash clogs engines and lava melts rubber tires.

• Put distance and terrain between you and the lava flow. Be aware of its flow path.

- Take the high road if you can. Lava and water flow downhill. Be aware of irregular water levels and flow paths.
- If you are in a safe facility, keep all the windows and doors tightly sealed to keep out as much ash as possible.
- Turn off the environmental system and close all vents.
- Close the fireplace flue.
- Listen to the radio for updates.
- Stay hydrated.
- Tend to any open wounds or burns immediately to prevent developing an infection.
- Stay inside until there is an announcement that venturing outdoors is safe.

AFTER

- Seek medical attention.
- Alert your loved ones to your status.
- Make sure you are cleared before heading back into the affected area.
- Take care of your physical needs: eat, sleep, stay hydrated, etc.

THE QUESTIONS TO ASK TO FORMULATE A TARGET SEARCH AREA

When searching for a missing person in any situation, you can quickly take the search from a "needle in a haystack" scenario to a highly specific, target-area search by asking intelligent questions.

- What time were they last seen?
- Is anyone else missing?
- If so, are they together?
- What is the average walking speed on this terrain?
- Draw a circle on the map with a diameter of that distance around the point where they were last seen.
- What is the direction they have most likely taken?
- Are they constantly walking or sometimes stopping?
- Do they have a history of taking off?
- What do they like: isolation or population? Are they introverted or extroverted?

- **What kind of clothing and shoes are they wearing?**
- **What is the local weather?**
- **Do they have knowledge of the area?**
- **Do they have any known health issues?**
- **Do they have survival skills?**
- **Do they have gear and/or supplies?**
- **What are the regional (terrain-based) boundaries?**

Shade the area inside the circle that fills all the criteria discovered by the answers to these questions and you will have your primary target area to search. You can change the search area with new information. Incredibly, 68 percent of lost people are found within a three-mile radius of their last known location, no matter how much time elapses.

It is far better to take the time to ask and answer these questions and narrow down a target search area than to head out blindly without a plan. The investment of time upfront might mean the difference between success and failure.

SURVIVING AN AVALANCHE

How many of us love snow sports? Skiing. Snowboarding. Snowmobiling. Snowshoeing. Winter hiking. Mountain climbing. Ice climbing. I know I do. I would rather ski than breathe. There is nothing I find as exhilarating as quietly slaloming down a sparsely populated trail. Sometimes at night, I lay awake for hours and listen to the sound of distant thunder. In actuality, that is the sound of an intentional and controlled avalanche. In an effort to prevent natural avalanches from consuming their customers, ski resorts the world over will detonate charges high up in the mountains at night to knock loose the precariously hanging snow. From a safe and comfortable distance, it is awesome and even beautiful to behold. But nothing strikes fear into the heart of even the most seasoned mountain climber like the idea of an avalanche.

Some years ago, I was doing some winter mountaineering in the Rockies. I had a snowmobile and was going through my paces, taking all the steepest and riskiest routes. After hours of maneuvers, I came to the top of the steepest terrain I had ever attempted. A local told me this sheer face was colloquially referred to as Suicide Hill. I asked why but he would not answer the question until I had successfully traversed down to the bottom. It was a white knuckle route. I could not brake for very long without fishtailing so I had to pump the brakes briefly and try to keep the snowmobile pointed in the right direction. When I got to the bottom, I was finally told that, the winter prior, a man and woman attempted this run on snowmobiles. They had been wearing helmet-mounted cameras and they had caused an avalanche. Both of them died and their own helmet cams had recorded their deaths, footage that is now used by forensics teams who study avalanche-related deaths.

Could anything have been done to prevent that avalanche? Could anything have been done to survive it? If the two snowmobilers had correctly read the signs that day, they could have prevented it by choosing a different route.

IF ANY OF THESE SIGNS ARE PRESENT, AVOID USING THE SLOPE BELOW THEM
- An overhang of wet snow
- Recent cracks
- The shady side of the mountain
- Steep terrain
- Recent rain
- A recent earthquake
- A recent avalanche
- Hollow-sounding snow
- Wind coming from behind a snowy overhang
- Backcountry and/or non-groomed terrain
- A foot or more of fresh snow on a steep face
- Local knowledge that the area is dangerous

THERE ARE DECISIONS YOU CAN MAKE IF YOU HAVE TO TRAVERSE THROUGH A RISKY AREA
- Traverse the slope as high up as you possibly can.
- Never go there alone.
- Connect yourself by rope to your teammates and do not let go.
- Pay attention to weather conditions: recent, current and forecast.
- Plan a route that will take you as close as possible to large, solid objects like boulders

and trees and stay uphill of them.
• Carry a cigarette lighter.

IF YOUR POWERS OF PREVENTION HAVE FAILED YOU AND YOU FIND YOURSELF CAUGHT IN AN AVALANCHE, HERE ARE THE TIPS THAT WILL GIVE YOU THE BEST CHANCE FOR SURVIVAL

• Jump uphill of any crack that forms in your presence.
• Get to the edge of the slope as soon as possible. The avalanche will funnel the snow down the center, trying to create or follow a trough.
• Kick off your skis, snowboard and snowshoes, and let go of your poles and backpack.
• Grab on to anything you pass, like a tree or a boulder.
• "Swim" perpendicular to the cascading snow in an effort to stay on top of it.
• If you feel yourself getting buried, cover your face with your hands and try to create space for a pocket of air.
• Try to make your body as big as possible to create as much space for wiggling as you can. Inhale to inflate your lungs. Spread your elbows apart. Nod your head back and forth in exaggerated movements.
• Light that lighter to determine which direction is up.
• Begin to dig and, if possible, punch your hand up as far as it will go to create a ventilation shaft.
• Do not fight or exhaust yourself. Conserve your strength until the avalanche has stopped and then use it to tunnel out.

Make no mistake, avalanches are killers. The best rule for all survival is prevention and avoidance. However, if you do find yourself in this dangerous situation, using these tips will maximize your chances of survival and rescue.

SURVIVING A GRENADE

There is no way that anyone can guarantee your survival of a close encounter with a grenade. However, if you should find yourself in that undesirable circumstance, following these simple steps will maximize your survivability.

Grenades explode upwards in a cone shape. Do you remember the difference between cover and concealment? Cover stops bullets. Concealment only hides you. Some examples of cover are: thick wood, granite, steel, concrete, brick, cement, trees and boulders. If cover is within three steps, run to cover. If not, move quickly and prepare to get as low as possible.

You will likely suffer injuries from the blast and the shrapnel, but carefully following this procedure will afford you the greatest chance of survival.

HOW TO DO IT

1. Take two giant leaping strides away from the grenade and hit the deck.

2. Point your feet toward the grenade to protect your head.

3. Lying on your stomach, cross your legs to protect the femoral arteries.

4. Open your mouth to prevent lung rupture.

5. Cover your ears, elbows tucked in tight, to protect your tympanic membranes from rupturing.

6. Close your eyes.

YOU'VE BEEN KIDNAPPED

How to prepare for the worst and hopefully live to tell the tale.

►► CLASSIC KIDNAPPING PRETEXTS

There are many ways criminals will initiate a kidnapping overseas. Some ways are more common than others, and knowing how to recognize them could mean the difference between ending your evening back at the hotel, or in captivity.

THE BUMP

Kidnappers will choose a target in a vehicle and follow the vehicle to an opportune location. The driver of the abduction vehicle will choose a point at which the target vehicle is stopped and gently bump their vehicle into the target's vehicle. Every driver's first instinct is to stop, put the car in park, get out and assess the damage. When they do so, the kidnappers act, taking the person and sometimes their vehicle, too.

YOUR STRATEGY Do not get out of the car. Drive away from the scene and head to a police station or embassy to assess the damage and make an official report. You are better off explaining the situation to the authorities and risking a fine or jail time than putting yourself at risk of being kidnapped.

THE GOOD SAMARITAN

When walking down the street in a foreign city or town, it is not unusual to be approached by people of any age seeking help. It could be a man, woman or child. They could be asking for money, food or help with anything else. That is a common pretext for kidnappers to be able to get close to their target.

YOUR STRATEGY Look around for any other people who appear to be connected with the supplicant or who are watching you. If you feel any unease, do not go with them. Politely but firmly refuse and depart the scene.

THE TRAP

Like the first scenario, this one happens in vehicles on the road. The target vehicle will be stopped or parked and suddenly surrounded on three sides by other vehicles. With no way out and nowhere to run, the kidnappers have their target trapped.

YOUR STRATEGY Think outside the box. There may be more ways to get away than staying in your lane. Push cars out of the way with your vehicle. Drive on the sidewalk. Use your horn to attract attention.

THE HOTEL GRAB AND GO

Kidnappers will use stairwells to gain accessibility to the closest rooms and wait for their target to come or go. Out of sight of the lobby and the front desk, they can pounce on their target and whisk them away via the stairwell and out a side door.

YOUR STRATEGY Regardless of whether or not you suspect you will be kidnapped, be sure to vary your routes when entering or leaving your room. If you use the stairs, keep your head on a swivel and your condition orange. Boost your situational awareness by looking as far up and down the staircase as you can and try to see things in advance. Keep your hands free and your knife, mace, tactical pen or other weapon within easy reach.

PHONY CHECK POINTS

Checkpoints are not uncommon overseas, especially in crisis areas. However, they can be faked with relative ease and kidnappers know that people are very reluctant not to stop for something that looks official. Once the target vehicle is stopped in what has become a choke point, the driver is trapped and easy to kidnap.

YOUR STRATEGY Do not stop at checkpoints in a country where kidnapping is a known problem. Continue through at a respectable speed and contact your embassy if you think you may have broken the law. Again, you are far better off explaining your situation to the authorities than potentially getting kidnapped.

BREAKING AND ENTERING

This can happen in a house, hotel, office or car. The kidnappers do their homework and surveil their target until they know that person's pattern of life. The kidnappers either sneak in quietly or kick the door down, take their target and go.

YOUR STRATEGY Live in condition yellow. Keep your doors locked and your weapon in reach. Be prepared to defend yourself. Pay attention to the local baseline and train yourself to notice anomalies. If you spot an anomaly, move from condition yellow to orange.

THE DIRECT APPROACH

Sometimes a solo kidnapper will approach a target and reveal a gun, forcing the person to go with them to a secondary location, where they will then rendezvous with the rest of the gang.

YOUR STRATEGY These are the sorts of moments that justify having trained in self-defense against an armed attacker. Do it now, before such a scenario has an opportunity to occur. Be prepared to fight back and remember your rabid chipmunk.

THE RUSE

This can be something as simple as someone tugging excitedly at your sleeve and telling you they have found money. They want to show it to you and they want you to come around the corner with them to see it. Do not go with them.

YOUR STRATEGY Remain aloof and seemingly preoccupied as you continue on your way without stopping to acknowledge what they want you to see. In reality, be focused on the potential threat.

DIVIDE AND CONQUER

This is often used when the target is a jogger. The kidnappers will station themselves out of sight at a point along the target's usual path. They will choose the best spot along the route for maximum concealment and split up, each covering a possible escape route. As the unsuspecting jogger passes in between them, they will converge and overpower their target.

YOUR STRATEGY Choose a route that gives you good lines of sight and yards of clear space on either side of your path. If someone tries to ambush you, it will take them a second to break cover and get to you. That will be all you need to grab your tactical pen and flip the script. If you're a strong runner, bolt away from your attackers and outdistance them until you can get to safety. Just make sure your chosen route avoids terrain that allows for hiding someone too close to the path.

FAKE ID

Kidnappers pose as workers of any sort to gain placement and access to their target. These false personas can be a plumber, a delivery person, an electrician, a caterer, a mail carrier, room service, maintenance personnel or anyone else who might have reason to knock on your door.

YOUR STRATEGY If you have not initiated a request for service, do not let them in. If you think they might be legitimate, call their company and verify their presence before allowing them entrance.

It is not my intention to teach you not to trust anyone, just to be situationally aware and use sound judgment. Remember, when something does not feel right, it generally is not right. Get off the X. Move to a safe location and trust your instincts.

➤➤ DEFEATING THE SHOCK OF CAPTURE

When kidnappers first lay hands on their target, they all have one thing in common. All kidnapping gangs, cartels, terrorists and rings will begin the relationship with their victim by a massive display of dominance. They will cause fear and intimidation in their victim by yelling, swearing, barking out orders and beating the person mercilessly. This is intended to produce immediate compliance on the part of the victim. It is also meant to put the victim into a state of shock and numbness, where they pay no attention to the details of the setting and situation.

Now is the time to remember advanced preparation of the battle space (pg. 13). Remember that the battle space is your mind. Now is the time to decide what you will do in such an event. This will only work for you if you spend a bit of time imagining getting caught in that scenario and imagining yourself taking action on your own behalf. Make a checklist and decide what you will do. Stick to it.

- Make a conscious effort to slow your breathing and your heart rate.
- Calm yourself down.
- Try to notice how many people there are.
- Note if they are male, female or, if there are multiple people involved, a mix.

- Note if they are armed and with what.
- Note the make and color of the vehicle into which you are being forced.
- Note the direction the vehicle is pointed.
- Pay attention to the direction of travel. You will either be hooded or pushed to the floor where you cannot see. That is OK—you can still pay attention to a few things. Orient the vehicle to a cardinal direction in your mind. Track with it as it makes turns and try to understand the direction of travel.
- Note how long it took to get from the kidnapping site to the secondary location.
- Note the smells and sounds when they take you out of the vehicle.
- How many steps are there from the vehicle to the inside of the structure?
- Did they take you up or down any stairs?
- Did you hear any other captives?
- Ask for water, food and a blanket.
- Humanize yourself to your captors.
- Make them aware of your medical needs.
- Be polite and respectful, never belligerent.
- Ask for time and space to pray.
- Show them compassion and demonstrate that you regard them as individual humans.
- Notice if any of the kidnappers seems uncomfortable with their job.
- Target that person regularly for compassion and humanization.

These are some of the things you can do immediately to force your mind to work, force yourself to pay attention and slip into the role of conqueror within the first moments of capture. Each of these things is a small victory. You are exercising your resiliency and setting yourself up for success. This helps you not to succumb to learned helplessness, despair or victimhood. Again, this will only work for you if you decide to do it now.

▶▶ NEVER NEGOTIATE AGAINST YOURSELF

If you should ever find yourself surviving a kidnapping situation, be extremely careful what you say to your captors. The one all-important piece of information they will want is the maximum amount of money your loved ones can pay for your safe return. If you talk about your bank accounts, sports car, vacation plans or any other assets, they will not settle for anything less than everything you have. No matter what happens or how scared you feel, never disclose financial information to your captors. You may think you can control the situation by revealing secret savings accounts, but the more you disclose, the longer they will hold you. They will not be satisfied until they have squeezed every last penny out of you, your family and your community.

However, bear in mind what kinds of things are public record. The amount in your savings account is not, but the properties and vehicles in your name are. Do not lie if your captors disclose to you what their research about you has revealed.

Instead of talking about your money and holdings, talk about yourself. Humanize yourself to your captors. Talk about your family, your life and your needs. Do not allow yourself to be drawn into negotiating for your own release against your family on the other end. Keep your financial knowledge secret.

» PROOF OF LIFE

When a loved one has been kidnapped for ransom, the very first thing to establish is proof they are still alive. The kidnappers are asked to produce some kind of evidence that their captive is alive and worth the ransom they are demanding. Cutting off a finger and sending it to the family is a popular scare tactic, but it will not work for proof of life. It only proves the identity of the person they are holding, not the fact that their hostage is still alive.

Proof of life is something that must be established on a regular basis throughout the ordeal. Kidnappers have been known to hold their victims for months and, in some cases, years. Proof of life must be updated regularly.

The first and best thing for which to ask is to be allowed to talk to the victim on the phone. You will know the voice of your loved one, even under tremendous stress. Carrying on a conversation with the captive proves that they are still alive. Kidnappers are very reluctant to grant this request and will usually say no because of their own security concerns. They do not want your loved one revealing anything sensitive to you.

Another method of proving the hostage is alive is releasing a video with the date and time embedded in it. If that is the method to which the captors agree, it only establishes that their captive was alive at the time and date on the video, but it is usually a very recently made video. It can be only hours old.

Kidnappers will usually make their victim express their demands in the video and plead with their own family to pay whatever is being asked and save their life. While it is relieving for the family to see their loved one alive, it is traumatizing to see them in that situation.

A third option for obtaining proof of life is to have the kidnappers take a photograph of their captive holding a daily newspaper. If you can read the date of the newspaper edition, that will prove that your loved one was alive on that day. It is not unreasonable to ask for that photo on the same day it is taken.

A popular proof of life request is to ask the kidnappers to ask your loved one a question to which only they would know the answer. Kidnappers will usually approve this method because there is no risk to them. In a proof of life video, photograph or phone call, there is risk of leaking data. In a relayed question and answer, there is less risk to them.

In order for this method to work, both the asker and the answerer must know the answer. The best way to ensure this is for you and your loved ones to establish now what your proof of life questions and answers will be. Each person should know the answers they are expected to give.

The final, usual method for obtaining proof of life is to tell the kidnappers that you want a photograph or a video of your loved one doing or wearing something very specific, something they could not anticipate and will have to create upon your request. For example, you could request a photo or video of your loved one wearing red shorts and a green shirt. Or, you could request a photo or video of your loved one kicking a soccer ball. Since they will have to go and create it after you request it, it will establish proof that your loved one is still alive.

ALL ABOUT TERRORISM

How to spot and deal with radical extremists of all stripes.

❯❯ ONLINE CLUES

If you pay close attention, there are ways you can detect a terrorist in the making. That said, please do not become paranoid. Be alert. Be vigilant. However, you cannot maintain condition orange or red for very long without it taking a significant toll on your mental health, physical health and overall morale. Of course, what I am advocating here is to truly live in condition yellow: relaxed but aware.

Everyone and anyone who uses the internet—friends, family, co-workers, classmates, fellow congregants, etc.—has ample exposure and opportunity to be radicalized. Does this mean it will happen to everyone? No, but there is a segment of the population that is susceptible to extremist propaganda. People who feel ostracized and abandoned by their own society are at high risk of being inculcated by terrorist groups. The Islamic State of Iraq and the Levant, a.k.a. ISIL, knows this well and uses this data masterfully in their recruitment efforts. They appeal to the young and emotionally volatile, people who are lonely and hurting, to rebels and to those who are looking for a cause to support. They have a robust recruitment program and, once a person has been drawn to their twisted ideals, that individual is given all the training and other resources they could possibly need to mount an attack anywhere in the world.

If someone you know begins to manifest these online signs, it is time to speak up and say something, by which I mean contact the police or the FBI:

- **Deleting true-name social media accounts.**
- **Setting up avatars and aliases.**
- **Downloading encrypted applications for mobile devices.**
- **Web searches about terrorism, bomb making or mass attacks.**
- **Changing phone numbers or carriers.**
- **Deleting profiles.**
- **Closing online accounts.**
- **Deleting search history.**
- **Deleting known email accounts.**
- **Setting up temporary accounts.**

If you see one or two of these signs, there is a chance the person in question may simply be increasing their own level of personal security. However, if you see many or all of these signs, it is painting a picture you cannot afford to ignore.

Pay attention. If you see something, say something. If you suspect you are dealing with a potential terrorist in the making, do not confront them. Bypass them and go directly to the authorities as soon as you see anything that genuinely worries you.

›› VERBAL CLUES

Listen when the people around you are talking. What do you hear? If they are saying any or all of these things, it is time to say something:

- Praising any violent extremist group's ideals.
- Showing sympathy or understanding for terrorist causes.
- Supporting violence as a means to an end.
- Showing an interest in traveling to war zones and conflict areas.
- Showing frustration at their own boring life.
- Showing contempt for their own society.
- A sudden interest in weapons and explosives.
- A disdain for their own geographic setting, usually coupled by a desire to relocate to a specific region.
- A desire to get involved in something exciting.
- An interest in a language they do not currently speak.

Again, watch for trends and patterns. Watch for multiple signs to emerge and begin to paint a picture.

›› BEHAVIORAL CLUES

A huge tell that something is wrong is the way a person begins to behave such as:

- Isolating themselves.
- Taking up with new and questionable friends.
- Becoming serious, ill-tempered or impatient.
- Altering their established routine.
- The inability to make eye contact when talking with you.
- Purchasing or stockpiling weapons and/or bomb-making components.
- Sneaking around.
- Refusing to talk about how they have been, what they have been up to and whom they

have been seeing.
- A loss of interest in the things they used to love.
- Strange/new/suspicious travel patterns.
- Training in combat styles, techniques or tactics.
- Buying one or several burner phones.
- Severing long-standing relationships.
- Laughing at things you would consider to be cruel, disturbing or graphic.
- Becoming fascinated with violence and blood.
- A religious conversion.
- Changing their diet.
- Changing their sleep habits.
- Insomnia.
- Emotionally checking-out.

Look for trends. These things do not usually happen overnight but occur gradually. Do not panic if you see one or two of these things, but if you see the whole list, it is time to pay attention and prepare to get the authorities involved if necessary. It is important to know the person's behavioral baseline so you are able to detect the changes.

» THE EIGHT SIGNS

What can you do once someone has been radicalized? Chances are you will not be able to change their mind and I am not suggesting you try. These individuals have chosen to align themselves with the bad guys. If you have not yet alerted the authorities, look for these tells and make the call.

There are eight classic signs you might see in someone who is actively planning to carry out a terrorist attack. If you are switched on and maintaining condition yellow, there is a very good chance that you will see one or more of these things if they are happening around you. As you stay situationally aware and know what to look for, you may be the one to spot the abnormal behavior, report it to the police and stop the attack in its planning stages.

1. SURVEILLANCE

Every operation starts here. There is a certain level of detailed intelligence that cannot be acquired by any means other than surveillance. If you see a person, or people, conducting surveillance on a site, facility or person, it is time for you to go into condition orange and watch them. They could be photographing, video recording, audio recording, note taking, dictating, reporting into a cell phone or radio or some combination of these. They will be especially interested in access and egress points, hours of operation, alarms, security personnel, shift changes, traffic patterns, population numbers of a particular site or building, routes traveled by individuals, schedules, dogs, proximity to the police department and getaway routes.

Naturally, as you may have guessed, there are some valid reasons for doing this in normal society. It could be a person or a crew making a video; the alarm company or site security company assessing their own vulnerabilities; the electric company, the water company or other utility company surveying for work; or the local government doing the same thing. That is why I recommend elevating your condition to orange and watching. Try to ascertain if they have a legitimate reason for being there and doing whatever it is they are doing. If you think not, observe their body language and facial expressions. Are they tense? Overly focused? Looking around furtively to see if anyone notices them? Are they communicating with anyone? What are they saying? Are they acting professionally? Does this seem routine or abnormal? Are they sweating?

Your senses will paint a picture for you and tell you if all is not right. If you are suspicious, report it.

2. INFORMATION GATHERING

This step is essentially meant to gather the same information as the surveillance did but to gather it differently. In surveillance, we learned that the information in which they are chiefly interested is: access and egress points, hours of operation, alarms, security personnel, shift changes, traffic patterns, population numbers of a particular site or building, routes traveled by individuals, schedules, dogs, proximity to the police department and getaway routes. When they conduct surveillance, they are trying to learn all of these things by direct observation.

In the information gathering phase, they will actually be asking questions of the local populace. There are many ruses people can devise in order to ask questions without raising suspicion. They might say that they are lost and ask you how to get from where they are to where they want to go. They might act as though they are taking a survey and ask questions about your level of satisfaction with the facility's security apparatus. They might pose as a utility worker and ask about access points. There are many possibilities but they are all designed to answer questions that could not be answered by direct surveillance.

3. TESTING SECURITY

The third sign is when the bad guys begin to actually test the security apparatus of their target. If their target is a facility, they will try to gain unauthorized access. They want to see how easy or difficult it will be to enter without a badge, ID, key card, escort, etc. If their target is a house, they might try to ring the doorbell and get themselves invited inside under any pretense. If their target is an individual, they will try to get close enough to touch the person and see how hard or soft a target they really are. All they are doing at this stage is testing how much they can do without raising alarms or suspicions, to see at what point the target becomes hard.

4. FUNDING

No one can carry out an operation without the funding to buy supplies and secure capabilities. Fundraising can come in many shapes and sizes. It could be someone soliciting you to give to a charity of which you have never heard, an online fundraising campaign, door-to-door candy sales, begging on the street corner, anything and everything that collects funds.

5. ACQUIRING SUPPLIES

We all know to be on the lookout for people who are acting uncomfortable when buying household cleaners and fertilizer. There are plenty of items which are legal to purchase that might be indicators of nefarious intent: pressure cookers, burner cell phones, nails and screws, diesel fuel, etc. These cannot be bought at the same store because hardware stores do not sell cell phones and grocery stores do not sell fertilizer. Sometimes these purchases are made online. If they are bought together, they should flag the system as suspicious. However, a smart criminal will scatter their acquisition methods over time and geographic area to avoid raising suspicion.

Should the individual in question wish to conduct a mass shooting or bombing, they will seek out weapons and ammunition. If a person is gathering all these things over a relatively short period of time, that is definitely suspicious behavior and it must be reported.

6. IMPERSONATION

This is when the criminal adopts a disguise in order to gain deeper access to their target. They might attempt to present themselves as a police officer, a delivery person, a utility worker, a first responder, an employee, the spouse of an employee, a construction worker, a visiting executive, a member of the military, a security officer or anything else you can conceive (really). This stage carries inherent risk to the criminal because it hinges on how well they present their assumed identity; in other words, if their cover is blown, their entire operation is ruined. This exceeds the step where they began testing security, as they could have claimed that they were simply in the wrong place. At this stage, they are nervous or stressed, making them more dangerous than before.

7. REHEARSAL

The seventh sign is when the criminal(s) begin to rehearse their attack. At this stage, they have acquired all the information and supplies they need and are now ready to start testing that information, equipment and their own capabilities. They would ideally do this in as much solitude as possible, but they might have to walk through their plan in broad daylight, trying to blend into the local populace. They will need to coordinate with each other so they will most likely be communicating by radio or cell phone, and will also need to gain access and move themselves into position, each one carrying out their own part in the plan according to the sequence of events.

8. DEPLOYMENT

If we have missed all seven preceding signs, whether through misjudgment or inaction, and have not yet intervened, then the eighth sign is deployment.

This is show time. Everything is in place and they are ready to act. They will show up, gain access, move into position, communicate (if there are more than one) and attack. They may or may not be nervous, hypervigilant or hyper focused. They may have tunnel vision and not notice (hear or see) anything but their intended target because they are confident in all their preparation and are fully concentrating on carrying out the attack. They will be in "mission mode" and moving with a purpose. If you see someone or multiple people acting this way, elevate your condition to red, get out of there and call the police. This is the time to enact Run-Hide-Fight (pg. 217).

» HOW TO DETECT A SUICIDE BOMBER

You can absolutely stay in condition yellow forever if you find that it suits you well. Doing so will not harm you. In fact, it might just save your life and the lives of those around you someday.

We have now crossed the threshold from spotting someone in the process of radicalization to recognizing someone who is about to commit an imminent attack on innocent lives. These individuals have gone beyond the point of no return, and now is decidedly not the time to reason with them. Here are some of the tells of a suicide bomber:

- Freshly-shaven body
- Hat
- Sunglasses
- Coat or jacket, no matter the weather
- Backpack or heavy-looking bag (may be concealed under clothing/coat/jacket)
- Multiple layers of bulky clothing
- Looking around to an abnormal extent
- Agitation
- Nervousness
- Sweating
- Wringing hands
- Fumbling fingers
- Clothing inappropriate for the weather or setting
- Moving with a purpose

- Mission focused
- Determined
- Clenched jaw
- Inability to make eye contact
- Vest
- Heavy belt
- Any visible wires whatsoever
- Cell phone ready
- Silent praying

Allow me to take a step back for a moment and humanize this person so you can better understand their dark mentality and anticipate their "tells." Obviously a suicide bomber is someone in a state of profound distress. They are in a crisis and are about to lose their life. Think of all the emotional signs and perhaps even microexpressions you would expect to see in such a person. Depending on their personality, however, their emotional signs may differ greatly. They may appear relaxed, peaceful, resolved, unhurried and clear-headed. There are those for whom accepting their imminent death imparts a peace and tranquility that it will all soon be over. All their planning and hard work are about to pay off. They are about to become a martyr for their cause and gain entry to an afterlife where they expect all their angst will be resolved.

Remember to put the emotional signs together with the physical signs. If you see a person manifesting many of these signs, DO NOT attempt to intervene. Get yourself and your loved ones far away as quickly as possible. Get off the X. Remember, survival is a byproduct of action.

AFTERWORD

I HOPE YOU have enjoyed this book and that it has added knowledge and skills to your own personal toolbox. It has been a pleasure to write. I only wish I could engage every reader in individual discussions and hear your thoughts.

Please do not let what you have learned here be forgotten or set aside. Now that you know what you know, you are responsible for what you do with it. Take some time to process. Go back over the things you want to remember. Move forward into even more capabilities.

Take yourself out of your comfort zone on a regular basis. Have courage. Try new things with the full expectation that you will fail at times. Be willing to fail and learn all the lessons that accompany failure. Be willing to succeed, too. Even success demands something of us. When you succeed, you have the right to demand more of yourself. That path has an ever-upward trajectory. This means there is no way you can predict where you will actually go, what you will achieve or what opportunities await.

As you risk failure outside of your comfort zone, be sure to do things that will engage your sympathetic nervous system, experiencing stress for the purpose of teaching yourself how to function properly under its effects. Most people can perform well when shooting a stationary target at a controlled range, where all the bullets are flying in the same direction and there are no bad guys. But how will those marksmanship skills hold up under less than ideal conditions?

What about when bullets are flying in many directions?

How about when the air is so cold your hands are slow and clumsy?

What happens when you or your target are moving?

In my training, we were routinely subjected to stress inoculations. That could mean anything from being yelled at and thrown against a wall to being dropped off three days from civilization with no gear. This was not designed to torture us but to force us to use the skills we had been taught to solve our problems and get to a better place. My first flight instructor used to say, "If you can run with weights, you can run without them." This means if you teach yourself to perform under stress and adverse conditions, you can most assuredly do well on quiet and calm days.

Stress is different for different people. What stresses the heck out of one person may not even register to another. Spend some time on self-evaluation and figure out your own stressors. Be willing to operate in that environment until you have taught yourself how to thrive there. You can inoculate yourself against allowing stress to take you down. This has a time limit, though. My stress inoculations from 20 years ago have long since worn off. If I am still relying on their potency, I will be sorely disappointed in my hour of need. So, go to the range. Take a scuba diving course. Get certified in Wilderness First Aid. Get trained in rappelling. Go sky diving. Do something you find both exhilarating and scary, something that will enable you with new capabilities and teach you new skills. Take what they teach you in the classroom and be prepared to carry out those tasks based on sound principles in a stressful environment. You will feel as accomplished as you have ever felt and you will watch your preconceived limitations evaporate. Never stop learning. Be curious. Always seek to add both skills and knowledge to your survival kit.

Remember to take care of yourself and invest in all three categories of your fulcrum every day: physical, spiritual and emotional. Put yourself into forward CG and live there ready to take whatever comes. Conquer and thrive.

FURTHER READING

THE OLDER I get, the more I am keenly aware of how much I do not know. But I have discovered the secret to being effective at what I do: I surround myself with high quality subject matter experts. While I cannot always have them on staff, I can follow their teachings and use their resources. Below is a list of books and one amazing survival gear manufacturer whose insights have helped keep me informed and focused on a broad array of disciplines ranging from hostage negotiations to social engineering and from spycraft to survival.

- *An Astronaut's Guide to Life on Earth* BY CHRIS HADFIELD

- *Between Silk and Cyanide* BY LEO MARKS

- *How to Win Friends and Influence People* BY DALE CARNEGIE

- *Kidnap for Ransom* BY RICHARD P. WRIGHT

- *Krav Maga: Combat Mindset and Fighting Stress* BY EYAL YANILOV

- *On Killing* BY DAVE GROSSMAN

- *Out of the Mountains* BY DAVID KILCULLEN

- *The Body Keeps the Score* BY BESSEL VAN DER KOLK M.D.

- *The Freedom Line* BY PETER EISNER

- *The Rise of Superman* BY STEVEN KOTLER

- Grim Survival Workshop Tip Cards (*GRIMWORKSHOP.COM*)

INDEX

ABOUT THE AUTHORS

CHECK FREEDMAN is the COO of Captive Audience Prevention Training and Recovery Team. She has decades of operational experience including executive protection of clients in overseas locations, surveillance, counter surveillance, survival, evasion, resistance, escape, armed and unarmed combat. Freedman holds black belt and/or instructor rank in 11 martial arts styles and is currently training in her 14th style. She is a technical scuba diver, a multi-engine instrument pilot, crisis hostage negotiator, private investigator, Certified Missing & Exploited Child Investigator, Critical Incident Stress Debriefer, Emergency Medical Response Instructor, Search and Rescue Ground Team Leader and travel security specialist. Freedman is currently the NHQ, Senior Program Manager for Critical Incident Stress Management and Resiliency for the United States Air Force Auxiliary (Civil Air Patrol).

BILLY JENSEN is the CEO of Captive Audience Prevention Training and Recovery Team. He is a Personnel (Hostage) Recovery Professional and honorably retired Special Forces Soldier (Green Beret). During active duty, he served more than a decade as a Special Forces Intelligence NCO. Jensen has worked as an anti-terrorism instructor and is highly trained in terrorist and criminal network analysis. Since retiring from Special Forces Billy was trained as a Crisis Hostage Negotiator, Critical Incident Stress Debriefer, private investigator, locksmith, martial artist, master scuba diver and Certified Missing & Exploited Child Investigator. Billy has a Bachelors in Science and Masters of Arts Graduate of Norwich University and is currently pursuing a Doctorate in Community Counseling and Traumatology.

JACK CAMBRIA is a former member of the NYPD who contributed 34 years of exemplary service. He has served in various ranks and assignments including patrol, the Emergency Service Unit and the Hostage Negotiation Team, of which he is their longest tenured commander. He now teaches negotiation, de-escalation and active shooter survival strategies for corporations at the local, national and international level.

ACKNOWLEDGMENTS

WE WOULD LIKE to thank Dr. Sam Bernard who has helped us, supported us and been our biggest cheerleader since day one. Dr. Bernard is our Director of Mental Health and oversees the psychological stabilization of every client, student and team member associated with the unique and difficult mission of Captive Audience. Dr. Bernard is a trauma-informed psychologist with a heart to relieve the mental anguish which often accompanies ordeals like kidnapping, captivity and rescue. He believed in us and in our mission when Captive Audience was still a pipe dream. His unflagging support and dedication has led him to advocate for us and for our work all over the world. We could not have done this without him. Thank you, Sam.

We would also like to thank Scott Trager of Northeast Off Road Adventures in Ellenville, New York. Scott embraced us as soon as we met and caught our vision early. Scott has hosted many training courses at his adventure school in the Catskills and continues to advocate for us and our work tirelessly by throwing the weight of his good name behind everything we have done. The connections he has made for us have been a godsend and we look forward to many more years of working side by side with him in this endeavor. Thank you, Scott.

ABOUT CAPTIVE AUDIENCE

NGOS, MISSIONARIES, DOCTORS and all humanitarian aid workers are at an all-time high risk of being the victims of violence, kidnapping for ransom, trafficking and murder. These kind-hearted people leave their homes and their families and travel great distances to the farthest reaches of the globe to render aid to people in need. Regrettably, the population of unsavory groups (terrorists, gangs, organized crime rings, despots, criminals, etc.) is on the rise. The political instability of entire geographic locations has given rise to more of these groups than the world has ever seen before. In precisely the same places where humanitarian aid is most desperately needed, these opportunistic, criminal elements are flourishing. Additionally, every natural disaster is a canvas upon which the opportunistic criminal mind paints. Well-meaning people, who arrive on the scene of a disaster to render assistance, are prime targets for kidnap-for-ransom groups. They are seen as easy money because the assumption is made that their families are wealthy and will pay anything to get their loved ones back. We may know that to be the farthest thing from the truth, but that does not change the reality that kidnapping for ransom has become a booming business in many regions of the world. It has moved from merely a crime of opportunity to a structured, strategic business model for making large sums of money. Kidnapped workers are viewed as a commodity, frequently sold at auction to the highest immediate bidder, and will be held for as long as it takes to extract the highest price from the victim's family or organization.

That's why we created Captive Audience: Prevention, Training and Recovery Team.

If you or your organization are planning on traveling overseas for the purposes of rendering humanitarian aid to any population in need, we offer training at a variety of levels to maximize your chances for success while minimizing your exposure. Our training courses and services offer multiple tiers including pre-deployment readiness, crisis planning and response and post-incident help.

If you would like to learn more about **Captive Audience** or are interested in participating in one of our courses, please visit our website: *captiveaudienceptrt.com.*

SOME OF OUR OFFERINGS INCLUDE...

- Survival on air, land or sea
- Urban survival
- Desert survival
- Mountain survival
- Jungle survival
- Arctic survival
- Water survival
- Basic navigation
- Advanced navigation
- Personal protection
- Third-party protection
- Risk assessments
- Threat vulnerability assessments
- Virtual threat vulnerability assessments
- Geopolitical risk analysis
- Vulnerability detection and mitigation
- Site security
- Decision making
- 360° situational awareness
- Surviving captivity
- Self-rescue
- Surveillance detection
- Counter kidnapping
- Psychology of captivity
- Hostage negotiation
- Proof of life
- Crisis planning for families
- Acting and compliance
- Radical religious action and survival
- Cross cultural communication
- SERE combatives
- Counter rape

- Improvised weapons
- Found object fighting
- Mindset
- Combatives
- Restraint escape
- Evasion
- Crisis negotiation support
- Crisis planning support and consultation
- Crisis consultation
- Investigations
- Surveillance and counter surveillance
- Left of Incident investigative support
- Interagency and international crisis support liaison activities (Diplomatic, Law Enforcement, Military)
- Hostage rescue liaison activities and planning support
- Isolated person recovery from politically sensitive, hostile or inhospitable areas
- Air operations planning for expeditions or to support persons in remote areas
- Cross cultural liaison and support activities in the Middle East, Eastern and Western Europe, North Africa, Central Africa, the South Pacific, Southeast Asia, Central America and South America
- Other specialized technical support to support the recovery of clients available upon request

Media Lab Books
For inquiries, call 646-838-6637

Copyright 2021 Topix Media Lab

Published by Topix Media Lab
14 Wall Street, Suite 4B
New York, NY 10005

Printed in Canada

ISBN-13: 978-1-948174-74-9
ISBN-10: 1-948174-74-X